# Guide
# North Country National Scenic Trail in Minnesota

Editors
Susan Carol Hauser
Linda D. Johnson

Map Illustrator
Todd "Tman" McMahon

North Country Trail Association
Arrowhead Chapter, Itasca Moraine Chapter,
Laurentian Lakes Chapter, Star of the North Chapter

Trails Books
BOULDER

Copyright © 2014 by the North Country Trail Association
All rights reserved. No portion of this book, either text or photography, may be reproduced in any form, including electronically, without the express written permission of the publisher.

Published by Trails Books
a Big Earth Publishing company
3005 Center Green Drive, Suite 225
Boulder, Colorado 80301
1-800-258-5830
E-mail: books@bigearthpublishing.com
www.bigearthpublishing.com

Cover and text design: D.K. Luraas
Production Manager: Mira Perrizo
All photos used with permission

9    8    7    6    5    4    3    2    1

Library of Congress Control Number: 2014936209
ISBN: 978-1-934553-47-3

North Country Trail Association
229 E. Main Street
Lowell, MI 49331
(616) 897-5987
(866) 445-3628 toll-free

Acknowledgement: The story "Tamarack and Chickadee" is from the story collection *When Beaver Was Very Great: Stories to Live By*, Anne Dunn, Midwest Traditions, 1995. Reprinted with permission.

Cover photograph: Matthew R. Davis
Cover inset photograph: Marcus Schaffer

Please Note: Risk is always a factor in backcountry hiking. It is the responsibility of the users of this guide to plan hikes with care and to exercise caution on the trail. The author and publisher disclaim any liability for injury or other damage caused by hiking the North Country Trail in Minnesota. The author has exercised due diligence in reporting accurate information in this guide. For updates, including trail routing, visit northcountrytrail.org/mnguidebook

Printed in the United States of America

*"I have been told that when we walk the land our breath falls to the earth and in that place we are remembered always. Therefore, on a certain fragrant day, I considered all who had climbed these hills before me, stepped through fallen leaves and walked beneath the pine. I thought of those who were coming, too. Surely they will remember that our living breath has fallen in this place and cannot be removed from our good and ancient land."*
—Anne M. Dunn, Anishinabe Grandmother Storyteller

*For those who keep their feet on the ground by following a path through the forest.*

# Contents

**Foreword** ............................................................................. 7
**Welcome to the Trail** .......................................................... 8
**Acknowledgments** ...............................................................
**Introduction to the North Country
National Scenic Trail (NCT)** ............................................... 11
    The Trail and Its History   11
    The NCT in Minnesota   13
    Volunteer for the NCT   13
**Accessing and Using the NCT in Minnesota** ................. 15
    Getting on the Trail   15
    Trail Markings and Path Dimensions   15
    Rules and Regulations   16
    Camping along the Trail   16
    Leave No Trace Principles   17
    Invasive Species   17
    Permits and Fees   18
    Private Lands   18
**Using this Guide** .............................................................. 19
**FAQ (Frequently Asked Questions)** .............................. 20
**Abbreviations & Terminology** ....................................... 24
**Overview Maps** ............................................................... 27

**1 Majesty, Beauty, Biodiversity** .................................... 28
    Seasons   28
    Vegetation   30
    Wildlife   33
    Geology   35
    Tamarack and Chickadee   27
**2. Safety on the Trail** ...................................................... 39
    Calling for Help   39
    Injury   39
    Staying in Touch   39
    Weather   40
    Wildlife   40
    Poison Ivy   41
    Bugs, Ticks, and Tick-borne Illnesses   42

    Dangerous People  44
    Hunting and Trapping  44
    Water Sources and Treatments  45
    What to Carry with You: Ten Essentials  46

**3. Maplewood and Itasca State Parks** ....................................... 47
    Introduction and Recommendations  47
    Maplewood State Park  48
    Itasca State Park  50

**4. Fort Abercrombie, North Dakota, to Tamarac National Wildlife Refuge** ....................................... 54
    Mostly road walking with some off-road trail hikes. Trail and locator maps.
    80.8 miles
    Overview trail descriptions
    Service town information

**5. Tamarac National Wildlife Refuge through Chippewa National Forest near Remer** ....................... 66
    Contiguous, off-road hiking trail through the center of Minnesota.
    163.3 miles
    Detailed trail maps
    Mile-by-Mile trail descriptions
    Points of interest
    Service towns
    Winter use
    Driving directions to trailheads
    Alerts
    Trail stories
    History, biology, botany, and geology notes

**6. Chippewa National Forest near Remer to Jay Cooke State Park** ....................................... 200
    Paved bicycle trail and road walking (Remer to Ely); contiguous rugged footpaths, some traversing remote wilderness (Ely to Jay Cooke State Park).
    558.3 miles
    Locator maps
    Overview trail descriptions
    Resources including trail guides, associations, contacts

**7. West and East of Minnesota** ....................................... 213
    North Dakota  213
    Wisconsin  214
    Onward to New York  214

**Appendices** ..................................................................................215
    A. Map Index and Hiking Checklist  215
    B. Camping, Campsites, Campgrounds  218
    C. Service Towns  224
    D. Loop Trails for Easy-Access Shorter Hikes  233
    E. Winter Use  237
    F. Restricted-Use Areas  239
    G. Recommended Reading  241
    H. Meetup groups, Social Media, Contacts  244
    I. Editorial Team  247

**Acknowledgments** ....................................................................249
**Index**..........................................................................................251
**Journal/Notes** ..........................................................................253

# Foreword
Will Weaver

"Something there is that doesn't love a wall ... that wants it down" ("Mending Wall"), wrote Robert Frost. But the opposite is true about trails. Everybody and every living thing loves a path.

For animals, trails are the logic of nature. The "path of least resistance," sometimes suspect, is a good thing in the wild—a key part of animal survival. Deer and other large mammals conserve energy by getting to and from sources of food, water, and shelter in the most efficient manner. Small critters hunt along them. And trails are preferred by those creatures who need not walk them—birds, for example. The "partridge trail" provides a flying channel for partridge, small hawks, owls, and songbirds, as well as a handy food source for ground-feeders.

For humans, trails carry a similar but more complicated value. While trails make our hiking easier, and occasionally provide us food via hunting or berry picking, their value reaches deep into the human condition. There is something extraordinarily comforting about walking where others have gone before. Trails offer assurances that we will not get lost; if you have experienced it, there is no greater sense of panic than being "turned around," and no greater sense of relief than finding the trail once again.

Trails also provide an interconnectedness between humans, a shared experience that we can speak to: that trail's vista, that other trail's boggy slog. The trail makers, then, participate in an ancient ritual: one tied to survival, but also woven into our spiritual well-being.

In another poem, "The Road Not Taken," Robert Frost advised taking "the [path] less traveled by." This is good advice metaphorically, but sometimes a well-marked, actual trail is just what we humans need.

*Author Will Weaver writes from his lifelong experience of hiking and hunting in the vicinity of the North Country Trail. His book* The Last Hunter *and the movie* Sweet Land, *based on a short story by Weaver, plumb the sometimes quiet, sometimes volatile changes in rural midwestern life in the twentieth century.*

# Welcome to the Trail

Go out in the woods today ... *Your adventure starts nearby.*

Take a lunch break along the shore of a beautiful, undeveloped lake; stand in awe within a majestic stand of old-growth pines; listen to the call of loons on a misty summer morning; observe the wonder of throngs of spring migrating waterfowl; catch a glimpse of a pack of wolves while snowshoeing on a sunny -20°F winter day; backpack and camp for the first time with your kids; and catch a walleye from shore at a backcountry fishing lake. These are just some of the wondrous experiences to be had on the North Country National Scenic Trail (NCT) in northern Minnesota.

At 4,600 miles in length, the NCT is the nation's longest footpath, one of only eleven National Scenic Trails in the U.S., and is the only one located within the state of Minnesota. The NCT's route includes 775 miles between the Red River of the North at Fort Abercrombie, ND, and Jay Cooke State Park south of Duluth. Many experienced NCT hikers say the best scenery of the entire trail is found within the North Star State—Minnesota.

This guidebook features mile-by-mile descriptions of the 163.3-mile contiguous segment from Tamarac National Wildlife Refuge near Detroit Lakes through the Chippewa National Forest near Remer. Other NCT segments in Minnesota—North Dakota to the Tamarac, and the Kekekabic, Border Route and Superior Hiking trails—are introduced and useful resources are highlighted. Experienced hikers, thru-hikers, casual hikers, and new hikers will all find the *Guide to the North Country National Scenic Trail in Minnesota* to be a comprehensive resource. NCT volunteers have walked every inch of this trail and provided the descriptions. The guide and the trail are ready for you!

—**Matthew R. Davis,** North Country Trail Association
Regional Trail Coordinator for Minnesota and North Dakota

Welcome to the North Country National Scenic Trail in Minnesota! Uniting America's northern heartlands, the North Country Trail is America's longest national scenic trail, meandering 4,600 miles from its western terminus at Lake Sakakawea, North Dakota through seven states to wind up at Crown Point, New York. Along the way the Trail tells the story of the people of the North Country—past and present—and how the northern landscapes and Great North Woods shaped their experiences.

The Gopher State hosts some of the best hiking and backpacking on the entire Trail—and this step-by-step guide is brought to you by those who know it best—the volunteers who build it, maintain it and tell its stories. We like to call ourselves the Red Plaid Nation, and we invite you to hike with us—see you on the Trail!

—**Bruce E. Matthews**, Executive Director, North Country Trail Association

This guidebook is an indispensable resource. It not only offers critical how-to information—including detailed route descriptions, maps, and town services—but it also provides extensive context about the landscape, such as geological features, tree types, and human history.

—**Andrew Skurka**, North Country Trail Thru-Hiker and National Geographic "Adventurer of the Year"

Anyone who enjoys the outdoors will benefit from this guide! It provides the seasoned hiker the chance to cross Minnesota from North Dakota to Wisconsin, or the casual hiker the chance to jump onto any segment of the North Country Trail within Minnesota. Whether planning a leisurely afternoon hike or a walk across Minnesota, this guide will reveal to the reader the natural treasures found across our state's section of this national trail.

—**Connie Cox**, Lead Park Naturalist, Itasca State Park

The North Country National Scenic Trail is an incredible asset to our rural areas in Minnesota, and helps to enhance economic development and tourism opportunities in the regions it passes through. Trails help attract visitors and preserve open space, and they offer many benefits to those who are seeking places to exercise and spend time in nature.

—**Collin C. Peterson**, U.S. House of Representatives, Minnesota Congressional District Seven

*Hikers in a guided group enjoy a summer day in the woods. Photo by Matthew R. Davis.*

# Introduction to the North Country National Scenic Trail

### The Trail and Its History

The North Country National Scenic Trail, at 4,600 miles, runs through seven states and is the longest of eleven U.S. National Scenic Trails. The next longest national trail is the Continental Divide, at 3,100 miles. The most well-known trail, the Appalachian, is 2,181 miles. The North Country Trail, or NCT as it is commonly known, is the only National Scenic Trail in Minnesota.

| North Country National Scenic Trail States, West to East | U.S. National Scenic Trails by Length in Miles |
|---|---|
| <ul><li>North Dakota</li><li>Minnesota</li><li>Wisconsin</li><li>Michigan</li><li>Ohio</li><li>Pennsylvania</li><li>New York</li></ul> | <ul><li>North Country, 4,600</li><li>Continental Divide, 3,100</li><li>Pacific Crest, 2,650</li><li>Appalachian, 2,181</li><li>Florida, 1,400</li><li>Ice Age, 1,200</li><li>Pacific Northwest, 1,200</li><li>Arizona, 807</li><li>Potomac Heritage, 700</li><li>Natchez Trace, 695</li><li>New England, 220</li></ul> |

On March 5, 1980, Congress passed legislation that authorized the North Country National Scenic Trail, culminating efforts that began even before the National Trails System Act of 1968, which established the first trails—the Appalachian and Pacific Crest National Scenic Trails. For additional history of the NCT, visit <northcountrytrail.org/trail/history>.

Besides its length, the NCT offers diversity of place, including:
- Tall-grass prairie and wide open spaces of North Dakota
- Old-growth forests in Itasca State Park and elsewhere
- Boundary Waters Canoe Area Wilderness
- Shores of the Great Lakes
- Downtowns of major cities, including Duluth, MN and Dayton, OH
- New York State's Adirondack Mountains

The NCT stitches together these diverse landscapes, inviting hikers today to walk alongside America's past: "... the NCT is deeply connected with American history, following the footsteps of the country's first peoples, voyageurs, surveyors, soldiers, canal boaters, sailors, lumbermen, runaway slaves, miners, and aeronauts, as well as a few less savory characters here and there." (Bruce E. Matthews in Ron Strickland, *The North Country Trail*)

## The NCT in Minnesota

Day to day management of the NCT is handled by volunteers of the non-profit North Country Trail Association (NCTA) working in conjunction with the NCTA staff, National Park Service staff, and local trail partners, including land managers, commercial and private landowners, and local governments. There are currently four chapters working on the North Country Trail in Minnesota:
- Laurentian Lakes Chapter: Becker and Clearwater Counties, from near Frazee to the middle of Itasca State Park.
- Itasca Moraine Chapter: Hubbard and Cass Counties, from the middle of Itasca State Park to Cass County 125 near Longville in the Chippewa National Forest.
- Star of the North Chapter: Cass County, from Cass County 125 near Longville to just north of Remer in the Chippewa National Forest.
- Arrowhead Chapter: Cass County, from just north of Remer to the East Forest Boundary, and Arrowhead re-route from near Remer to the Kekekabic Trail near Ely.

Future chapters in Minnesota may include:
- Otter Tail and Wilkin Counties from Frazee through Maplewood State Park and west to the Red River and North Dakota.
- Ely area, Kekekabic Trail southwest toward Grand Rapids, known as "the Ely gap," to meet up with the Arrowhead Chapter.

## Volunteer for the NCT in Minnesota

NCT chapters have responsibility for the construction, maintenance, promotion, and protection of their trail sections. They work in close partnership with local land managers and partnering government agencies, trail-hosting private landowners, and the NCTA and National Park Service. Chapters typically have trail adopters who are responsible for maintenance on specific segments of the NCT, including mowing the path and clearing away trees that have fallen across the path.
<northcountrytrail.org/Minn>

In Minnesota, the NCT shares trail with three other non-profit organizations:
- Kekekabic Trail Club
- Border Route Trail Association
- Superior Hiking Trail Association

These organizations are responsible for nearly 400 of the 775 NCT miles in Minnesota. The shared trails showcase scenic highlights of Minnesota's NCT and, from Ely to Jay Cooke State Park, also offer rugged wilderness hiking challenges unrivaled elsewhere on the NCT from North Dakota to New York.

# Accessing and Using the NCT in Minnesota

**Getting on the Trail**

The easiest way to access the NCT is to drive to a designated trailhead parking area. Designated trailheads offer safe, off-road parking. The NCT crosses many roads but only rarely is there room to park safely at these junctures.

Many trailheads feature kiosks with maps and brochures, detailed trail information, and a register where trail users can leave comments. For locations of trailheads see the Appendix A: Map Index and Hiking Checklist, and individual maps throughout the book. For winter access, see Appendix E: Winter Use. Also see northcountrytrail.org/trail/hike-planning/

To sample the NCT, try a loop trail, one that utilizes the NCT but leaves from and returns to a designated parking area. These are described in Appendix D: Loop Trails and in Chapters 4, 5, and 6.

*The NCT emblem that marks trail and trailheads.*

**Trail Markings and Path Dimensions**

The NCT is typically marked with a decal of the official NCT emblem, usually located on a Carsonite (flexible fiberglass) post.

The official blaze (marking) for the NCT is blue and is usually a two-inch by six-inch rectangle painted on a tree at eye level. Blazes are painted alternately on opposite sides of a tree so they can be seen from both directions. Typically, blazes are visible from one to the next, looking forward or back on the trail. Additional signage is frequently used at confusing intersections and at most road and trail crossings.

Double blazes are used to mark direction changes in the trail and to indicate the direction of the change. The lower blaze indicates the trail. A blaze above it and to the right indicates that the trail turns to the right, and vice versa for left turns. These are especially useful when the NCT crosses another trail or a road: the directional blazes indicate where to look for the trail's reentry into the woods.

The NCT treadway is maintained as a corridor four feet wide with an overhead clearance of eight feet. Volunteers keep it mowed, cleared of trees, and with trailside brush lopped back. Diligent maintenance can be quickly undone by storms, wind, and illegal or improper use. Damage or the need for maintenance can be reported by email. See Appendix H: Meetup groups, Social Media, Contacts.

### Rules and Regulations

*Foot Traffic Only.* Generally speaking, the North Country Trail treadway is open only to foot traffic. This includes walking, hiking, backpacking, trail running, bird watching, cross-country skiing, snowshoeing, hunting, fishing, geocaching, nature observation, photography, and related activities. Certain sections of the NCT may be open to other non-motorized uses such as mountain biking, road biking, or horseback riding at the discretion of the local landowner or land manager. All motorized vehicle use by the public is prohibited, including use of four-wheel drive vehicles, dirt bikes, ATVs, and snowmobiles.

*Camping.* See Camping along the Trail, below.

*Pets.* Pets are allowed everywhere on the North Country Trail except within Greenwater Lake Scientific and Natural Area. For the pets' protection, they should always be in sight of their owners and under their control, ideally using a leash. Pets can be endangered by hunters, trappers' traps, and some wildlife.

*Damage/Vandalism.* Willful damage to all natural and/or cultural resources found along the NCT should be avoided. Reports of damage should be made by phone or email. See Appendix H: Meetup groups, Social Media, Contacts.

### Camping along the Trail

Hikers are encouraged to use designated campsites when they are available (see Appendix B: Camping, Campsites, Campgrounds). These sites are designed and built to withstand the impacts from camping and also feature amenities such as dependable water sources, campfire rings, and wilderness privies. Dispersed backcountry camping (outside of designated campsites and campgrounds; no amenities) is allowed on most public lands along the NCT, and Leave No Trace principles (see below) should be adhered to, e.g., camp and dispose of human waste at least 200 feet from a water source. Campfires are allowed, unless no burning restrictions are in place (see www.dnr.state.mn.us/forestry/fire/fire rating_restrictions.html). Hikers should contain campfires within a rock fire ring and completely extinguish the fire and embers before moving on.

Dispersed camping is not allowed within the Tamarac National Wildlife Refuge, Greenwater Lake Scientific and Natural Area (SNA), and state parks, including Maplewood, and Itasca.

**Leave No Trace Principles**

The North Country Trail Association endorses Leave No Trace (LNT) outdoor ethics and its seven principles, designed to minimize the impacts that outdoor recreationists have upon the natural environment and other recreationists. All NCT users are asked to adhere to the seven LNT principles:
- Plan Ahead and Prepare
- Travel and Camp on Durable Surfaces
- Dispose of Waste Properly
- Leave What You Find
- Minimize Campfire Impacts
- Respect Wildlife
- Be Considerate of Other Visitors

(The member-driven Leave No Trace Center for Outdoor Ethics teaches people how to enjoy the outdoors responsibly. This copyrighted information has been reprinted with permission from the Leave No Trace Center for Outdoor Ethics <www.LNT.org >.)

**Invasive Species**

Invasive species are non-native plants, animals, and micro-organisms that damage the lands and waters that native plants and animals need to survive. Trails like the North Country National Scenic Trail and its users are a common vector for the spread of invasive species. Everyone needs to be part of the fight against invasive species.

By following these four easy steps, together we can stop the spread of invasive species:
- Arrive with clean gear
- Burn local or certified firewood
- Stay on the trails
- Before leaving, remove mud and seeds

The NCTA supports and contributes to efforts to limit the spread of invasive species, and partners with other agencies to install boot brushes at selected sites, including some on the NCT.

---

*Help Prevent the Spread of Invasive Plants and Animals*
*Learn more at www.PlayCleanGo.org*

**Is it a porcupine?**
No ... if you see a funny-looking brush contraption at an NCT trailhead, don't be afraid ... use it! Several NCT land management partners have installed boot brush stations and interpretive signs at trailheads so NCT hikers can clean seeds or other plant materials from their boots. The stations consist of stiff bristle brushes facing each other with a space between them for your boot. These help minimize the likelihood of hikers spreading invasive plants via the NCT.

---

## Permits and Fees

Generally, no permits or fees are required for using the North Country Trail or camping along it. However, there may be fees associated with entering, parking at, or camping within certain areas, such as state parks, including Maplewood and Itasca. Special regulations are posted on trailhead kiosks.

## Private Lands

Many private landowners host segments of the NCT on their lands with only a "handshake agreement" for which they receive little or no compensation. While most private lands along the trail are posted, some are not. When ownership of land is not clearly public, NCT users should respect the rights of private landowners: stay on the trail, observe posted regulations (e.g., no hunting, fishing, or trapping), camp and have campfires only in designated sites, pack out trash, close gates, and avoid other unnecessary impacts. When hikers exhibit neighborly behavior, they acknowledge the gift of private land use and help protect NCT relations with private landowners, thus helping to protect the trail.

# Using this Guide

The guide is mostly self-explanatory. When using the maps in Chapters 4, 5, and 6, it might help to keep in mind the following:
- The guide is written from west to east.
- Mileage in the reverse, from east to west, is given in parenthesis.
- The mileage numbers track the distance within each map.
- Directions to trailheads and access points are given in the Mile-by-Mile entries.
- Trailheads have designated parking areas for NCT hikers.
- Access points do not have designated parking areas. It is the responsibility of hikers to exercise caution when parking vehicles at access points.

Before using the trail, please review Chapter 2: Safety on the Trail.

Definitions of specialized words can be found in the Abbreviations and Terminology chapter that follows.

Take a look at the appendices. They include lists of campsites, service towns, loop trails, winter access trailheads, and recommended reading.

There are checklists in Appendix A: Map Index and Hiking Checklist, and Appendix D: Loop Trails. Record your accomplishments!

Notice that most chapters begin with an image of a blue blaze, the NCT official trail marker. Watch for it when you are on the trail. The blazes can usually be seen from one to the next and can keep you headed in the direction you intend to go. Especially attend to blazes at trail and road crossings.

Armed with knowledge and desire, you are bound to enjoy the trail: *Your adventure starts nearby.*

---

Send feedback, questions, corrections, trail stories to MNguidebook@northcountrytrail.org. We'd love to hear from you.

---

# FAQ
# (Frequently Asked Questions)

**Q:** How hard is it to hike the trail? Are there a lot of hills?
**A:** From Abercrombie, North Dakota, through the Chippewa National Forest, the NCT is blessed with long stretches of gently undulating terrain. There are occasional ascents and descents that might be challenging for less-experienced hikers. These are described in Chapters 4 and 5 of the guide. When the trail turns northward, after the Chippewa National Forest near Remer, elevation increases. The affiliate trails from Ely to Jay Cooke State Park, which pass through the Boundary Waters Canoe Area and along Lake Superior, are generally more difficult and can be challenging even for experienced hikers. See Chapter 6.

**Q:** Will I be able to use my cell/mobile phone on the trail in Minnesota?
**A:** It depends on your phone, your service provider, and the section of the trail.
- North Dakota to Tamarac National Wildlife Refuge: Signals are usually available in and near towns and major highways.
- Tamarac National Wildlife Refuge through Chippewa National Forest: Quality of the signal varies from absent to strong and can change in short distances. However, most of the time a signal is available.
- Chippewa National Forest to Jay Cooke State Park: Signals are usually available in and near towns and along major highways. They are especially scarce on the Kekekabic Trail, the Border Route Trail, and the northern end of the Superior Hiking Trail.

Signals can vary over short distances. If there is no signal, try moving forward or back on the trail, or in the direction of a roadway, especially a major highway. If the signal is weak, text messages might get through even when a call will not go through.

**Q:** How do I access the trail? Where are the trailheads?
**A:** The quickest way to find a trailhead is to look at the maps in Chapters 4, 5, and 6. Directions to trailheads and related information follow each map. The Map Index in Appendix A is also useful. Appendix E: Winter Use has information on trailheads in winter.

**Q:** I would like to try out the trail by taking a short hike. How do I know which sections to try?
**A:** See Appendix D: Loop Trails for Easy-Access Shorter Hikes. These trails range from 0.5 to 4 miles. They return to their starting point—and your vehicle. Also, read trail descriptions in Chapters 4, 5, and 6.

**Q:** I worry about getting lost in the woods. How do I stay on the trail?
**A:** The North Country Trail uses a blue blaze, two inches by six inches, placed six feet above the ground on trailside trees. Blazes are painted for travel in both eastbound and westbound directions, alternating from one side of the tree to the other and at a distance so they can be seen from one to the next going either direction on the trail. A second blaze is used to indicate a change in trail direction. The lower blaze is the trail marker. A second blaze above and to the right means the trail continues to the right, and vice versa for the left.

---

Blue blazes are the key to not getting lost on the trail. Keep them in sight and you will be able to stay on the trail. See Accessing and Using the NCT in Minnesota, Trail Markings.

---

**Q:** Can I camp along the trail?
**A:** Yes, in most sections. See the maps in Chapters 4, 5, and 6; Appendix B: Camping, Campsites, Campgrounds; and Appendix F: Restricted-Use Areas.

**Q:** Is the trail open in the winter?
**A:** The trail is open year-round. However, not all trailheads are maintained in the winter. See Appendix E: Winter Use.

**Q:** How would I plan for a hike from North Dakota to New York?
**A:** Visit northcountrytrail.org/for-long-distance-hikers/; contact the NCTA headquarters; and contact local NCT chapters.

**Q:** Am I safe on the trail?
**A:** Generally speaking, hiking on the NCT is a safe activity. For information on trail safety, see Chapter 2: Safety on the Trail.

**Safety**
One of the best protections while hiking the trail is to make certain that someone knows specifically where you are going and when you expect to return.

**Q:** I've heard about Minnesota mosquitoes. Are they a problem on the NCT?
**A:** There are mosquitoes on the trail and it is important to protect yourself from them. See Chapter 2: Safety on the Trail.

**Q:** How can I avoid ticks on the trail?
**A:** Stay on the path, i.e., do not wade through vegetation. See Chapter 2: Safety on the Trail.

**Q:** I would like to talk to someone who knows the trail. Who can I contact and how do I reach them?
**A:** NCTA chapters and volunteers love to talk about the trail. See Appendix H: Meetup groups, Social Media, Contacts for information and connections.

**Q:** Are there guided hikes on the trail? I feel more comfortable hiking in a group.
**A:** The NCT chapters sponsor guided hikes throughout most of the year. See Appendix H for information on meetup.com, a website where chapters post invitations to their hikes along with directions to starting points and features of the trail to be hiked. Appendix H also has contact information for the chapters.

**Q:** I am staying at Itasca State Park or Maplewood State Park. How do I access the NCT in the park?
**A:** For Maplewood, see Chapter 4 maps 1 and 1-A. For Itasca, see Chapter 5 maps 13 and 13-A. For both state parks, see Chapter 3: Maplewood and Itasca State Parks, and also Appendix D: Loop Trails for Easy-Access Shorter Hikes.

**Q:** What do NCT volunteers do?
**A:** Volunteers assist or work independently to construct, maintain, promote, and/or protect the North Country Trail. Trail projects are coordinated through NCTA Chapters. See Appendix H: Meetup groups, Social Media, Contacts.

**Q:** What do adopters do?
**A:** Adopters—persons or groups—take responsibility for maintaining a particular section of the NCT. They ensure that the trail is in good condition and a pleasure to hike. Trail work is coordinated through NCTA chapters. See Appendix H: Meetup groups, Social Media, Contacts.

**Q:** How do I volunteer?
**A:** Contact local chapter leadership. See Appendix H: Meetup groups, Social Media, Contacts.

**Q:** What does it cost to use the NCT?
**A:** There is no fee for hiking the NCT. However, permits are required to park at the trailheads in state parks, including Maplewood and Itasca.

**Q:** I want to support the trail. How do I join the NCT Association?
**A:** Visit the website and sign up! www.northcountrytrail.org.

**Q:** Are there really 10,000 lakes in Minnesota?
**A:** Actually, there are more than 11,842 lakes that are more than ten acres in size. The NCT passes by hundreds of lakes in Minnesota.

# Abbreviations & Terminology

**Abbreviations**

ARW: Arrowhead Chapter, NCTA
BRT: Border Route Trail
BRTA: Border Route Trail Association
FR: Forest Road
ITM: Itasca Moraine Chapter, NCTA
KEK: Kekekabic Trail
KTC: Kekekabic Trail Club
LLC: Laurentian Lakes Chapter, NCTA
NCT: North Country National Scenic Trail or North Country Trail
NCTA: North Country Trail Association
SHT: Superior Hiking Trail
SHTA: Superior Hiking Trail Association
STN: Star of the North Chapter, NCTA
WMA: Wildlife Management Area

**Terminology**

Access point: A road that accesses the NCT but does not have a designated parking area. Usually it does have adequate space for roadside parking, except in winter.

ATV: Motorized all-terrain vehicle, also known as four-wheeler.

Benched-in: A construction technique for creating a trail on the side of a hill by trenching into the side slope. It requires significant effort to construct but results in a sustainable pathway.

Blaze: A mark on a tree to indicate a trail (*American Heritage Dictionary*).

Blue blaze: The trail marker for the North Country National Scenic Trail.
Bushwhack: To break trail or hike off-path.

Campground: A campground is a collection of campsites with additional amenities, usually including bathrooms and water. See also *Campsite* and *Tent site*.

Campsite: A campsite is a designated space, sometimes developed, for one or more tents. See also *Campground* and *Tent site*.

Carsonite post: A printed trail marker made of fiber-reinforced material. It is brown and usually a few inches wide by four feet high.

Day-hiker: A person who is hiking the NCT for part or all of a single day, leaving the trail at night and returning to their home (or civilization). See also *Section-hiker* and *Thru-hiker* (distance-hiker).

Dispersed camping: Camping outside of designated campsites and campgrounds with no amenities.

Esker: A long, narrow ridge of coarse gravel deposited by a stream flowing in or under a decaying glacial ice sheet (*American Heritage Dictionary*).

Fire ring: A designated spot at a campsite for building fires, usually ringed with stones. Most campsites on the NCT in Minnesota have fire rings. A few have fire grates. These are usually constructed of cement blocks and have an iron cooking grate above the fire bed.

Hunter walking trails: Mowed trails on public land for hunting and recreational hiking.

Kame: A short ridge or mound of sand and gravel deposited during the melting of glacial ice. (*American Heritage Dictionary*)

Kettle: A depression left in a mass of glacial drift, formed by the melting of an isolated block of glacial ice. (*American Heritage Dictionary*)

Laurentian Divide: A north-south divide separating the waters of the northern midwestern United States from the waters of eastern and southern Canada. The NCT in Minnesota generally follows this divide. (wikipedia.org)

Laurentian Shield: Also called Canadian Shield, Laurentian Plateau, Laurentian Highlands. A highland region of Canada that reaches from the Great Lakes to the Arctic Ocean and extends southward into the United States. (*American Heritage Dictionary*)

Laurentide Ice Sheet: A massive ice sheet that covered most of Canada and the northern United States several times between c. 95,000 and c. 20,000 years before the present day. (*American Heritage Dictionary*)

Moraine: An accumulation of boulders, stones, or other debris carried and deposited by a glacier. (*American Heritage Dictionary*)

NCT, NCTA: The official trail name of the NCT is the North Country National Scenic Trail, placing it in the league of other National Scenic Trails. Commonly, it is called the North Country Trail and its official abbreviation is NCT, in the way that the Appalachian National Scenic Trail is known as the Appalachian Trail and is abbreviated AT. The NCTA is the North Country Trail Association, the National Park Service's official non-profit partner in building, maintaining, promoting, and protecting the NCT.

Norway pine: In Minnesota, the commonly used name for red pine, *Pinus resinosa*.

Puncheon: An engineered board walkway that rests on a series of sills and is usually less than a foot above surrounding wetland. In comparison, a puncheon is supported by posts driven or anchored into the bottom of the wetland, similar to a dock and, also like a dock, can be two to three feet above the water. (National Park Service *Handbook for Trail Design, Construction, and Maintenance*)

Section-hiker: A person who hikes and camps on the trail for several days at a time. See also *Day-hiker* and *Thru-hiker*.

Single-track trail: Narrow footpath that contrasts with a wider, multiple-use trail.

Sprinkle road: An early twentieth-century logging road that was sprinkled with water in winter. The water turned to ice, making it easier for horses to pull the monstrous log sleds out of the woods.

Tamarac vs. tamarack: "Tamarac" is the spelling used in the name of the Tamarac National Wildlife Refuge (ending with "c"). The tamarack tree is spelled with a "k" at the end. Etiology unknown.

Tent site: A cleared space where a tent can be pitched. See also *Campground* and *Campsite*.

Thru-hiker (distance-hiker): A person who is hiking the NCT from the western to the eastern terminus (or vice versa) in one calendar year, usually camping on the trail at night. See also *Day-hiker* and *Section-hiker*.

Trailhead: An official entry point to the NCT that includes a designated parking lot and usually also has an information kiosk.

Tread or treadway: A dirt path, such as the NCT's, that is level, cleared of rocks and other tripping hazards, and drained to prevent erosion.

Wilderness privy: A pit toilet with no walls, maybe with a privacy screen.

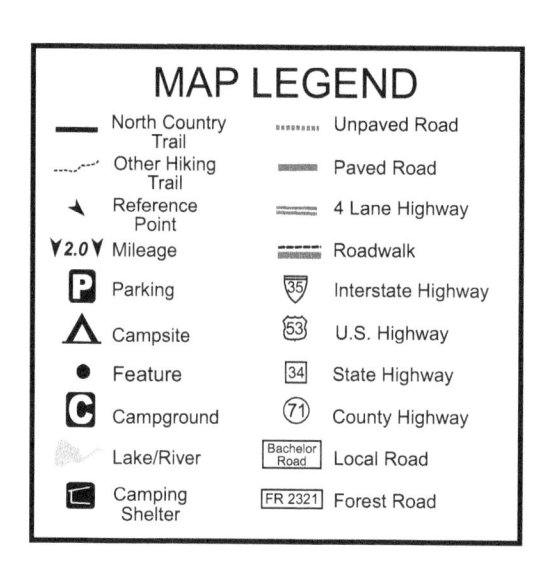

## MAP LEGEND

|  |  |  |  |
|---|---|---|---|
| ──── | North Country Trail | ▪▪▪▪▪ | Unpaved Road |
| ‑‑‑‑ | Other Hiking Trail | ▬▬▬▬ | Paved Road |
| ◄ | Reference Point | ══════ | 4 Lane Highway |
| ▼2.0▼ | Mileage | ===== | Roadwalk |
| P | Parking | (35) | Interstate Highway |
| △ | Campsite | (53) | U.S. Highway |
| ● | Feature | (34) | State Highway |
| C | Campground | (71) | County Highway |
|  | Lake/River | Bachelor Road | Local Road |
| ▰ | Camping Shelter | FR 2321 | Forest Road |

## Overview Maps

Abercrombie, North Dakota, to Jay Cooke State Park, Minnesota/Wisconsin
- For an index of the map sections, see Appendix A: Map Index and Hiking Checklist.
- For map and trail details, see Chapters 4, 5, and 6.

### Abercrombie, North Dakota, to Itasca State Park

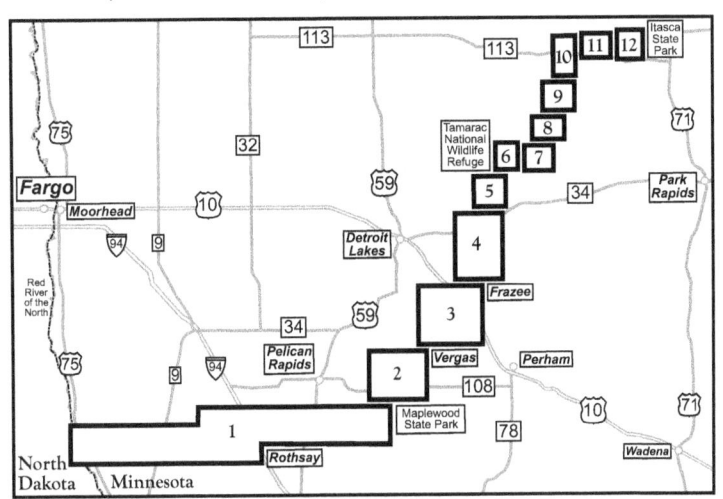

### Itasca State Park to Remer

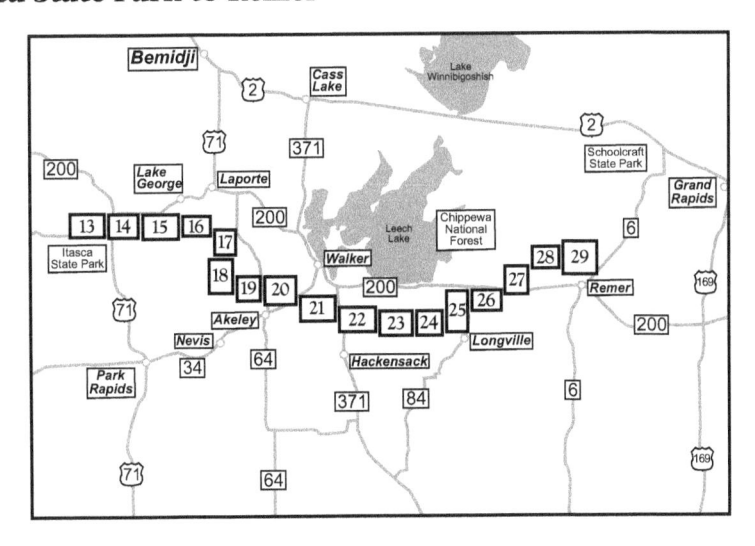

### Remer to Jay Cooke State Park/Wisconsin

See Chapter 6, maps 30, 31, 32, 33.

# Chapter 1
# Majesty, Beauty, Biodiversity

*The first four entries here are essays written by experts in their fields who are also hikers on the NCT in Minnesota. Their contributions offer both fact and fancy, addressing the natural history of the trail and the experience—the meaning, emotions, and values—of being on the trail. A traditional Ojibwe story follows the essays. It offers a life lesson as well as an understanding of interdependence in the forest.*

**The Seasons**
**Bob La Fleur**

Those who are familiar with the yearly cycle in the north country understand that four equal divisions into seasons isn't the way nature works. What we experience is more like this:

Spring doesn't arrive for a month or more after it's expected.
Summer is an undependable visitor.
Autumn runs headlong into winter before its time.
Winter is the guest that arrives too soon and stays too long.

Spring

Trees budding, a thin canopy, early flower blooms, morel mushrooms, frosty mornings, cool days and evenings, squirrels about their business, migratory birds returning. There are now 5,500 trumpeter swans returning to Minnesota each spring. You may see them nesting in the ponds along the trail. Look for loons too, but don't disturb them. A flower that blooms early and is prevalent throughout the region is the large-flowered bellwort. A less common flower that is the prize of many a hiker to observe is the lady's slipper. The yellow variety is most common. Bears, wolves, and wild cats, including the lynx, though present, are rarely seen. It's enough to know they are here and you the hiker are privileged to share in this grand performance of nature. For the serious hiker there is nothing in the human experience that can match sighting such an animal, not just in spring, but throughout the year.

Summer

Like spring, summer doesn't conform to the calendar. It can be long, hot, and humid or it can be short with a few hot days and nights and many cool days and nights. Rainfall varies greatly as well. The foliage in summer is dense and the high canopy lets in little light. Consequently, in the deep woods, there isn't a thick understory of brush and young trees to obstruct the view. Summer is the season of insects and they can be more than an annoyance. Wood tick bites are uncomfortable. The smaller deer tick can cause serious illness. Ticks are most common from very early spring to mid-summer. Though the season has its drawbacks, a hiker shouldn't avoid the opportunities summer offers: a chance to see cygnets (young swans), a fawn, a porcupine (no, they don't shoot their quills), or catch a glance of something intensely red in among the branches overhead—a scarlet tanager, our most tropical of birds.

Autumn

This beautiful season of the year is the most pleasant time to be outdoors. It is also the most forgiving of seasons, with few of the extremes Minnesotans take for granted other times of the year. The colors are spectacular because of the variety of trees, each having its own trademark hue. The sugar maple turns fire-red. The quaking aspen and poplar turn golden yellow. The oak turns reddish-brown and hangs on to its leaves through winter. Another autumnal contribution to the sense of wonder nature has to offer is (we were taught) that conifers don't drop their needles. But one unusual one does. The needles of the tamarack turn golden yellow before dropping to the ground, leaving the tree to stand bare and colorless through winter. By late October, the display of color is over, and in November hunters emerge to ramble through fallen leaves and the first snowfall in pursuit of deer.

Winter

Two seasons long it seems, and the season least willing to give up its reign. The sun is low in the sky and the days are short. Animals are about to go, or have gone, south, or are in hibernation. Skiing and snowshoeing are favorite ways to get about. Winter is blessedly free of insects of all sorts, but not entirely. If you are a careful observer you may see a hardy survivor—a mosquito—walking on top of the snow on a warm January day. Some live through winter by building up a store of natural antifreeze in order to survive the cold and be ready to breed (and ouch! sting) in early spring. Though winter often gets a bad rap for being cold and colorless, it is as full of wonder and mystery as any season. Look for the panorama of colorful lichens on a rock topped off with a white snow cap; tufts of snow and clinging frost, like Christmas ornaments, on a still-green pine; oak leaves dancing in the wind, the same wind that will usher in spring and begin the cycle of seasons all over again.

*Bob La Fleur is an anthropologist, writer, and woodsman. His writing has appeared in a number of publications. He lives off-grid in a cabin in the Minnesota north woods within a short distance of a segment of the North Country Trail, which as a volunteer he helped lay out and clear, and now maintains as an adopter.*

## Vegetation of the North Country Trail
## Harvey Tjader

Trees

As you walk through the woods on a quiet day, notice that the leaves of one species of tree will flutter in the slightest breeze. That species is quaking aspen (*Populus tremuloides*). The reason for the flutter is its flattened leaf stalk (petiole), which gives it great flexibility. The trunks are light-colored and start out smooth, with the bark becoming furrowed near the base of the tree as it ages. Quaking aspen is the most common tree you'll see along the trail.

Another aspen that is often seen along gravelly ridges is the bigtoothed aspen (*Populus grandidentata*). Its leaves are nearly twice as large as quaking aspen's and have large teeth. The bark on the upper trunk may take on a faintly bronze or peachy blush.

Paper birch is easily identified by its white papery bark. It often grows in clumps, sprouting from the stump of its parent tree.

Two pine species are common. Red pine (*Pinus resinosa*), better known as Norway pine, is Minnesota's state tree. Named for its red bark, its needles are long and borne in clumps of two. Eastern white pine

(*Pinus strobus*) has dark bark and bears its needles in clumps of five. It is moderately shade tolerant and often becomes established in the understory below the aspen or Norway pine. Minnesota's third native pine is jack pine (*Pinus banksiana*). It has dark, flaky bark, similar to black cherry, and a wild, ragged appearance. Its needles are shorter than the red or white pine, are clumped in twos and are twisted. It is less common along the trail, but may be seen on areas of droughty sand.

Sugar maple, red maple, basswood, northern red oak, and bur oak are also common but less frequent.

Ironwood (*Ostrya virginiana*) is a small tree or tall shrub that has leaves similar to an elm's, but they are velvety soft. The male flowers are catkins similar to birch or aspen, but the female flowers look like hops. A small tree with leaves still holding on late in the fall or in the winter is either a northern red oak or an ironwood.

Shrubs

The most common shrub species is beaked hazelnut (*Corylus cornuta*). Named for the beaked appearance of the husk that surrounds the nut, beaked hazel is nearly ubiquitous and sometimes nearly impenetrable to off-trail walking. The nuts aren't available long because they are eaten quickly by squirrels in late August to early September. A pliers is handy for cracking the hard shells.

Chokecherry shrubs (*Prunus virginiana*) produce flowers in long clusters in late May or early June. The fruit is too bitter for humans to appreciate, but birds like it. It ripens in late July or early August. If you add lots of sugar, it makes a distinctive and delicious jelly.

Juneberries (*Amelanchier* sp) are another fruiting shrub found along the North Country Trail. Also called serviceberry, the four species that grow in this area are rather tricky to distinguish from each other. The fruit is classified as a pome (like apple), but it is berry-like with juicy flesh and a core that is not very noticeable.

If you are hiking in early summer and stop to smell the downy arrowwood flowers, you may be surprised that they resemble the stench of a rotting carcass. Just to prove that being the "stinky kid" can be a successful tactic, downy arrowwood (*Viburnum rafinesquianum*) hosts pollinating insects that are attracted to its foul smell. Its flowers assemble in rounded or flat clusters, turning to blue fruits that aren't eaten by humans. Its leaves have an opposite arrangement on the stem and turn a beautiful muted red in the fall.

Bush honeysuckle (*Diervilla lonicera*) is a low shrub with long, pointed, opposite leaves that have teeth along the leaf margin. It superficially resembles a true honeysuckle, which does not have teeth on its leaf margins.

Non-woody Plants

Large-leaved aster (*Eurybia macrophylla*) is probably the most common non-woody plant along the trail and maybe throughout northern Minnesota. Sometimes called lumberjack toilet paper, it has large downy, sharply toothed leaves. When it grows in sunny locations, it can reach three to four feet tall and produce clusters of violet flowers. It was used by the Algonquins and Iroquois in numerous ways for food and medicine.

Wild sarsaparilla (*Aralia nudicaulis*) is also common. Alternatively known as parachute plant, the leaf grows straight from the ground and divides into a whorl of three stems which branch up and out, each forming three to seven (most often five) pinnately compound leaflets. If picked and tossed into the air, the compound leaf floats like a parachute to the ground. Its small white flowers are borne on a separate stalk, probably a hundred of which are arranged in a perfect sphere. Its root can be used in making root beer. Sometimes mistaken for poison ivy, it's easily distinguished by having fine teeth on its leaf margin.

Canada mayflower (*Maianthemum canadense*) is also known as wild lily of the valley. It grows up to six inches tall and has one or two lily-like leaves. Its narrow cluster of four-petaled flowers blooms in May and June and eventually produces one-eighth inch round, dull red fruits.

Rose twisted stalk (*Streptopus roseus*) is one of several plants that are said to look like Solomon's seal, having an arching stalk lined by stalkless, lanceolate leaves. It can grow from one to three feet tall. Rose twisted stalk is easily distinguished from the others by having a fringe of short hairs (eyelashes) along its leaf margins. It bears one flower at each leaf node that becomes a round red fruit. Although the fruit is reported to be edible, another name for the plant is scootberry, which refers to the laxative effect of eating too many of them.

Another plant that is said to look like Solomon's seal is the large-flowered (or yellow) bellwort (*Uvularia grandiflora*). Large-flowered bellwort is easily identified by its perfoliate leaves (the base of the leaf completely surrounds the stem). Growing up to twenty inches tall, its large, yellow, bell-shaped flowers bloom in early spring. The seeds form in three-sided capsules.

Bracken (*Pteridium aquilinum*) is a common fern along the North Country Trail. The triangular mature fronds have a shape reminiscent of an eagle's wing, from which comes the species name—*Aquila* being

Latin for eagle. It is the largest triangle-shaped fern in northern Minnesota. It is inedible, containing carcinogenic compounds.

Wood anemone (*Anemone quinquefolia*) is a delicate little plant that has two different appearances, depending on whether it is sterile or fertile. The sterile individuals appear as a single, three-parted, irregularly toothed leaf. Fertile plants are twice compound, splitting into three to five stems, each bearing a compound, irregularly toothed, lobed leaflet. A single one-inch flower, usually white, typically has five petal-like sepals and blooms in early spring. It is also called windflower or nightcaps.

Bluebead lily (*Clintonia borealis*) has many common names, including yellow clintonia, which seems more apt when it is blooming: it bears three to eight yellow, bell-shaped flowers. The name bluebead comes from its round, blue fruit, which are bitter and mildly toxic. The three to five lily-like leaves are edible when just a few inches tall. The root has been used in folk medicine.

Sweet-scented bedstraw (*Galium triflorum*) is a scrambling perennial that grows along the ground or crawls up on other plants. It has whorls of six leaves and clusters of three tiny flowers. The little fruits are bristly. Due to hairs on the plant, it may be coarse enough to stick to a cotton shirt, but not to a nylon jacket. It is said to smell like vanilla, especially when dried.

*Harvey Tjader has been a Minnesota DNR forester for 35 years. He currently leads the Ecological Land Classification program in the northwestern quarter of the state, mapping native plant communities and monitoring adaptive management projects. He helped lay out and construct the North Country Trail from Minnesota 64 to Itasca State Park.*

## Wildlife
**Barry Babcock**

There are many field guides and other writings available for examining the natural science of wildlife that resides along the North Country Trail in Minnesota. But infrequently do we have the opportunity to see wildlife as the traditional Ojibwe have for untold centuries.

Red Lake Healer and Elder, Chi Maringa (Great Wolf—Larry Stillday) teaches that "There are many lessons to learn from the natural world, that's where the Great Spirit put all the lessons we need to fulfill our earth journey. We are to look deep into nature to have a better understanding of everything."

The "Teachings of the Seven Grandfathers" were given to the Anishinaabe as their spiritual foundation. Each teaching or law, is represented by a spiritual animal Grandfather.

The Teachings of the Seven Grandfathers are (as taught to me by Larry Stillday):

*Courage/Bravery* is represented by *Makwa,* the Black Bear.
In its home, the bear shows us the spirit of courage. The bear is a gentle creature, but threaten its cub and it becomes fearless in defense of its offspring. The virtues taught us by Makwa are power, industriousness, instinctive healing, gentle strength, introspection, and dreams. The bear is closely connected to the Grand Medicine Society (GMS) as a teacher. Midewiwin, GMS members, are said to "follow the bear path." Because of its claws that are good for digging, the bear pays attention to healing herbs that many other animals pass up.

*Truth* is represented by *Mikinaak*, the Snapping Turtle.
When the Great Spirit gave the Anishinaabe these laws, the turtle was present to ensure that the laws would never be forgotten or lost. The 13 markings on the back of the turtle denote the 13 moons that represent the truth of one cycle of the earth's rotation around the sun. There are also 28 markings on Mikinaak's back to denote one cycle of the moon around earth. These signs are evidence of the truth that the turtle represents: self-containment, Mother Earth (*Gidakiiminaani*), and knowledge.

*Respect* is represented by *Mushkode-Bizhiki*, the Buffalo.
Every part of the buffalo provided Native People's with some valuable tools for life: shelter, clothing, food, utensils, and even fuel for fire—its dung. "Through giving its life and sharing every part of its being, the buffalo shows the deep respect it has for people." Bizhiki teaches us we must respect all life and the interconnectedness between us all.

*Wisdom* is represented by *Amik*, the Beaver.
"To know and understand wisdom is to know that the Great Spirit gave everyone special gifts to be used to build a peaceful and healthy community ... it uses its sharp teeth for cutting trees and branches, a special gift received from the Great Spirit."

*Love* is represented by *Migizi*, the Bald Eagle.
The eagle in Anishinaabe creation stories was a savior for man by showing his love for them before the Great Spirit. Migizi is the one animal that can reach the highest in bringing vision to the seeker. Migizi's val-

ues are divine spirit, clear vision, great healing powers, courage, sacrifice, and connection to the Creator.

*Humility* is represented by *Ma'iingan*, the Wolf, "an animal guide for true teaching."

The wolf represents loyalty, perseverance, courage, stability, teaching, and intuition. Practicing humbleness means we always consider our fellow humans before ourselves. In the natural world, the wolf expresses this humbleness with great clarity: "The Wolf bows his head not out of fear but out of humbleness; he humbles himself in our presence." A wolf that has hunted food will take the food back to the den to eat with the pack before he takes the first bite or he regurgitates all he has for the pups.

*Honesty* is represented by *Masaba*, the Wilderness Man or Bigfoot. Masaba is honesty and innocence. "The Elders say, 'Never try to be someone else: live true to your spirit, be honest to yourself, accept who you are and the way the Great Spirit made you.'"

When you again hike the beautiful wilds of the NCT, which are home to the wide diversity of plant and animal communities we share this beautiful earth with, think hard and listen carefully to the heartbeat of thousands of life forms as complex and beautiful as ourselves and appreciate the interdependence and joint tenancy that we share in this place called *Gidakiiminaani*—Mother Earth.

*Barry Babcock has been an environmentalist and wilderness enthusiast for his entire adult life. His efforts in the late 1990s promoted development of the North Country Trail west of the Chippewa National Forest. He is also active in addressing issues critical to the stewardship of public lands, including the regulation of off-road vehicles, and protection of Minnesota's unique species and watersheds.*

## Geology
**James Cotter**

*John McPhee, author of many books about geology, wrote: "Rocks are records of events that took place at the time the rocks formed. They are books. They have a different vocabulary, a different alphabet, but you learn how to read them."*

*The Minnesota North Country Trail provides access to a beautiful "book" about glacial geology and glacial history. That book is called the Itasca Moraine.*

*Each rock and landform that you will encounter on the NCT is a product of past glacial activity. The purpose of this portion of the guidebook is to provide you with a lesson in "reading" those rocks and landforms.*

***

From the Tamarac National Wildlife Refuge to Remer, near the eastern edge of the Chippewa National Forest, the NCT traverses the Itasca Moraine, which was laid down about 15,000 years ago. A moraine is a ridge constructed by a glacier. A glacier is an ice sheet that moves by sliding and flowing, propelled by its own weight. As it moves, it incorporates material that it transports to its margin in the form of a ridge. The rocks and sediments of the Itasca Moraine indicate the position of the ice-sheet edge where the glacier dumped or pushed its cargo, forming the ridge. The Itasca Moraine is one of the largest (in terms of relief) in Minnesota.

In order to best "read" the landscape and history of the Itasca Moraine it is best to learn the two most important phrases in the glacial "vocabulary": geologic scale and geologic time.

The formation of a moraine the size of the Itasca Moraine requires glacial processes on a geologic scale—you have to think big! For instance, at the time the moraine was deposited at the margin of the ice sheet, the glacier would have been 500 feet thick in what is now Bemidji, and 2,000 feet thick at the Canadian border. (At its thickest, the Laurentide ice sheet was over two miles thick.) Although the Itasca Moraine includes some rugged terrain, it is actually small in comparison to the ice sheet that formed it.

Geologic time scales are equally immense. Many of the rocks (such as the fossil-rich, white-colored limestone from the Winnipeg area) have been transported over 100 miles, and several (like the grey sandstone with unique pits of the Omarolluk formation of the Belcher Islands in Canada) have traveled over 1,000 miles. How can this be, if glaciers only flow a few feet per year? The ice sheet that formed the Itasca Moraine existed for over 10,000 years and continually incorporated rocks into its mass and transported them southward.

There is one last lesson in learning to successfully read the geology of the NCT—your imagination. Envision great blocks of ice broken off of a glacier, then imagine the glacier, as it inches along, burying those blocks with sediment. Many geologists call the resulting landforms "inverse topography." For example, the lakes of the Lake George area were once large blocks of ice buried by glacial sediment. As these blocks melted, along with the glacier, they left behind a void or depression that became a "kettle" or "ice block" lake.

In a second variation of glacial topography, the Milton Lake esker near Remer is made up of river sediment that was deposited in a tunnel at the base of the ice sheet. Once the glacier melted, these river deposits were left standing above the surrounding area as a beautiful winding ridge.

Finally, in a third glacial topography variation, the series of small, parallel ridges that the NCT crosses southwest of Walker are the result of a collision of two ice margins, one flowing southward and the other flowing southwestward from the Lake Superior region. Can you envision the power of the geologic forces so many years ago?

The geologist and adventurer John Wesley Powell wrote: "All about me are interesting geologic records. The book is open and I read as I run." The glacial landscape that is crossed by the NCT is both beautiful and inspiring. Take time to "read" its history—it may help you enjoy your hike even more. Enjoy the trail!

*James Cotter is a Distinguished Teaching Professor of Geology at the University of Minnesota, Morris, where he has taught for thirty years. His field of expertise is Glacial Geology and he has conducted research on glacial deposits throughout North America, Ireland, Italy, Brazil, and Antarctica. In 1990, Cotter was awarded the University of Minnesota, Morris, Alumni Award for outstanding contributions to undergraduate education and, in 2000, was awarded the Presidential Award for Excellence in Science Mentoring (PAESMEM Award) by President Clinton. Cotter regularly brings his students to the NCT to study glacial deposits.*

## Tamarack and Chickadee
**Anne Dunn**

It happened in the long ago that Tamarack was evergreen, like the red pine. The Ojibwe say its beautiful, green, cone-shaped form graced the woodlands all through the winter.

One day during a terrible storm, Chickadee was injured. He was nearly dead from cold. The little bird struggled through the blowing snow until he stood at the foot of the tall Tamarack.

"Please drop some of your lower branches to shelter me from the storm," Chickadee cried. "Oh, that I might live!"

"I should say not," Tamarack quickly replied. "I did not grow beautiful green branches to break them off for you. I'm sorry, but I prefer to keep my fine form."

So Chickadee pulled his small battered body to the root of the tall Red Pine.

"Please drop some of your lower branches to shelter me from the storm," Chickadee cried. "Oh, that I might live!"

Red Pine pitied Chickadee and quickly dropped enough branches to shelter the little bird.

Now, Great Spirit saw what had happened and said to Red Pine, "From this day, you will always drop your lower branches to remind others that you paid a high price so a small bird could live."

When Tamarack heard this, he was glad he had not dropped any of his branches.

"Now," he thought, "I will keep my fine form."

"Yes, Tamarack," Great Spirit said, "you will keep your fine form. But from this day, your needles will begin to turn brown, then they will fall off. Soon you will die and be forgotten."

Tamarack wept. "The punishment is too harsh," he cried.

Chickadee had crept out from under the red pine branches lying on the snow. He pitied Tamarack.

"Oh, Great Spirit," Chickadee prayed. "Please don't let Tamarack die and be forgotten."

"Very well," Great Spirit said to Chickadee.

Then turning to Tamarack, Great Spirit added, "You will not die and be forgotten. But every autumn, your fine green needles will turn brown and fall off. Then you will stand naked in the forest all winter, as a reminder to others that it is always better to be kind and merciful than it is to be vain and selfish."

*From* When Beaver Was Very Great: Stories to Live By. *Anne M. Dunn is an Anishinabe Grandmother Storyteller.*

*Majestic pines shade the NCTpath. Photo by Matthew R. Davis.*

# Chapter 2
# Safety on the Trail

Generally speaking, hiking is a safe activity. There are, however, things that NCT hikers should be aware of to ensure that their safety remains at the forefront of their experience on the NCT in Minnesota.

**Calling for Help**

Dial 911 on your cell phone. If you do not have a signal, move farther along or back on the trail and try again. The signal is usually stronger close to state or county highways, so move in that direction if possible. Sometimes moving a short distance along the trail can change reception. If the signal is weak, try sending a text message to someone—texts sometimes go through when calls will not. Keep trying. Use the maps in this guide to relate your location to the 911 dispatcher. GPS coordinates are included in trailhead descriptions.

**Injury**

Hikers should always carry a basic first aid kit with them—even on day hikes—because injuries can occur from trips, falls, and other accidents. People who spend significant amounts of time on the trail should consider taking part in a wilderness emphasis First Aid course or reading one of the many excellent books on this topic.

**Staying in Touch**

You should leave a detailed itinerary of your hike with someone you trust back at home and ask that person to contact the local authorities if you don't check in with them after your hike. Be sure they know where you are, who your contacts are for the hike and how reach them.

Sample hike itinerary to leave with family or friends:
I'll be hiking the North Country Trail from XYZ trailhead to XYZ trailhead from X-day through X-day.
If you think I am lost or might need help, contact the XYZ Ranger Station at (555) 555-5555 or the XYZ Sheriff's Department at (555) 555-5555.

- Day 1 – Park at the XYZ trailhead and hike to ABC campsite
- Day 2 – Hike from ABC campsite to DEF campsite
- Day 3 – Hike from DEF campsite to GHI trailhead and get picked up by Jane Doe (555) 555-5555.
- A map showing my hike section is found at www.xxx.xxx (or is attached).

## Weather

Mother Nature can throw a lot of challenging weather at hikers in northern Minnesota in all months of the year. Winter obviously brings frigid temperatures, dangerously cold windchills, and winter storms. Spring and fall can bring sudden, drastic changes in temperatures as weather systems move in or out of the area. These seasons also provide the greatest chance for hypothermia-inducing cold rains. Summer can bring high temperatures, high humidity, bright sunshine, and powerful thunderstorms. Hikers need to be especially aware of electrical storms and the dangers posed by lightning. The best place to ride out an electrical storm is in a low spot, away from tall trees or high spots. Ditch your trekking poles and other metal objects at least 100 feet away from where you are. If lightning is striking immediately around you, the safest position is a low crouch on the balls of your feet with your feet together and your head lowered. Do not lie flat on the ground.

NCT hikers should consult the local weather forecast before embarking upon a hike and should change their plans respective to significant storms or extreme temperatures. Consider always bringing along a change of clothing, a winter hat (yes, even in the summer), and good rain gear.

## Wildlife

The NCT passes through some pretty remote country and the animals that live there are wild and generally not habituated to humans. Because of this, wildlife should exhibit a healthy fear of you if you are lucky enough to encounter them while on the trail. Fortunately, there are few animals that pose actual threats to hikers in northern Minnesota.

Care should especially be taken to protect oneself from black bears—present all along the NCT in north-central Minnesota. Never put yourself between a sow and her cubs. In fact, if you encounter cubs on the trail you should assume that their mom is nearby and you should quickly depart. When backpacking and in camp, you should be extra careful with your food as this is the most common cause for human/bear interactions. Ideally, you would cook, eat your meals, and wash your dishes at least 200 feet from your tent. In addition, you should either hang your food bag in a tree (at least 15 feet from the ground and 10 feet from the tree's trunk) or use a bear-proof canister.

Mountain lions or cougars do not officially reside in Minnesota although several wandering young males have been spotted in recent years. There have not been any recent documented cases of cougar attacks in Minnesota. If you were to be lucky enough to encounter a cougar along the NCT, you should face the animal directly, make yourself big, and make lots of motion and noise. If attacked, you should attempt to fight back by hitting the animal in the face and head. Do not play dead or attempt to run away.

**Poison Ivy,** *Toxicodendron rydbergii*

Hikers should know how to identify poison ivy (rule of thumb: "leaves of three, let it be") and must take care to avoid it on the NCT. Although it is an allergen, it is not deadly. Still, as most people know, exposure to the plant's oils can cause major skin irritation that can easily ruin a hike. For more information, visit the National Institute of Health website <www.nih.gov> and search for poison ivy, or check with your pharmacist. If you are exposed to the plant's oils, and you are near a lake or river, washing with copious amounts of water within ten minutes of exposure can dilute the oil and reduce the severity of a reaction. A cold or hot poultice made of dirt or cloth can bring temporary relief from itching.

*Toxicodendron radicans, Poison Ivy. Sometimes called Western Poison Ivy. Drawing by Pearson Scott Foresman*

Learn more about poison ivy at medical websites and from *A Field Guide to Poison Ivy, Poison Oak and Poison Sumac,* Falcon Guides. (Disclaimer: The *Field Guide* is written by co-editor for this guide, Susan Carol Hauser.)

## Bugs, Ticks, and Tick-borne Illnesses

The prevalence of bugs (mosquitoes and deer flies) and ticks (wood ticks and deer ticks) can be one of the biggest challenges on the NCT in the spring, summer, and fall. Generally speaking, these are the seasons when these critters are at their worst in northern Minnesota.

- Mosquitoes make their appearance typically in mid-late May to early June (depending upon spring's arrival) and usually wane by mid-late summer.
- Deer and horse flies typically make their appearance in early-mid July and stick around through early fall.
- Ticks are typically active beginning right after snow melt through mid-summer, and then again in late summer and early fall (i.e., during the seasons when they take a blood meal from a mammal).

Tick-borne Diseases: When to Seek Medical Care

While mosquitoes and flies can be a nuisance, ticks can infect humans with serious diseases including Lyme disease, human anaplasmosis, babesiosis, Rocky Mountain spotted fever, Powassan virus, and tularemia. If you become ill after hiking in the woods, review your symptoms carefully. If no one else has similar symptoms, seek medical care. If you have left Minnesota, inform your medical professional that you have been hiking in tick country. Do not delay seeking treatment. With Lyme disease, early symptoms abate and then return later and are harder to treat. For more information on tick-borne diseases, visit the Minnesota Department of Health website <www.health.state.mn.us/divs/idepc/dtopics/tickborne/diseases.html>. For additional information on ticks, visit < www.cdc.gov/lyme/prev/on_people.html>.

Precautions against Bugs

Carry a headnet, an item that is considered essential in June, July, and August by experienced Minnesota hikers. Flies and mosquitoes sometimes command the air. Use bug repellant.

What Kind of Tick Is It?

Black-legged tick (*Ixodes scapularis*), also called deer tick and Lyme tick: In its larval (first) stage, it is essentially invisible but does not usually transmit germs. In its nymph (second) stage, it is visible but is much smaller than a sesame seed. In its adult (third) stage, it is usually about the size of a sesame seed or smaller with a brown collar on a reddish body

American dog tick (*Dermacentor variabilis*), also called wood tick: Usually larger than a sesame seed, it is a bit rounder in appearance than a black-legged tick and browner in color. A male has "suspenders": two series of white dots down the back. A female has a "necklace": a half-circle of dots on the shoulders (as in this image). The black-legged tick does not have these dotted features. (Images courtesy of the Centers for Disease Control <www.cdc.gov>)

Precautions against Ticks

- Wear light-colored long pants and shirt, so you can see the ticks.
- Tuck your pant legs into your socks while hiking, to cover your skin.
- Wear gaiters, to keep ticks from getting under your clothing.
- Stay on the trail.
- No matter what you use for repelling ticks, check yourself for ticks, especially embedded ticks, each day after finishing your hike. Check at your hairline, behind your ears, at your waistline, sock line, and armpits.
- Scientists have determined that the mouth parts of a black-legged (deer) tick must be embedded in a human for 24–36 hours in order to pass on the bacterium that causes Lyme disease. If you remove an imbedded tick within that time, you would be unlikely to have contracted the germ.
- If you find an embedded tick, do not squeeze it when you remove it. Use a tweezers to grasp it close to the skin and pull firmly outward.
- If you can, determine if the tick is a wood tick or a black-legged (deer) tick. Lyme disease is carried by the black-legged tick.
- Spray your clothing with Permethrin, Buzz Off or a similar solution containing Permethrin, or purchase clothing items pretreated with Permethrin. Permethrin is a good tick repellant and pesticide. DEET (up to 30% solution) also provides some protection against ticks.
- If you have been bitten by a black-legged tick, consult with your medical professional about precautionary treatment.
- Learn more about ticks at medical websites and from *A Field Guide to Ticks*, Falcon Guides. (Disclaimer: The *Field Guide* is written by co-editor for this guide, Susan Carol Hauser.)

## Dangerous People

People can be one of the biggest threats to your safety while on/near the NCT. Hikers should be aware of other people on the trail and "trust your gut instincts." Nearly all NCT users are harmless but the potential exists for encounters with odd individuals. Carry yourself confidently, don't divulge too much information about your plans ("I plan to camp at point X tonight"), and don't hike alone if you can avoid it.

## Hunting and Trapping

Hunting and trapping are institutions in northern Minnesota ... particularly hunting whitetail deer. The biggest danger posed to NCT hikers occurs during the one- to three-week deer rifle season in November. (See below for information on tribal hunting seasons on Reservation land.) Hikers should avoid the NCT during this time and should absolutely wear blaze orange if they choose to go out on the trail.

There are a variety of other fall hunting seasons that impact the NCT in north-central Minnesota from September through January, including turkey, grouse, and bear seasons.

For more information on State of Minnesota hunting and trapping seasons, visit www.dnr.state.mn.us/hunting/index.html. For hunting season dates in the Tamarac National Wildlife Refuge call the Refuge: 218-847-2641.

### Hunting Allowed

Hunting is allowed on most of the NCT in Minnesota. Hikers should wear the required amount of blaze orange during the fall while enjoying the NCT. This includes a blaze orange vest, an orange baseball cap or winter hat, and possibly a blaze orange bandana tied to your daypack/backpack. As noted above, it is best to stay off the NCT during the one- to three-week deer season in November.

### Tribal Hunting Seasons

There are special hunting and trapping regulations (including longer deer rifle seasons) that apply within the White Earth and Leech Lake Ojibwe Reservation boundaries. This includes the NCT roughly from Tamarac NWR to Itasca State Park and from Cass County 50 to the Boy River. Hikers should wear the requisite blaze orange while using the NCT in these areas starting in early September and lasting through January 1st. For detailed information on these seasons, visit whiteearth.com/ and www.llojibwe.org/.

## Water Sources and Treatment

Water is necessary for human life and even more necessary during participation in active sports like hiking or backpacking. Most hikers need to drink at least a couple of liters or quarts of water each day while hiking and more for summertime hiking when a lot of water is lost through sweating.

---

**Consuming Water on the NCT in Minnesota**
Unless signed potable (safe to consume), all water sources found along the NCT should be considered non-potable and the water should be treated to avoid water-borne illnesses (e.g. giardia, cryptosporidium, etc.). Snow and rainwater are generally safe to consume without treatment.

---

Fortunately, water is abundant along the NCT in north-central Minnesota. However, these are not water spigots from which potable (drinkable) water flows. The typical water sources found along the NCT include lakes, beaver ponds, wetlands, and streams. Snow is another popular source of water for winter trail use when other sources are frozen solid and inaccessible.

Water obtained from these sources must be treated before drinking because of the risk for water-borne pathogens. These include bacteria, viruses, and protozoa. Common ones are giardia and cryptosporidium, both of which cause a very unpleasant gastrointestinal illness. Water treatment options include:
- Boiling
- Use of iodine
- Use of chlorine
- Filtering or purifying
- Treating with ultraviolet light

Each method has its advantages and drawbacks. For more information, visit <www.americanhiking.org/water-purification>.

## What to Carry with You: Ten Essentials

The American Hiking Society (www.americanhiking.org/10essentials) recommends ten items that should be carried on every hike, no matter its length or familiarity with the trail:
- Appropriate footwear
- Map and compass/GPS
- Extra water and a way to purify water
- Extra food
- Rain gear and extra clothing
- Safety items—something to start a fire with, a light, and a whistle
- First-aid kit
- Knife or multi-purpose tool
- Sunscreen and sunglasses
- Daypack or backpack

Also recommended by the NCTA in Minnesota:
- Space (emergency) blanket
- Garbage bag (for hauling out trash, for lining your backpack during a rainstorm, or for use as an emergency rain poncho)
- Bug spray and/or headnet (for summer hiking)

*A campsite alongside the NCT in the Chippewa National Forest. Photo by Matthew R. Davis.*

# Chapter 3
# Maplewood and Itasca State Parks

*The NCT in Minnesota passes through numerous state parks. Maplewood (Chapter 4) and Itasca (Chapter 5) are featured here. For information on the many state parks between the Chippewa National Forest near Remer and Jay Cooke State Park, check out resources listed in Chapter 6.*

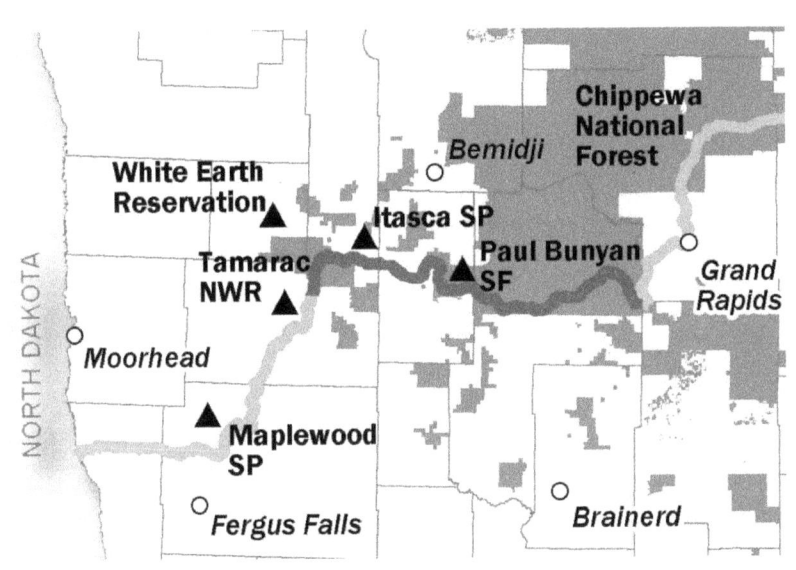

**For Visitors to Maplewood and Itasca State Parks**
- Campers and day-users are invited and encouraged to check out the NCT for new and delightful hiking experiences. The NCT connects with other trails within both parks.
- Visitors are encouraged to check out loop trails connected to the NCT. Appendix D identifies each loop's map number. The maps are followed by driving directions to the trailheads. Loop trails offer easy-on/easy-off circle pathways that bring hikers back to

47

their cars. These trails vary in length from approximately 0.5 mile to 4 miles. In general, the terrain is level with some gentle undulations. Loop trails are an excellent way to sample the NCT in Minnesota. Appendix D: Loop Trails includes an "I Hiked It!" checklist. How many loops can you complete during your stay in the north woods of Minnesota?

**The Editors Recommend**
- Appendix D: Loop Trails. Learn about modest hikes with easy access and direct return to your vehicle.
- Appendix H: Meetup groups, Social Media, Contacts. From photos and the words of hikers, discover what it looks and feels like to hike the NCT in Minnesota.

## Quick Look: Services at the Parks
- Maplewood: Park office, interpretive exhibits, campsites, campgrounds, camper cabins, RV sites, loop trails, boat rentals, and a gift shop.
- Itasca: Most of the services found in a small town, including restaurants, camping supplies, campsites, campgrounds, lodging, interpretive exhibits, boat and bike rentals, gift shops.

## Maplewood State Park and the North Country Trail

www.dnr.state.mn.us/state_parks/maplewood/
- 5.5 NCT miles
- Due north of Fergus Falls and southeast of Moorhead
- GPS Coordinates, Park Office: 46.538643, -95.953164

## Quick Stats, DNR
- 10,279 acres
- 119,317 annual visits
- 19,109 overnight visits

Maplewood State Park is located at the intersection of tall grass prairie and deciduous (hardwood) forest biomes. The North Country Trail's route runs south to north through the park. See Maps 1 and 1-A for routing details.

The idea of establishing a park in the area goes back to 1923 when it was originally proposed at the state legislature. A later study concluded that this hilly, lake-dotted terrain was better suited to recreation than to farming. In 1963 the park became a reality when Maplewood State Park was established by the Minnesota Legislature.

The varied terrain of Maplewood hosts 150 breeding bird species, 50 species of mammals, and 25 kinds of reptiles and amphibians. The park also hosts sites for colonial nesting birds, including American coots. Human habitation in the area dates back at least 6,000 years. Artifacts found in the park give evidence of both prairie and woodland cultures. Most

---

**Fall Colors**

Maplewood State Park is one of the best places in Minnesota for viewing spectacular fall colors. The many hills are intensely covered with hardwoods, including maples, of course, that turn brilliantly gold and red during the autumn transition. Climb or drive to a hilltop and enjoy the scene!

---

*Maplewood State Park lives up to its name with summer vistas and autumn views, as in this scene. Photo by Matthew R. Davis.*

artifacts, however, indicate that the site was occupied 900 to 1,200 years ago and that the residents were primarily hunters during that period.

Maplewood lies on a series of hills in the Leaf Hills Landscape Region near the eastern edge of the level Red River Valley. These hills, part of the Alexandria Glacial Moraine, were deposited during the last ice age. The Lake Lida basin was probably formed when the last glacier retreated 20,000 years ago and left ice stranded in the valley. The ice melted, exposing the basin and allowing the present lake to form.

Amid the farmlands that surround the park, Maplewood sits on a series of tree-covered hills—the highest approach 1,600 feet—that provide visitors with striking vistas of small, clear lakes nestled in deep valleys. Wildflower lovers will find flowers and grasses representative of both the prairies and forests. Spring through fall, the park is dressed with displays of trillium, hepatica, bloodroot, yellow lady's slipper, wild onion, prairie rose, and showy milkweed. (*Adapted from* www.dnr.state.mn.us/state_parks/maplewood/)

---

**Stay safe during hunting seasons!**
Avoid hiking the NCT during rifle seasons, wear blaze orange all through the fall, and check for hunting season dates at www.dnr.state.mn.us/state_parks/hunting.html.

---

## Itasca State Park and the North Country Trail

www.dnr.state.mn.us/state_parks/itasca/
- 9.4 NCT miles
- Southwest of Bemidji and north of Park Rapids (not on above map)
- Jacob V. Brower Visitor Center, GPS Coordinates: 47.194586, -95.165115

## Quick Stats, DNR
- 33,235 acres
- 550,599 annual visits
- 107,200 overnight visits

*Hernando DeSoto Lake, Itasca State Park. Photo by Bart Smith.*

## Itasca State Park: Headwaters of the Mississippi River

Deane L. Johnson

Itasca State Park is located deep in Minnesota's north woods. The North Country Trail runs west to east through the park.

Park visitors and North Country Trail hikers have much to enjoy in the park, which protects over 33,000 acres of forestland, 49 miles of hiking trails, 16 miles of paved biking trails, and 28 miles of groomed cross-country ski trails. The park holds constructed treasures such as Douglas Lodge, dedicated in 1905, the Forest Inn, and other classic log and stone structures that the Civilian Conservation Corps (CCC) built from 1933–1942. Although most of the half-million visitors per year use the recreational facilities on the developed east side of Lake Itasca, the rest of the park is dominated by backcountry trails and wild places. Wilderness Drive loops around the interior of the park, enclosing the Itasca Wilderness Sanctuary Scientific and Natural Area, where natural processes are left on their own to the fullest extent possible. The NCT traverses the backcountry area on the south side of the park, passing through extensive stands of old-growth pines interspersed with mature maple, basswood, aspen, and birch that sprouted a century ago in logged-over areas.

The Minnesota Legislature established Itasca State Park in 1891. The timber industry, the driving economic force in Minnesota at the time, hotly contested the bill, which passed by a single vote and included only a minimal 60-day appropriation. Jacob V. Brower, surveyor and archeologist, completed the initial survey of the watershed of the Mississippi headwaters and fought vigorously with his time, political connections, and his own financial resources to acquire land and protect the stands of old-growth red and white pine and oak. In the end, despite extensive logging from 1901 through 1919, over 40 percent of the old-growth trees, some dating back 300 years, remain intact.

Itasca is part of the Pine Moraine biome, a mixed hardwood and pine forest covering the end moraine of a glacier that stagnated for centuries before it finally receded more than 11,000 years ago. Within Itasca's boundaries, the glacier left behind a varied terrain of hills, wetlands, and over 100 small lakes. Located near hardwood forest and prairie to the west, Itasca has great diversity of plant and animal species within its boundaries, many of which depend on its undisturbed expanses of virgin forest.

### Finding the Lodge, Campgrounds, Headwaters, and Services

*See also Maps 13 and 13-A, page 109.*

Take time to explore Itasca State Park and to enjoy the variety of experiences that it offers:

To get to Douglas Lodge (open Memorial Day into early October) and Jacob V. Brower Visitor Center (open year-round) from the NCT, entering the park from the west: take Deer Park Trail 4 miles northeast to the lodge and the center. On the way, watch for the Aiton Heights Fire Tower, 0.5 mile west of Deer Park Trail. It provides a panoramic view from 100 feet above one of the highest hills in the park.

*A campsite with shelter on the NCT. Photo by Matthew R. Davis.*

To get to Douglas Lodge and Jacob V. Brower Visitor Center, entering the park from the east: take the Ozawindib Trail 3 miles north to the lodge and the center.

From Douglas Lodge, use a State Park map or Map 13-A in this guide to explore the many sites and sights at Itasca, including:

- Brower Trail that skirts Lake Itasca and wends through the iconic sights of Preacher's Grove and Peace Pipe Vista
- Bear Paw Campground, register at the Campground Office. Some campsites can be reserved, but others are first-come, first-served, including several walk-in tent sites. Showers and indoor facilities are available except in winter, when Bear Paw is closed.
- Pine Ridge Campground, open all year
- Lodging at Douglas Lodge or in one of many cabins
- Mississippi Headwaters Hostel
- Swimming beach, picnic grounds
- Bike rentals, camping supply shop, gift shops.

**Do not forget!**
Walk to the headwaters where you can teeter across a submerged rock "dam" or walk across a split-log bridge and say, "I walked across the Mississippi River!"

*Deane L. Johnson grew up in Grand Forks, North Dakota, and has lived and traveled throughout northern Minnesota. Drawn to the lakes and woods of Park Rapids, Minnesota, in 1980, he has lived there ever since, and has hiked the NCT during all seasons. Retired from family medicine, he was a founding member of the Jackpine Writers' Bloc and a co-owner of Beagle Books of Park Rapids with his wife, Jill. He supplied the photographs for Jill's book,* Little Minnesota: 100 Towns Around 100, *and is the writer and photographer of a guidebook to Itasca State Park, The Best of Itasca: A Guide to Minnesota's Oldest State Park, Adventure Publications. Deane is a member of the Itasca Moraine Chapter of the NCTA.*

# Chapter 4
# Fort Abercrombie, North Dakota, to Tamarac National Wildlife Refuge

*For alerts, corrections, updated maps and additional map resources:*
*northcountrytrail.org/mnguidebook/.*

**Distance: 80.8 Miles**
**Route:** Mostly road walking with some off-road trail hikes.

◄ **Map 1**
**Fort Abercrombie State Park, North Dakota Border to Park Office in Maplewood State Park, Minnesota**

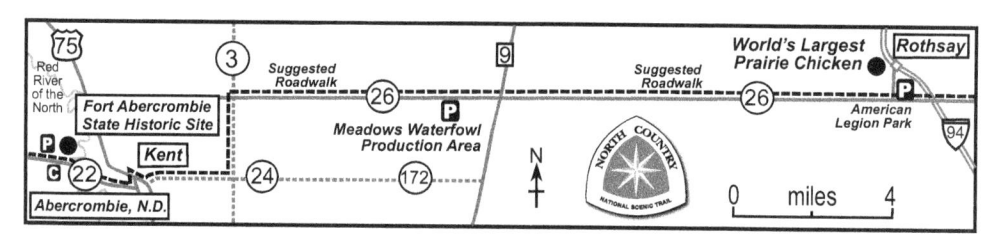

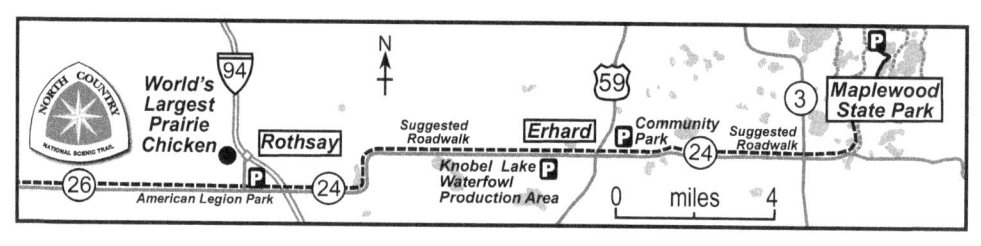

**Distance:** 43.9 Miles
**Official Route**

The NCT's official route for this section is defined in the National Park Service's 1982 Comprehensive Plan for the Management and Use. It calls for eventually using abandoned railroad grades from Breckenridge east to Fergus Falls, then north to Erhard (as well as from Abercrombie south to Wahpeton).

### Recommended Alternative Route

The NCTA recommends an alternative route for the NCT section and thru-hikers. It takes a straighter route from Abercrombie to Erhard and then on to Maplewood State Park. This route utilizes some off-road trails, and overnight camping is available. Hikers will pass by large farms where sugar beets, corn, soybeans, sunflowers, and/or potatoes are grown using large agricultural equipment (e.g. combines that are 50 feet wide). Between Rothsay and Erhard, hikers will also notice that small pothole lakes, remnants of the last glacier in the area, become more abundant. They are the beginning of the "lake belt" that is characteristic of northwestern Minnesota.

*Sky and land both offer room for reflection on a road walk section of the NCT from Fort Abercrombie, North Dakota, to Rothsay, Minnesota. Photo by Todd "Tman" McMahon.*

### ◀ Map 1A
### Maplewood State Park

**Distance:** 5.5 miles
**Maplewood State Park Information**

- Maplewood State Park Office, 218-863-8383 or maplewood.statepark@state.mn.us
- Maplewood State Park website at www.dnr.state.mn.us/state_parks/maplewood/

- Maplewood State Park Summer Park Map files.dnr.state.mn.us/maps/state_parks/spk00229_summer.pdf
- Maplewood State Park Winter Park Map files.dnr.state.mn.us/maps/state_parks/spk00229_winter.pdf

**Campsites**

- 71 tent sites
- Drinking water, showers, toilets
- Camper cabins

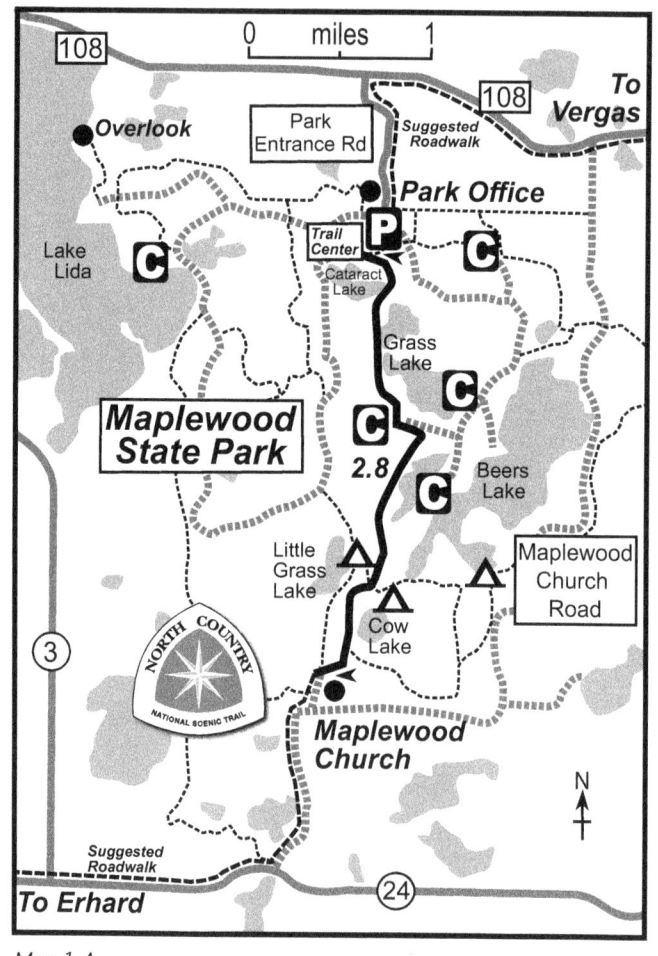

*Map 1-A.*

### Services

See Appendix C for services and amenities available in these towns.
- Abercrombie, ND
- Rothsay
- Off-trail: Detroit Lakes and Pelican Rapids

### Map 1A Mile-by-Mile

State Park's south boundary / Maplewood Church Road
- GPS Coordinates: 46.486648,-95.962906
- Driving Directions: From Erhard, east on CR-24 for 6.5 miles.
- Details: There is no parking at this intersection. The gravel road is plowed in winter from CR-24 to the church.

### The Trail

The NCT leaves the CR-24 road walk and heads north into Maplewood State Park. Hikers have an option of walking the gravel road north for 1.3 miles to the Maplewood Church or walking on a hiking/horseback riding (summer) and snowmobile trail (winter) that closely parallels the road. The trail is approximately 1.5 miles long. At the intersection, look for a trail heading off to the northwest and then an immediate right turn. *Note: this trail cannot be certified as the NCT route because of the motorized winter use by snowmobiles.*

### 0.0 (3.1) Miles

Maplewood Church
- GPS Coordinates: 46.502753,-95.958104
- Details: The Maplewood Church is an active country church that meets on Sundays most of the year.

### The Trail

The NCT leaves the church heading north, passes around a park gate and immediately turns right onto a trail (old road) heading downhill and east. The road quickly turns into a narrow trail, passes over a small bridge and crosses an open field with a small lake to the south.

## 0.2 (2.9) Miles

Trail Junction, water

### The Trail

The trail re-enters the woods and then comes to a juncture with the Park's Cow Lake loop hiking trail. Turn to the left (heading north) heading through a mixed hardwood forest and start climbing with views of Cow Lake off to the east. Water is available from Cow Lake via the short spur trail heading east at this intersection.

## 0.6 (2.5) Miles

Trail Junction, Grass Lake campsite, side trail to Cow Lake campsite

### The Trail

The NCT reaches a confusing, four-way trail intersection and continues ahead (heading northeast—watch for blazes). A horseback/hiking trail runs north and southeast. Past this intersection the NCT winds over a couple of high hills and follows a ridge above Bass Lake strewn with boulders before descending very steeply (imagine going down that hill on cross-country skis). Hikers can catch a good view across Bass Lake from a dam before climbing to cross an old field that is reverting to forest.

### State Park Backcountry Campsites and Campgrounds

- The Grass Lake campsite is located immediately to the west at this intersection (privy, fire ring, log lean-to, picnic table).
- The Cow Lake campsite (privy, fire ring, picnic table) is located at the end of a short spur trail off the Cow Lake loop (horseback/hiking) trail that heads southeast, 0.2 mile from the intersection.
- Fees are charged and reservations are accepted for these very popular campsites. For more information on making campsite reservations, call 1-866-857-2757 (TTY: 952-936-4008), or visit www.dnr.state.mn.us/state_parks/reservations_campsite.html.

> Maplewood State Park's hilly terrain is part of the Leaf Hills Moraines, which are sometimes locally called the Leaf Mountains. These gravel deposits left by the last glaciers rise 100–350 feet above the surrounding landscape. According to nineteenth-century missionary Joseph Alexander Gilfillan, the Ojibwe name for the natural feature was Gaaskibag-wajiwan, which means "Rustling Leaf Mountains."

## 1.7 (1.4) Miles

Road intersection

### The Trail

The NCT reaches, turns left, and follows a gravel road leading west to the Knoll Loop Campground. Along the way, the NCT passes by the southern shore of Grass Lake before entering the campground loop (stick to the right). The campground features a water pump and a privy. Leaving the campground, look for signs for the Grass Lake Interpretive Trail / NCT heading northwest. The trail soon passes through an old field, passes by a spur trail to an overlook, and then descends a steep hill.

### Alert

Be careful on the short and hilly road walk as the road is narrow and is used by vehicles pulling campers and boat trailers.

### State Park Campgrounds

The Knoll Loop features vault toilets, 14 campsites (picnic table, fire ring, tent pad), and a Camper Cabin. More information is found at www.dnr.state.mn.us/state_parks/maplewood/camping.html.

## 2.0 (1.1) Miles

NCT leaves Road

### The Trail

The NCT leaves the campground in between campsite #53 and the

Camper Cabin on the Grass Lake Interpretive Trail and climbs an old road before entering an old field heading northwest. The NCT enters a young hardwood forest—watch for signs of beaver activity.

### 2.4 (0.7) Miles

Trail intersection, Grass Lake Interpretive Trail & Cataract Lake Trail

### The Trail

The NCT reaches a trail intersection where the Grass Lake Interpretive Trail turns right and the NCT continues straight ahead (heading north) on the Cataract Lake Trail through a mix of hardwood forest and old fields reverting to forest with a grassy wetland to the west.

### 2.7 (0.4) Miles

Trail intersection, Cataract Lake Loop Trail

### The Trail

The NCT reaches a trail intersection with the Cataract Lake Loop Trail. The NCT turns right passing around the east side of Cataract Lake before turning left and following along the shore of a grassy marsh and then climbing through an old field to the Trail Center.

### 3.1 (0.0) Miles

Trail Center Trailhead
- GPS Coordinates: 46.535691,-95.954373
- Details: The Trail Center trailhead features ample parking, a pit toilet, small warming building with nature information inside, and outdoor deck with picnic tables and a charcoal grill.

### The Trail

From the Trail Center (which is the end of the certified and signed/marked segment of the NCT within Maplewood) the trail's route follows the gravel park road and Park Entrance Roads heading north 1.2 miles to State Highway 108. Hikers will pass the Park Information Station/Office.

Another option with less road walking is to turn right at the trail intersection just east of the Park Office and head east 1.0 mile on the horseback riding/hiking/mountain biking and snowmobiling trail to Maplewood Church Road and then follow this gravel road north for 0.4 mile to Highway 108. *Note: the trail portion of this route cannot be certified as the NCT because of the winter use by snowmobiles.*

### Alert

The latter option will save 2.3 miles of paved road walking. Use caution on Minnesota 108: shoulders are narrow. From the intersection of Maplewood Church Road and Minnesota 108, it is 3.1 miles east to the intersection with County 41, which heads north toward Vergas.

State Park's northern boundary / Highway 108 and Park Entrance Road
- GPS Coordinates: 46.54994,-95.954484
- Details: The entrance road to Maplewood State Park is located 7.4 miles east of Pelican Rapids via State Highway 108.

## ◀ Map 2
## Maplewood State Park Office to Vergas

**Distance:** 14.1 Miles

**Route:** This road walk segment crosses the water-rich northeast corner of Otter Tail County, which has over 1,000 lakes. Along the way, the NCT passes through a mixture of small farms, small woodlots, tree plantations, and typical northern Minnesota rural scenery. Several of the lakes are surrounded by resorts, seasonal recreational cabins, and year-round lake homes.

### Services

See Appendix C for services and amenities available in these towns.
- Frazee
- Rochert
- Vergas
- Off-trail: Detroit Lakes

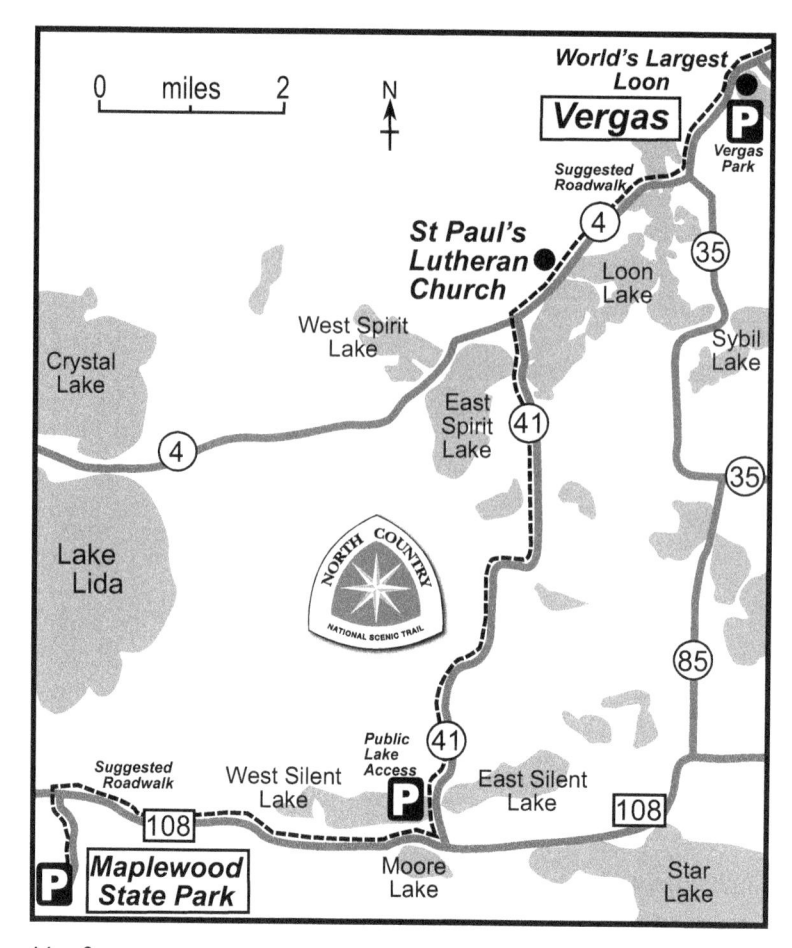

Map 2.

*The prairie gives way to forest on this road walk section between Rothsay and Frazee. Photo by Todd "Tman" McMahon.*

## Maplewood State Park to Tamarac National Wildlife Refuge

From Maplewood State Park, long-distance NCT hikers road walk for approximately 34 miles to reach the next off-road trail segment within Tamarac National Wildlife Refuge. Hikers should plan their own route to tie together the communities of Vergas, Frazee, and Rochert. The roads pass through an area studded with lakes making it a popular summer recreation area, particularly on weekends.

◀ **Map 3**
**Vergas to Frazee**

**Distance:** 8.4 Miles

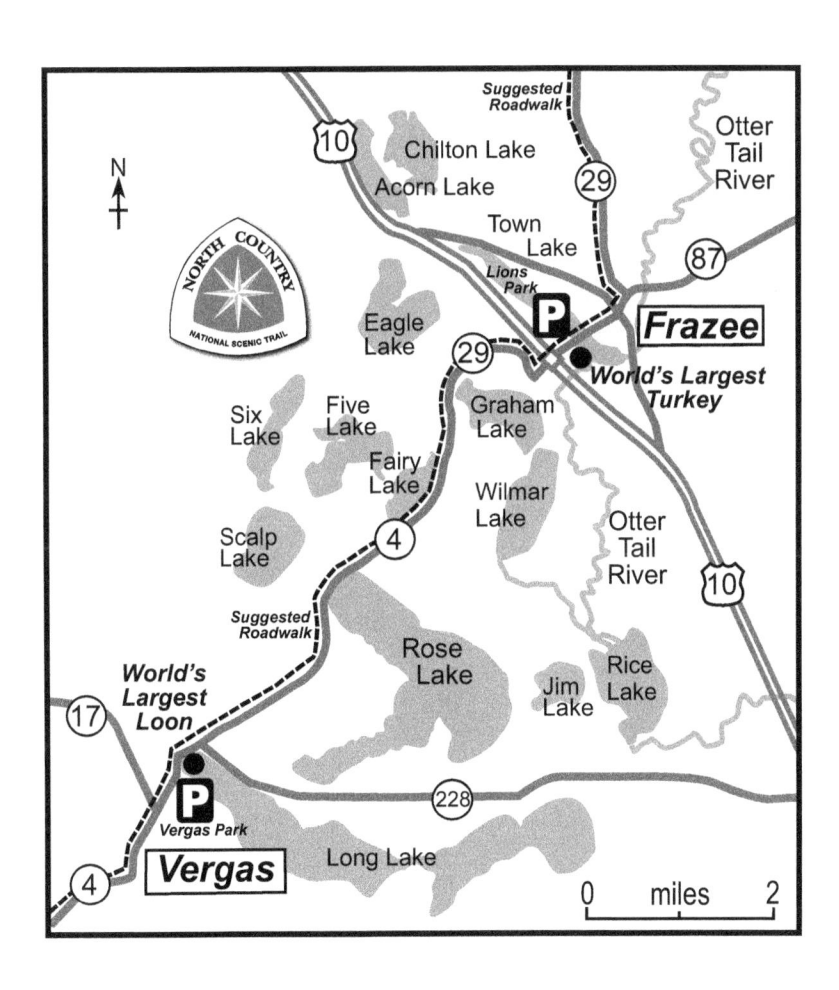

**Route:** This road walk segment crosses from Otter Tail County into the city of Frazee in Becker County and continues through more northern Minnesota rural scenery, including farm fields, small woodlots, and lakes. The NCT is marked through Frazee and several historic marker signs are included along its route. At one time, Frazee had the world's largest sawmill. White pine logs were floated south to the mill via the Otter Tail River.

## Services

See Appendix C for services and amenities available in these towns.
- Vergas
- Frazee
- Off-trail: Detroit Lakes

◀ **Map 4**
## Frazee to Tamarac National Wildlife Refuge

**Distance:** 14.4 Miles

Route: Frazee to "Four Corners" (intersection Otter Tail County 29 and Minnesota 34). This road walk segment passes through an agricultural area that becomes more heavily forested on the east side of the Otter Tail River. "Four Corners" (not a town) to Boundary Road Trailhead within Tamarac National Wildlife Refuge: Head north on Otter Tail County 29 for 1.8 miles, then east on Hubbel Pond Road. Follow Hubbel Pond Road for 3.2 miles where it becomes West Height of Land Drive. Follow West Height of Land Drive for 0.9 mile. Turn west on un-named township road (look for NCT signs) for 0.6 mile to NCT trailhead (GPS: 46.890371, -95.646685) at Boundary Road. Alert: This section is under development. For updates on routing of this section, visit northcountrytrail.org/trail/mnguidebook/.

## Services

See Appendix C for details on services and amenities available in these towns.
- Frazee
- "Four Corners" (not a town)
- Off-trail: Detroit Lakes

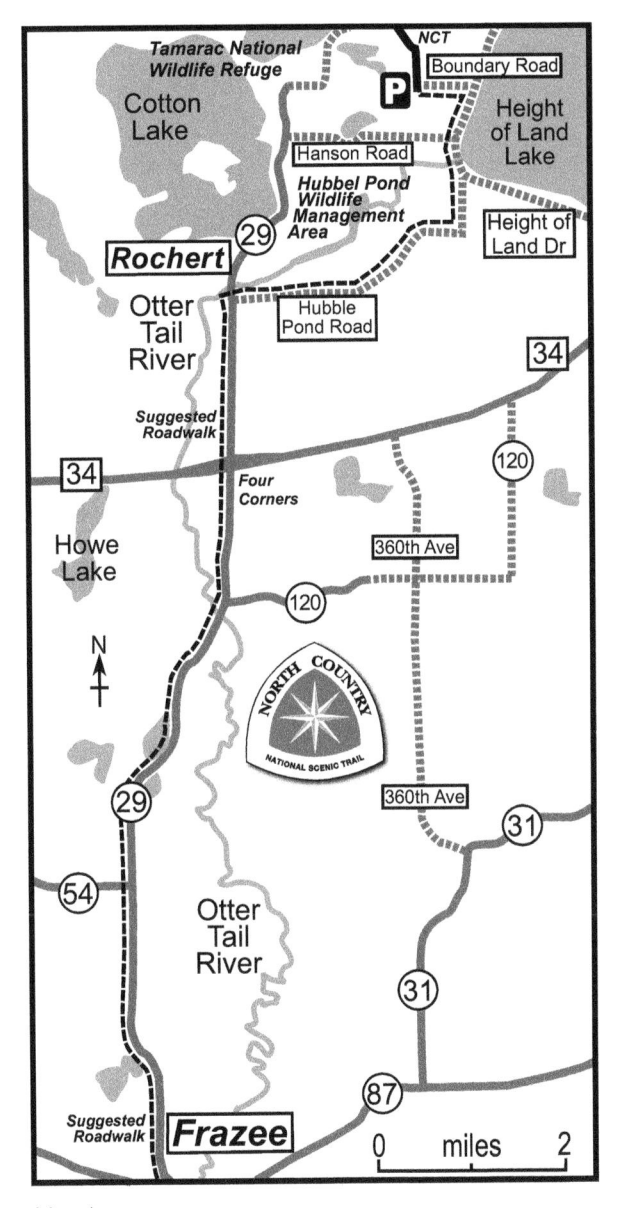

Map 4.

# Chapter 5
# Tamarac National Wildlife Refuge through Chippewa National Forest near Remer

*For alerts, corrections, updated maps and additional map resources:* northcountrytrail.org/mnguidebook/.

### Distance: 163.3 Miles

**Route:** Contiguous, off-road hiking trail through the center of northern Minnesota.

*Tamarac National Wildlife Refuge. See Appendix F: Restricted-Use Areas. See also Map 5-A, Optional Road Walk, Tamarack National Wildlife Refuge.*

### ◀ Map 5
### Boundary Road Trailhead to Blackbird Wildlife Drive Trailhead

### Distance

- 9.4 cumulative miles west to east, beginning to end of Map 5
- 163.3 reverse miles east to west, end of Map 29 to beginning of Map 5.

**Route:** The NCT rolls gently through the Tamarac National Wildlife Refuge. Occasional high ground offers excellent views of lakes, forest, and wetlands. Lowlands are sometimes bridged with puncheons. The forest ranges from old-growth pine to mixed hardwood to pine plantations. There is abundant wildlife, especially waterfowl during spring and fall migrations. In lowlands, watch for beaver dams, lodges, and runs.

### Campsites

Camping is not allowed in eastern National Wildlife Refuges. The NCT

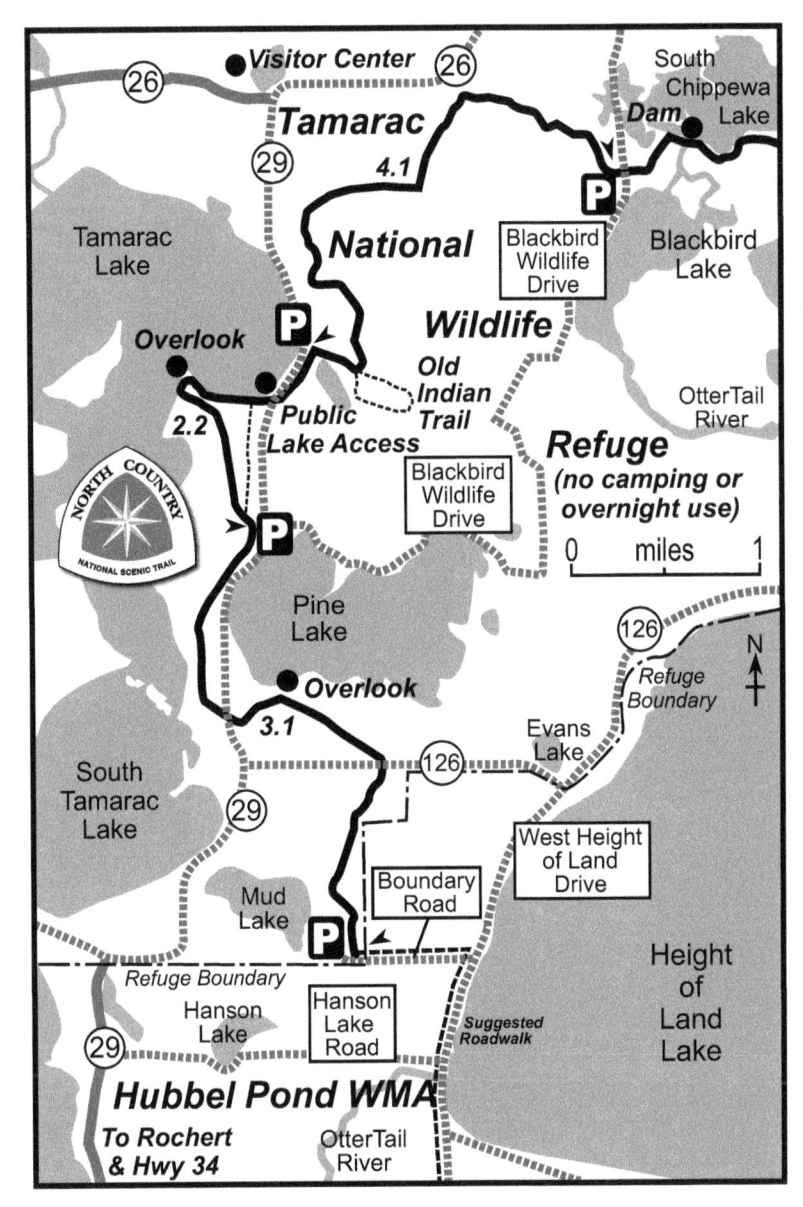

*Map 5. Boundary Road Trailhead to Blackbird Wildlife Drive Trailhead*

through Tamarac is 14 miles. Plan your overnights accordingly. The refuge is open from 5:00 a.m. to 10:00 p.m.

West boundary campsite, near Boundary Road: a wide spot at the end of the gravel road between the refuge and Hubbel Pond WMA. See Map 5 and Appendix B: Camping, Campsites, Campgrounds.

East boundary campsite: 390 feet northeast of the intersection of the

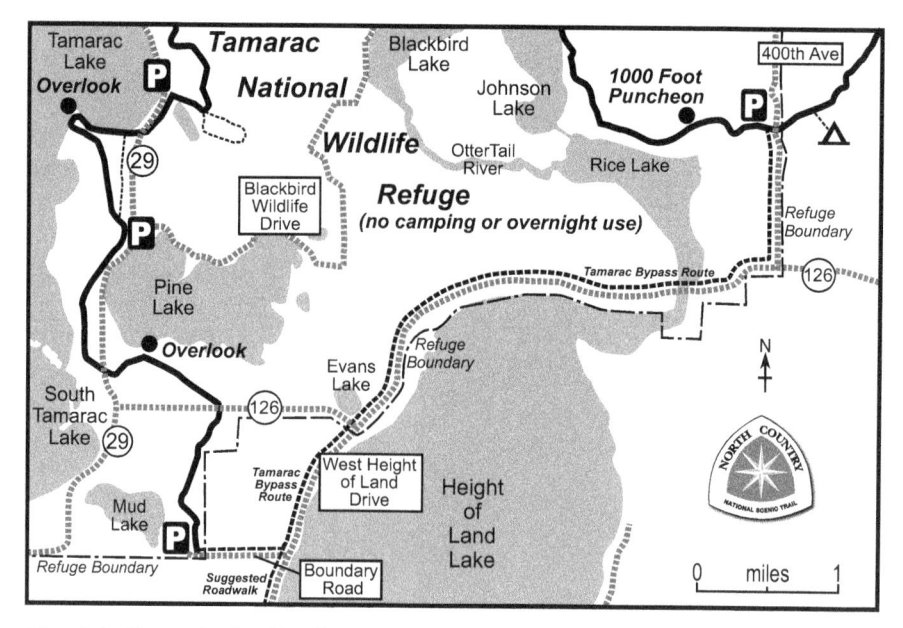

*Map 5-A. Alternative Road Walk*

NCT and 400th Avenue. See Map 7 and Appendix B: Camping, Campsites, Campgrounds.

See Alternative Road Walk, below, for a shorter passage through the Tamarac.

**Alternative Road Walk, Map 5-A**

Since camping is not allowed in the Tamarac, a 6.4-mile road walk is available. The road walk cuts off about 7.5 miles of 14 miles. From the NCT, take Boundary Road (Map 5) east to West Height of Land Drive; head north and pick up Becker County 126 east to 400th Avenue (Map 6); go north on 400th to the NCT.

### Services

See Appendix C for services and amenities available in these towns.
- Detroit Lakes

### Winter Use

- See Appendix E for winter parking at trailheads and groomed cross-country ski trails.

## Hunting Alerts
- See Chapter 2: Safety on the Trail.

## Water Sources and Treatment
- See Chapter 2: Safety on the Trail.

---

**Thru-Hiker "Strider"**
*From March 27 through October 13, 2013, Luke Jordan, trail name "Strider," thru-hiked the North Country Trail from North Dakota to New York, from the west terminus to the east terminus, 4,600 miles. He tells his story at www.stridernct.com/. The following excerpt is from his journal. Printed with permission from "Strider."*

**Sat. April 20**
**Trail Day 025**
**Miles hiked: 21**
**Private Home—Detroit Lakes, MN**
From Frazee it is a fourteen mile roadwalk to the beginning of the certified trail in Minnesota, and the beginning of a continuous segment of trail stretching from the southern border of Tamarac National Wildlife Refuge all the way to MN-6 just north of the town of Remer at the edge of the Chippewa National Forest. The roadwalk itself is very scenic; before long after leaving Frazee I can tell I am now in the northern woods. Pine trees are found in great abundance all around. I enjoy the smoked fish and the turkey jerky for lunch on the side of the road just before entering the refuge. I'm glad I stopped there on the side of a little hill free of snow because where I stand now, at the entrance to Tamarac National Wildlife Refuge, the trail is obstructed by at least two feet of snow. Oh boy, I will need the snowshoes for quite a while on this one.

---

## Map 5 Mile-by-Mile

### 0.0 (9.4) Miles

Trailhead, Boundary Road
- GPS Coordinates: 46.890349, -95.646726
- Driving Directions: From Detroit Lakes, go east on Minnesota 34 for 7.5 miles; then north on Becker County 29 for 1.8 miles and east on Hubbel Pond Road for 3.2 miles. Continue straight on West Height of Land Drive for 0.9 mile, then south onto the unnamed township road for 0.6 mile to trailhead.

*In Minnesota, the NCT footpath meanders through the northern forest. Photo by Matthew R. Davis.*

- Details: Parking area for 10 vehicles.

## The Trail

The NCT traverses open and wooded areas with some gentle elevations and changing vegetation, including fields, wetlands, forest groves, and pine plantations. It starts on and then exits an old logging road.

### 1.2 (8.2) Miles

Crossing, Becker County 126

### Winter Use

Groomed cross-country ski trail, Becker County 126 to near Tamarac Lake.

*See Map 5 for directions to the Visitor Center from the NCT.*

## What's at the Tamarac National Wildlife Refuge?
Visitor Center
35704 Becker 26, Rochert, MN 56578
GPS Coordinates: 46.117186384284004, -92.99793720245361

218-847-2641; tamarac@fws.gov
www.fws.gov/refuge/tamarac/

In addition to exquisite habitats and vibrant animal and plant life: Visitor Center, sanctuary area, hiking trails, picnic area, wildlife observation and photography, self-guided auto tour, fishing, hunting, cross-country skiing, bicycling, mushroom, nuts and berry picking, environmental education.

### Driving Directions
From Detroit Lakes, about 18 miles: Take Becker County 21/Richwood Road north to 270th Street/Becker County 26, about 10 miles; turn east on 270th to Visitor Center, about 7 miles. Watch signs to stay on 270th.

From Park Rapids, about 33 miles: Take Minnesota 34 west out of town to Minnesota 225, about 11 miles; turn north on Minnesota 225 and go about 9 miles to Ponsford; road name changes to Becker County 26 (270th street); continue for about 13 miles to the Visitor Center.

### The Trail

The NCT crosses Becker County 126 and enters the forest on a single-track trail heading northwest. It almost immediately intersects with Tamarac National Wildlife Refuge's Pine Lake cross-country ski trail, which it shares heading northwest through a hardwood forest. The NCT crosses through and by hardwood forest, pine plantations, and open fields. It also passes alongside an old road.

### 1.9 (7.5) Miles

Pine Lake
   Note: There is a public lake access at Pine Lake but it is open only for designated circumstances. General parking is not available.

### The Trail

From the public lake access, the NCT heads through a field with young white pine, passes by an old homestead, then reaches a forest road that it follows to a crossing of Becker County 29. (The Becker County 29 Trailhead is farther north.)

## 2.1 (7.3) Miles

Crossing, Becker County 29

### The Trail

The NCT crosses Becker County 29, heading west into mature hardwood forest still on the wide cross-country ski trail and roughly staying parallel to County 29 and skirting the edge of a wetland near the road.

## 3.1 (6.3) Miles

Trailhead, Becker County 29 at Pine Lake
- GPS Coordinates: 46.921017, -95.657498
- Driving Directions: From Detroit Lakes, head east on Minnesota 34 for 7.5 miles, then north on Becker County 29 for 6.9 miles. Large parking area is on the west.
- Details: Vault toilet and kiosk

### The Trail

The NCT passes alongside and through a variety of old fields, young forest, wetlands, and pine plantations. Watch for views of wetlands to the east and islands (designated wilderness) in Tamarac Lake, especially during spring and fall migrations.

## 4.3 (5.1) Miles

Overlook, Tamarac Lake, 1,800-foot Causeway

### The Trail

The bench at Tamarac Lake Overlook offers a great view looking west. From the overlook, the NCT follows the edge of the lake and then an ice ridge that runs parallel to and a few feet inland from the lake's edge. At the causeway the ski trail turns south and loops back to the Pine Lake Trailhead. The NCT trail continues onto an elevated, 1,800-foot causeway, a dirt structure built to protect potential cultural resources.

**Tamarac Lake Loop Trail**

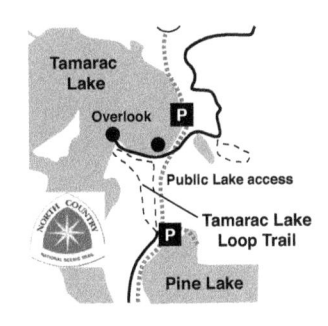

At the Becker County 29 Trailhead, go to the kiosk and continue west about 15 yards to the Tamarac Lake cross-country ski loop trail/NCT. Continue northward where the loop trail and NCT pass through open fields and intermittent forest of an old farm homestead. Views can be had of the large wetland located to the west, which is South Tamarac Lake. The trail quickly passes a spur trail going to the east and comes to a T intersection. Going to the left or west follows the loop trail and NCT. The trail to the right is the loop return trail. The joint trail eventually reaches the shore of Tamarac Lake. Going left or west the trail goes out to the Tamarac Lake Overlook. Going right or east the trail follows the lakeshore until it reaches the loop trail return to the south (small dotted line on Map 5). The NCT continues north-northeast and the loop return roughly follows Becker County 29 back to the trailhead. The terrain of the loop is mostly level.

---

The causeway ends at Becker County 29 where the trail continues to the north on the road past the boat landing. The NCT then goes into the forest on a single-track parallel to the road and soon intersects with the Old Indian Trail.

## 5.3 (4.1) Miles

Old Indian Trail Trailhead at Becker County 29
- GPS Coordinates: 46.938433, -95.654059
- Driving Directions: From Detroit Lakes, head east on Minnesota 34 for 7.5 miles, then north on Becker County 29 for 8.1 miles. Trailhead parking is to the west.
- Details: Parking for five vehicles; interpretive sign, historic marker; provides access to the NCT and to the Old Indian Trail loop.

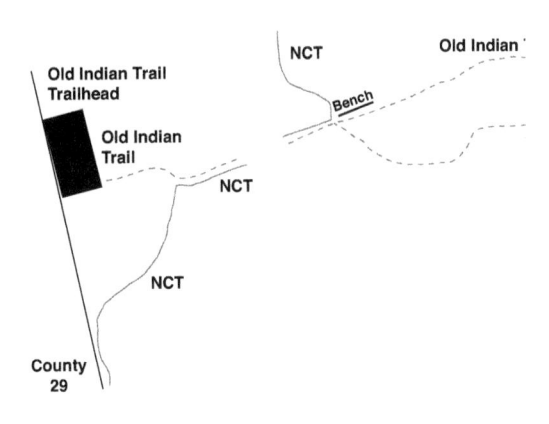

### The Trail

The NCT reaches the Old Indian Trail intersection. Heading northwest, the Old Indian Trail takes the NCT hiker 0.2 mile out to the Old Indian Trail trailhead on County 29. Turning east, the NCT follows the Old Indian Trail for 0.4 mile. Along the way, it undulates gently through old-growth deciduous, crowned trees. In summer, treetop foliage overlaps, shutting out sunlight and preventing dense undergrowth found elsewhere along the NCT.

> Ojibwe culture and beliefs tell that the Anishinabe, the Ojibwe people, migrated from the east to their current home in the upper Midwest by taking a route that is roughly followed by the North Country Trail.

### 5.7 (3.7) Miles

The NCT leaves the Old Indian Trail and heads north.

### The Trail

The NCT departs the Old Indian Trail at a point where the Old Indian loop starts by a bench. This is a potentially confusing intersection. Look for the NCT sign and blue blazes north on the NCT. The remainder of the Old Indian Trail, the loop, is scenic and worth a side trip.

### 7.5 (1.9) Miles

The NCT, now on an old trail, makes a 90-degree turn.

### The Trail

Heading almost due east on a widely cleared old trail, the NCT makes an abrupt 90-degree turn heading north-northeast. After leaving the forest, heading north-northeast, the NCT passes through young aspen invading a field edge.

### 7.9 (2.5) Miles

The NCT reaches a hilltop overlooking an old, large field.

## The Trail

Continuing along the field edge heading northeast, the NCT reaches the crest of a low hill with a sweeping view to the west-northwest. Here hikers overlook a fifty-acre grassland with several ponds holding nesting ducks and geese in the spring. A two-track field road leads northwest to Becker County 26 near the Tamarac National Wildlife Refuge Visitor Center.

### 9.4 (0.0) Miles

Trailhead, Blackbird Wildlife Drive

*Tamarac National Wildlife Refuge and Greenwater Lake Scientific and Natural Area. See Appendix F: Restricted-Use Areas.*

## Map 6
## Blackbird Wildlife Trailhead to 400th Avenue Trailhead

### Distance
- 4.5 miles Map 6.
- 13.9 cumulative miles west to east, beginning of Map 5 to end of Map 6.
- 153.9 reverse miles east to west, end of Map 29 to beginning of Map 6.

**Route:** In addition to passing through mixed pine and deciduous forest on a mostly level tread, the NCT crosses the Otter Tail River and traverses an extensive tamarack and black spruce bog on a 1,000-foot long puncheon.

### Campsites

None. Camping is not allowed in eastern National Wildlife Refuges. The NCT through Tamarac is 14 miles. Plan your overnights accordingly. The Refuge is open from 5:00 a.m. to 10:00 p.m.

### Alternative Road Walk

A 6.4 mile road walk is available, beginning on Map 5. See Map 5-A for details.

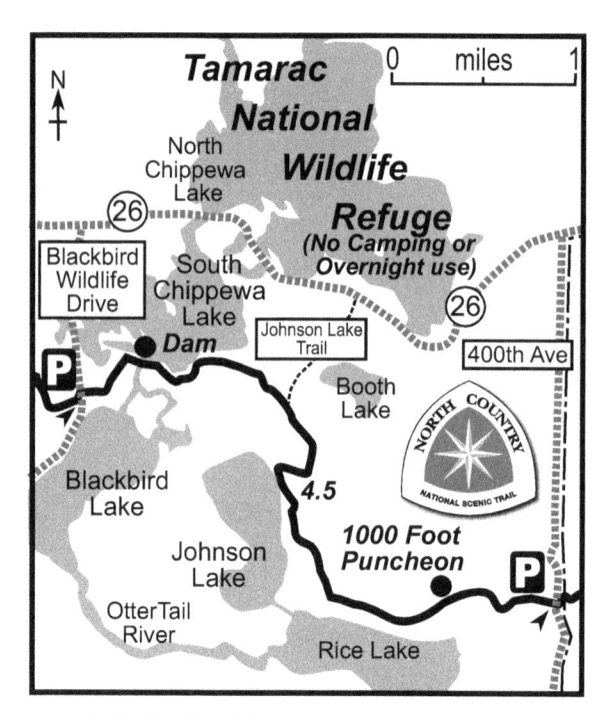

*Map 6. Blackbird Wildlife Drive Trailhead to 400th Avenue Trailhead*

### Services

See Appendix C for services and amenities available in these towns.
- Detroit Lakes

### Winter Use

See Appendix E for winter parking at trailheads and groomed cross-country ski trails.

### Hunting Alerts

See Chapter 2: Safety on the Trail.

### Water Sources and Treatment

See Chapter 2: Safety on the Trail.

**Out for a Stroll**
Saw two wolves cross the trail in front of us ...

## 🥾 Map 6 Mile-by-Mile

*This 1000-foot puncheon allows hikers to experience the mysteries of a black spruce–tamarack bog without injuring its fragile ecosystem. Photo by Marcus Schaffer.*

## 0.0 (4.5) Miles

Trailhead, Blackbird Wildlife Drive
- GPS Coordinates: 46.949003, -95.617576
- Driving Directions: From Detroit Lakes, go east on Minnesota 34 for 7.5 miles; turn north on Becker County 29 for 9.3 miles; continue straight on Becker County 26 for 2.1 miles; turn east on Blackbird Wildlife Drive for 0.7 mile. This trailhead can only be accessed from the north and Becker County 26.
- Details: Parking for 10 vehicles.
- Alert: Blackbird Wildlife Drive is a one-way road heading from Becker County 26 southwest to the Pine Lake Trail and then two-way out to Becker County 29.

## The Trail

The NCT passes through remote mixed pine and deciduous forest with mild to moderate hills, sometimes on single-track, sometimes double.

**0.5 (4.0) Miles**

Otter Tail River Dam, South Chippewa Lake

**The Trail**

The NCT crosses over a water control structure on the Ottertail River, with good views of the meandering river course and Chippewa Lake. East of the structure crossing, the NCT follows a gravel road (part of the dam's berm) and climbs a hill before re-entering the woods on the north. It traverses a steep side slope where the NCT is benched in before crossing the same gravel road (which leads from the dam out to County 26).

**1.7 (2.8) Miles**

The NCT comes out to and follows Johnson Lake Trail, a gravel road.

> The Otter Tail River is Minnesota's sixth longest river. It meanders 186 miles from its headwaters at Elbow Lake to its confluence with the Bois de Sioux River in Breckenridge. Historically, this river was used for travel between the valuable wild rice beds in the surrounding lakes by the Ojibwe, and for log transportation during 1870–1926, when the original forests of Norway and white pine were logged in this area. The dam at Chippewa Lake was built in 1941 by the U.S. Fish and Wildlife Service. Its walkway provides excellent viewing of abundant migratory birds as well as a view of the river valley.

**The Trail**

The NCT descends through tall Norway pine and then approaches the Johnson Lake Trail, a gated gravel road that leads south from County 26 to a carry-in public boat access on Johnson Lake. The NCT follows this road (heading south, west, and then south again) for 0.8 mile before reaching the Johnson Lake access loop. From the access loop, the NCT continues heading southeast on an old skid trail and crosses numerous low spots, some with puncheons. In early summer, watch for pink lady's slippers and blue flag irises.

**3.6 (0.9) Miles**

1,000-foot Puncheon, Tamarac and Spruce Bog

**The Trail**

This impressive 1000-foot puncheon was built by the Laurentian Lakes chapter of the NCTA. The heavy timbers used in its construction were hauled in by hand and with a powered wheelbarrow. Care was taken to disturb the bog as little as possible. The puncheon protects this special habitat while allowing hikers access to its mysteries and pleasures.

---

**Northern Tamarack Swamp Area of the North County Trail**
Nancy Brennan
*"Tamarac" is the spelling used for the Refuge (ending with "c"). The tamarack tree is spelled with a k at the end.*

In its passage through the Tamarac National Wildlife Refuge, the North Country Trail transects an unusual habitat: a tamarack and black spruce boggy swamp. To protect this special place, the Laurentian Lakes Chapter of the NCTA constructed a 1000-foot puncheon that elevates hikers' boots above the fragile terrain.

Tiny little hills, called hummocks, mark the path's descent toward the swamp through a sea of saturated soil and muck. This watery base creates a challenge for plants: it is hard for them to get enough oxygen and nutrients here to support growth. Sphagnum moss, which grows readily in the swamp, provides one solution: it soaks up and retains moisture, giving small plants, such as naked miterwort and bunchberry, a place to grow. When these plants complete their natural cycle and die, the hummocks provide oxygen to bacteria and fungi that decompose their tissues. These tissues in turn add to the hummock, making it bigger each year.

Tamarack trees use a different strategy to survive in the swamp. Their seeds can germinate in sphagnum moss, and as they grow, instead of reaching down into the earth, their shallow roots spread out widely, sometimes wider than the height of the tree, to access the more oxygen-rich top layers of soil. Tamaracks are an unusual conifer in that they shed their needles each winter, which helps them tolerate extremely cold temperatures.

Each biotic layer of this swamp is marked by plant communities that have adapted to life in wet and cold places through intricate means. Human adaptation is also evident here. Old, cut logs near the puncheon are leftover from a corduroy road that was used to access a duck hunting camp before this area was part of the refuge. Corduroy roads, constructed from logs laid parallel to each other in tight formation, have been used for centuries to facilitate passage over boggy, swampy areas. Puncheons also offer passage, but without disrupting the specialized life patterns of the plants and trees that inhabit this wondrous environment.

*Nancy Brennan is a retired librarian with a botany background, a certified Master Naturalist, and a Tamarac National Wildlife Refuge environmental education team volunteer. She received Tamarac NWR's 2013 Volunteer of the Year award for surpassing 1,000 hours of volunteer work.*

**4.5 (0.0) Miles**

Trailhead, 400th Avenue

Note: The NCT exits the main parcel of the Tamarac National Wildlife Refuge at 400th Avenue. A secondary, small parcel is crossed soon after 400th Avenue.

◄ **Map 7**
**400th Avenue Trailhead to Becker County 35 Trailhead**

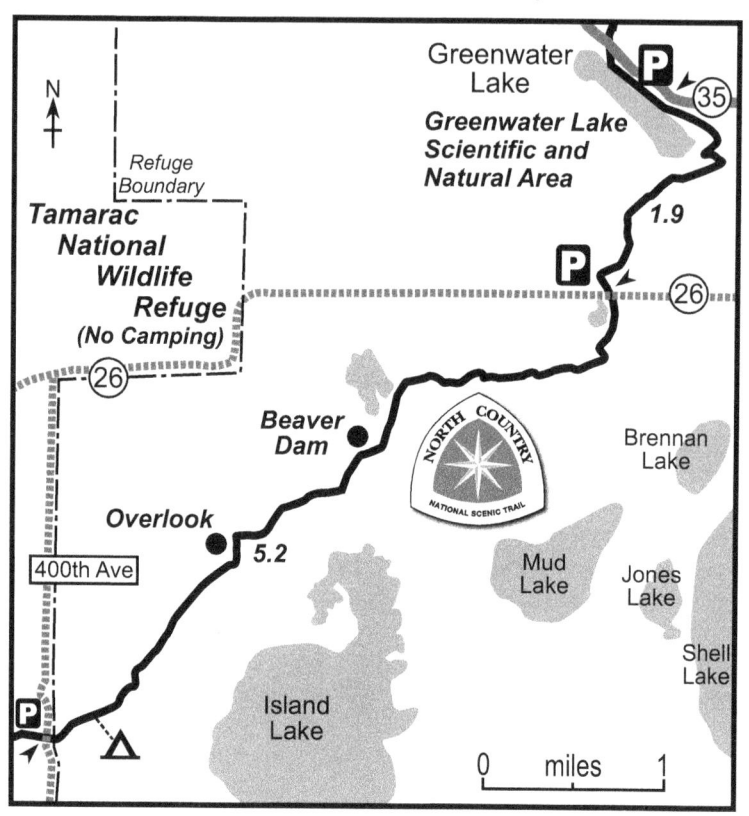

*The NCT enters and exits Greenwater Lake Scientific and Natural Area (SNA). See Appendix F: Restricted-Use Areas.*

**Distance**
- 7.1 miles Map 7.
- 21.0 cumulative miles west to east, beginning of Map 5 to end of Map 7.
- 149.4 reverse miles east to west, end of Map 29 to beginning of Map 7.

**Route:** The NCT wends through a variety of forest types as well as recent timber harvests. This section is level and an easy hike. Greenwater Lake Scientific and Natural Area hosts rare wildlife and plants.

## Campsites

See also "Camping along the Trail" in Accessing and Using the NCT in Minnesota in the front of this book, and Appendix B: Camping, Campsites, Campgrounds.
- 400th Avenue

## Services

See Appendix C for services and amenities available in these towns.
- Detroit Lakes
- Ponsford

## Winter Use

See Appendix E for winter parking at trailheads and groomed cross-country ski trails.

## Hunting Alerts

- See Chapter 2: Safety on the Trail.
- Hunting is not allowed in the State Scientific and Natural Areas.

## Water Sources and Treatment

See Chapter 2: Safety on the Trail.

## Alerts

- Near the center of this trail segment, the NCT crosses an isolated parcel of land owned and managed by Tamarac National Wildlife Refuge. It is identified by signs.
- Also near the center of this segment, the NCT crosses a parcel of private land. Camping is not allowed. Please stay on the trail and honor rules and regulations.

## 🥾 Map 7 Mile-by-Mile

*Trillium grandiflorum, large-flowered trillium, carpets the spring woods along this section of the NCT in northern Minnesota. Photo by Florence Hedeen.*

### 0.0 (7.1) Miles

Trailhead, 400th Avenue
- GPS Coordinates: 46.9367, -95.562633
- Driving Directions: From Detroit Lakes, head east on Minnesota 34 for 15.7 miles; north on Becker County 37 for 2.3 miles; west on Becker County 126 for 2.6 miles; then north on 400th Avenue for 1.2 miles.
- Details: Parking for 5 vehicles.

### The Trail

Glacial Laurentian topography continues to dominate the NCT, as evidenced by the gradual transition from hardwoods to boreal conifers. The forest also is intermixed with Norway and white pine, sugar maple, basswood, aspen, birch, and oak. The NCT crosses 400th Avenue, enters private land (obey signs), passes a short spur to a campsite, and soon begins climbing up to a noticeable ridge, partly on single-track trail and partly on an old road (within an isolated parcel of Tamarac NWR).

**History**

The trail passes through three major biomes in close proximity: tall grass prairie, northern hardwood forest, and coniferous forest (sometimes called taiga). It was perhaps the many wetlands, lakes, and ponds in the area that prevented prehistoric prairie fires from advancing to the east. The many boulders along the trail—called erratics—were transported here by the glaciers from as far away as northern Canada. The NCT continues along the top of an ancient Wisconsin Age glacial formation called the Alexandria Glacial Moraine, identified in part by irregularly shaped ridges of glacially deposited soil. Island Lake was also shaped by the glacier and lies in the Red River of the North basin along a north-south divide. Surface water runoff from this forest flows back north toward the source of the glaciers that shaped the area.

### 0.1 (7.0) Miles

400th Avenue Campsite
- Three tent sites, fire ring, privy.
- From the 400th Avenue Trailhead, cross 400th Avenue directly to the east. Campsite is 390 feet east on the trail.
- Campsite is located on private property. Please be respectful.

### 1.5 (5.6) Miles

Overlook, Chippewa Lake

**The Trail**

The NCT reaches the end of the old road, turns, and climbs up to the ridge top (elevation 1,730 feet) featuring a vista with a great view looking off to the northwest. In the spring and fall you can often hear abundant waterfowl on Chippewa Lake about two miles to the west.

**Tracking—NCT Adopter/Volunteer**

"One winter day, I saw two sets of tracks in the snow. One was a deer, the other a wolf. The tracks included big dashes from the deer's hooves and long slides from the wolf. I did not see evidence of the outcome of the race. Many times I have seen lone animal tracks in the snow on a lake."

## 2.7 (4.4) Miles

Beaver Dam

### The Trail

On the west side of the creek crossing, note a massive beaver dam, about 10 feet tall and 150 feet long. The dam is overgrown with vegetation and the dam pool is mostly silted in, so the dam must have been there for a very long time. It is a testimony to the engineering prowess of beavers.

## 4.2 (2.9) Miles

Forest road crossing

### The Trail

The NCT crosses a wide overgrown forest road thick with blackberries and raspberries, then almost immediately crosses another forest road. Here, the NCT is close to the Mud Lake Forest Road, which is used for timber harvesting and as a snowmobile trail in the winter.

## 5.0 (2.1) Miles

Small lake

### The Trail

The NCT passes by a small lake with a single white pine along the shore. Farmland is visible across the lake and occasionally hikers can hear cows mooing, which seems strange given the dense forest cover.

---

**Where the Water Goes**

Approximately from the Greenwater Lake Scientific and Natural Area to the Minnesota 113 Trailhead (Maps 8 through 10), the NCT runs south to north along a continental divide. To the west the flowage is into the Red River of the North, which empties north into Hudson Bay. To the east the flowage is into the Mississippi River, which empties south into the Gulf of Mexico. Overall, the trail is level or gently undulating with no steep changes in elevation.

---

## 5.2 (1.9) Miles

Access Point, Becker County 26
*Access to Greenwater Lake Scientific and Natural Area*
- GPS Coordinates: 46.969467, -95.497772
- Driving Directions: From Detroit Lakes, head east on Minnesota 34 for 15.7 miles; north on Becker County 37 for 8.0 miles; then west on Becker County 26 for 1.3 miles.

**Reflection—NCT Adopter/Volunteer**
"The Greenwater Lake SNA is a remote location. One can feel entirely alone [here] and enjoy the solitude."

### The Trail

After crossing a snowmobile trail, the NCT immediately crosses County 26 on a gravel approach used for a log landing (access point parking, not maintained). To the north, it passes through a recently logged area before entering an area with dense, older aspen and then a recently thinned oak stand. Notice the black signs of fire on the oaks' lower trunks.

## 5.8 (1.3) Miles

NCT South Boundary, Greenwater Lake Scientific and Natural Area
*All life in the SNA is protected, including plants.*

### The Trail

Approximately 0.6 mile past the access point, the NCT enters Greenwater Lake Scientific and Natural Area through a gate (walk around it) on an old road. The trail makes several turns while following additional old forest roads. As it rounds Greenwater Lake and heads north, traffic can be heard at the Becker County 35 Trailhead. The terrain is hilly with old-growth oak, basswood, and maple, with a series of beaver houses and ponds—watch for deep beaver runs in the bank leading down to the lake. Several uncommon butterfly species are found here. About 50 feet into this section, watch for an old porcupine den on the east side of the trail. It is noticeable by a large dung pile that accumulated over the years.

**Greenwater Lake Scientific and Natural Area**

The Greenwater Lake SNA has 815 acres. Greenwater Lake is a pristine, spring-fed lake, dominated by a single species of diatom (a type of algae) that occurs only rarely in other lakes. The Minnesota DNR Scientific & Natural Areas program preserves natural features and rare resources of exceptional scientific and educational value. SNAs are open to the public for nature observation and education, but are not meant for intensive recreational activities. www.dnr.state.mn.us/snas

### 7.1 (0.0) Miles

Trailhead, Becker County 35, Greenwater Lake Scientific and Natural Area (SNA)

◄ **Map 8**
**Becker County 35 Trailhead to Camp Six Forest Trail Trailhead**

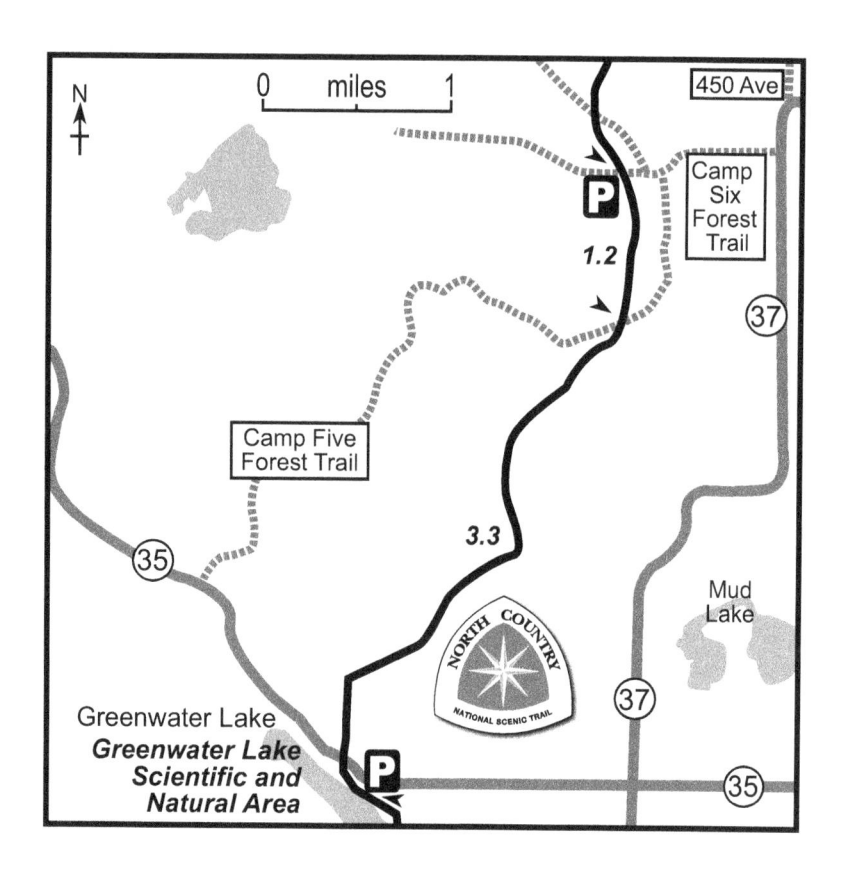

*NCT exits Greenwater Lake Scientific and Natural Area*

## Distance
- 4.5 miles Map 8.
- 25.5 cumulative miles west to east, beginning of Map 5 to end of Map 8.
- 142.3 reverse miles east to west, end of Map 29 to beginning of Map 8.

**Route:** This mostly level section starts near the north boundary of the Greenwater Lake Scientific and Natural Area. Much of it is wetland. The trail passes by several beaver dams and there are seven puncheons in the 4.5-mile section.

## Campsites

See also "Camping along the Trail" in Accessing and Using the NCT in the front of this book, and Appendix B: Camping, Campsites, Campgrounds.
- No designated campsites.

## Services

See Appendix C for services and amenities available in these towns.
- Detroit Lakes
- Ponsford

## Winter Use

See Appendix E for winter parking at trailheads and groomed cross-country ski trails.

## Hunting Alerts

See Chapter 2: Safety on the Trail.

## Water Sources and Treatment

See Chapter 2: Safety on the Trail.

## 👣 Map 8 Mile-by-Mile

**0.0 (4.5) Miles**

Trailhead, Becker County 35, Greenwater Lake Scientific and Natural Area (SNA)
- GPS Coordinates: 46.984419, -95.490301
- Driving Directions: From Detroit Lakes, head east on Minnesota 34 for 15.7 miles; north on Becker County 37 for 9.1 miles; then west on Becker County 35 for 1.2 miles.
- Details: Parking for 10 vehicles

**The Trail**

At the trailhead, the NCT continues heading northwest parallel to Greenwater Lake before turning north and crossing Becker County 35 after .25 mile.

---

**Solitude—NCT Adopter/Volunteer**
"From County 35 to Elbow Lake Road the NCT is wonderfully remote. There is only one road crossing. The 'egg carton' terrain can be challenging: it passes through areas of hummocks, beaver ponds and dams, and old-growth forest."

---

*The NCT opens from forest trail to forest view. Photo by Matthew R. Davis.*

**0.7 (3.8) Miles**

NCT North Boundary, Greenwater Lake Scientific and Natural Area

**The Trail**

Shortly after crossing Becker County 35, the NCT continues along an old, gated road that exits Greenwater Lake SNA before reaching the top of a hill and descending to cross a wetland on a puncheon. There are six additional puncheons within the next 2 miles as the NCT traverses a large forested wetland complex. There are a variety of plums, wild grapes, and mushrooms, a black ash bog, and lots of wildlife, including bears, wolves, wild turkeys, trumpeter swans, otters, and warblers. Eventually, the NCT turns north, following a north-south ridge that is the Laurentian Divide.

### 3.3 (1.2) Miles

Crossing, Camp Five Forest Trail

**Bedtime Story—NCT Adopter/Volunteer**
"I have seen deer beds and wolf beds not more than 225 feet apart, the grass pressed down in circles with tracks around them."

### The Trail

The NCT continues through mixed pine, hardwood, and aspen stands to Camp Six Forest Trail. There are many lovely vistas along this stretch. The "Camp" roads were established by logging camps in the early 1900s. They are used today by ATVs and snowmobiles and for hunting.

### 4.5 (0.0) Miles

Trailhead, Camp Six Forest Trail

# Map 9
# Camp Six Forest Trailhead to Elbow Lake Road Trailhead

### Distance
- 5.7 miles Map 9.
- 31.2 cumulative miles west to east, beginning of Map 5 to end of Map 9.
- 137.8 reverse miles east to west, end of Map 29 to beginning of Map 9.

**Route:** This section of trail follows a watershed divide. The topography is generally small rolling hills and ridges with a general decrease in elevation on both sides of the trail. It is completely forested with a wide variety of trees and undergrowth, including interspersed hardwood and conifer.

### Campsites

Flooded Woods

### Services

See Appendix C for services and amenities available in these towns.
- Detroit Lakes
- Park Rapids

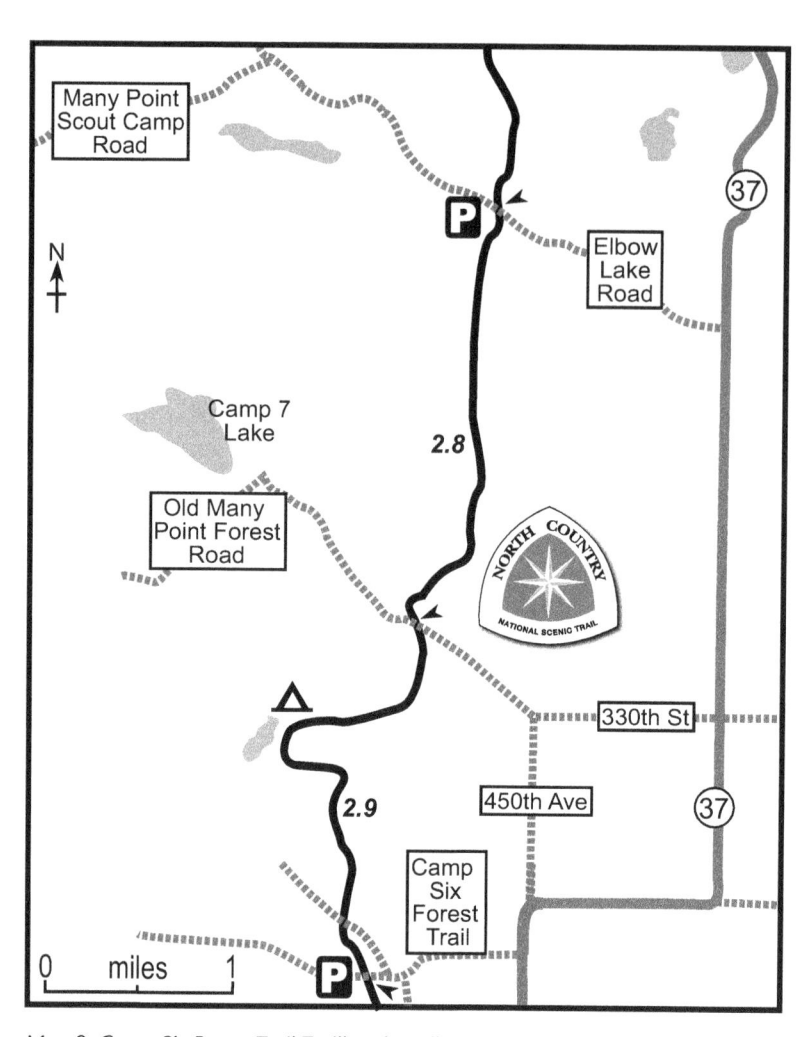

*Map 9. Camp Six Forest Trail Trailhead to Elbow Lake Road Trailhead*

**Winter Use**

See Appendix E for winter parking at trailheads and groomed cross-country ski trails.

**Hunting Alerts**

See Chapter 2: Safety on the Trail.

**Water Sources and Treatment**

See Chapter 2: Safety on the Trail.

*Hikers meander through spring woods on the NCT. Photo by Beth Trout.*

## 🥾 Map 9 Mile-by-Mile

### 0.0 (5.7) Miles

Trailhead, Camp Six Forest Trail
- GPS Coordinates: 47.03061, -95.46617
- Driving Directions: From Detroit Lakes, head east on Minnesota 34 for 15.7 miles; north on Becker County 37 for 12.7 miles; then west on Camp Six Forest Trail for 1.0 mile.
- Details: Parking for 6 vehicles; kiosk

### The Trail

The NCT crosses several trails and wends through pine, spruce, and maple groves. It follows the south edge of a wetland complex that extends about 0.5 mile. A series of puncheons keep the NCT high and dry.

---

**Preservation Area**

Parts of this section of the NCT pass through the Becker County Forest Preserve Area. Established in 2003 by the Becker County Board of Commissioners, dispersed tracts of old-growth Norway and white pine forest are brought under the blanket protection of the Preserve Area so their natural beauty can be enjoyed now and into the future. The nineteen Preserve Areas are each marked with a sign that encourages visitors to "take only memories; leave only footprints." The areas are open to hiking, cross-country skiing, hunting, and wildlife and plant observation. The Preserve is sponsored by the Becker County Natural Resources Management Department and the Resource Stewardship Association.

---

### 2.0 (3.7) Miles

Campsite: Flooded Woods
- Take spur trail to campsite on west side of trail
- Two tent sites, fire ring, privy
- View of Flooded Woods wetland complex, good for watching birds and waterfowl

### The Trail

The NCT crosses an old logging skid trail as it enters an area known as Flooded Woods, a wetland complex. Overall, the trail is level or gently undulating with no steep changes in elevation. In several places you can see old troughs in the soil from earlier logging operations.

## 2.9 (2.8) Miles

Crossing, Old Many Point Forest Road

### The Trail

The NCT continues through mostly level terrain and mixed forest, dropping down to a puncheon across a low area, winds east, crosses a power line opening and then arrives at Elbow Lake Road. Between Old Many Point Forest Road and Elbow Lake Road, hikers will see evidence of the great 1995 blowdown. Notice that the trees lying across the trail all face in the same direction and that the forest is reestablishing itself. Watch for a spur trail to Elbow Lake Road.

### Note

Old Many Point Forest Road is also known locally as Camp Seven Forest Road.

## 5.7 (0.0) Miles

Trailhead, Elbow Lake Road

## Map 10
### Elbow Lake Road Trailhead to Clearwater County 39 Trailhead

### Distance
- 9.1 miles Map 10.
- 40.3 cumulative miles west to east, beginning of Map 5 to end of Map 10.
- 132.1 reverse miles east to west, end of Map 29 to beginning of Map 10.

### Reflection—NCT Adopter/Volunteer

"I have hiked this segment of the North Country Trail many more times than I can count and it never fails to impress me with its striking beauty and majesty and biodiversity. From the large and tall to the infinitely small, it speaks to that which is nature within. It's like a spiritual friend and adviser. This is especially the way it feels when one hikes alone and communes in solitude with the abundant gifts nature so freely gives."

**Route:** Vistas include a river valley on the east that flows into the Mississippi River and one on the west that flows into the Red River of the North. Excellent wildlife viewing: water birds including swans, loons, ducks; beaver mudslides; occasional lynx and fisher; tracks of wolf, deer, coyote, bobcat; wildflowers—bellwort to orchids. Trail is often narrow, heavily forested with mixed hardwood, pine, and birch; rolling hills. Spectacular scenery including undeveloped lakes, beaver activity, biodiversity, and historic features. Mostly rolling hills with some steep ascents and descents. Puncheons sometimes used in occasional low areas.

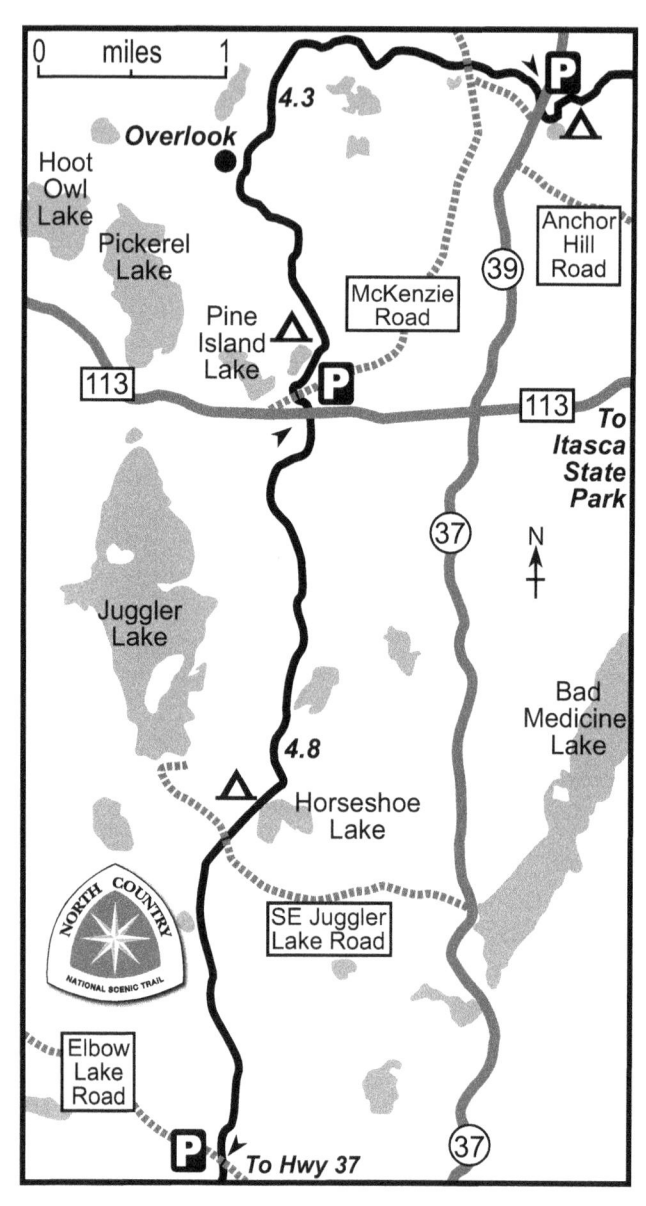

*Map 10. Elbow Lake Road Trailhead to Clearwater County 39 Trailhead*

## Campsites

See also "Camping along the Trail" in Accessing and Using the NCT in Minnesota in the front of this book, and Appendix B: Camping, Campsites, Campgrounds.
- Horseshoe Lake
- Pine Island Lake

## Services

See Appendix C for services and amenities available in these towns.
- Detroit Lakes
- Itasca State Park
- Park Rapids

## Winter Use

See Appendix E for winter parking at trailheads and groomed cross-country ski trails.

## Hunting Alerts

See Chapter 2: Safety on the Trail.

## Water Sources and Treatment

See Chapter 2: Safety on the Trail.

## Map 10 Mile-by-Mile

### 0.0 (9.1) Miles

Trailhead, Elbow Lake Road
- GPS Coordinates: 47.087929, -95.449398
- Driving Directions: From Detroit Lakes, head east on Minnesota 34 for 15.7 miles; north on Becker County 37 for 16.9 miles; then west on Elbow Lake Road for 1.6 miles.
- Details: Parking for 4 to 5 vehicles; a short spur trail leads south to the NCT.

Between the Elbow Lake Road Trailhead and the Clearwater County 39 Trailhead (Map 10), the NCT is on a ridge that runs north-south and is a watershed boundary. Because of the height and steep sides of the ridge, it is easy to imagine that precipitation falling there would flow downhill either to the east or west from along the top of the ridge.

*Children love the NCT! Photo by Matthew R. Davis.*

### The Trail

A mix of young and mature hardwood forest, spruce, and pine. At one point it follows a ridge with marsh on both sides. The trail progresses to rolling hills under a dense oak canopy but also passes by or through clear-cuts and plantations. Multiple trail crossings.

To access the Elbow Lake Road trailhead, watch for a short spur trail heading north to the trailhead. The NCT continues northeast, crosses under a power line, and then reaches Elbow Lake Road

**Recommended**

North of a forest road crossing, the trail passes through a magnificent, mature maple and basswood forest that is especially spectacular during fall colors.

### 2.0 (7.1) Miles

Crossing, Southeast Juggler Road

### The Trail

Watch for evidence of an old sugar bush (maple syrup) camp—rusted cans, tubs, and other remains. Mature, crowned forest.

**Best of the Trail—NCT Adopter/Volunteer Trail-Builders**
"The Elbow Lake area is an especially scenic, mature, old-growth forest. The trail goes around and up and down and through crowned hardwoods—there is little to no undergrowth. The land slopes off and the topography is glacial kames [hills] and kettles [holes]. It is an enchanted forest, often rising high and yielding tremendous views. It has a special feeling—gives you a different feeling of satisfaction and solitude that you don't have other places."

### 2.3 (6.8) Miles

Campsite, Horseshoe Lake
- Take spur to campsite.
- Two tent sites, fire ring, privy.

### The Trail

The NCT progresses to rolling hills under dense oak canopy, gradually shifting to mature poplar and birch, then to younger pine. It passes by a power line clearing. A puncheon takes the NCT over a marsh into a mix of pine and hardwood forest. The NCT ascends then quickly descends approximately 120 feet in elevation. Look for beaver activity at Horseshoe Lake.

### 4.8 (4.3) Miles

Trailhead, Minnesota 113
- GPS Coordinates: 47.144339, -95.437096
- Driving Directions: From US 71, head west on 113 and go 14.3 miles to the trailhead on the north side of road.
- Details: Parking for 6 to 8 vehicles; bench; kiosk

### The Trail

The NCT approaches the Minnesota 113 Trailhead through an area of mature white pine, some as tall as eighty feet and more than six feet in circumference. The trail here enters majestic country that is rich in biodiversity and natural beauty. Shortly past the trailhead, the NCT crosses McKenzie Forest Road (southerly juncture). The trail drops down onto an old Nichols-Chisholm railroad grade that leads to Elbow Lake, where harvested logs were off-loaded into the lake and then floated down the Otter Tail River to the Frazee sawmill. The NCT follows this railroad grade several times between McKenzie Forest Road and Itasca State Park. The NCT crosses McKenzie Forest Road twice, here and 8.5 miles north of Elbow Lake Road.

### 5.4 (3.7) Miles

Campsite, Pine Island Lake
- Two tent sites, fire ring, privy, bench/table.
- There is a short spur trail between the NCT and the campsite.

### The Trail

This campsite is on the west side of the trail a short distance past the McKenzie Forest Road. Privy is on the east. From the campsite, the NCT slowly gains elevation to a summit with an overlook.

### 6.6 (2.5) Miles

Overlook, Laurentian Divide, Elevation: 1,730 Feet

### The Trail

A spectacular view toward the northeast over a logged-off area with young re-growth. A ridge of coniferous trees can be seen about 2 miles away with a higher skyline ridge beyond. There is a bench—have a seat and enjoy the view. Can you spot the Tim-Don-Del Overlook, the highest point about 8 miles to the east-northeast? (Map 15, mile 6.3) As the trail leaves the ridge, it descends and turns east.

### 8.5 (0.6) Miles

Crossing, McKenzie Forest Road

### The Trail

The trail goes through a young Norway pine plantation and continues to weave through mixed forest with mild elevation changes.

### 9.0 (0.1) Miles

Crossing, Clearwater County 39

### The Trail

The NCT crosses an ATV trail, and then climbs up to cross Clearwater County 39 (which is Becker County 37 south of the county boundary) and then descends into a stand of mature white pine. Watch for a short spur trail that leads to the trailhead. On the spur trail, a puncheon crosses a spring-fed stream.

### 9.1 (0.0) Miles

Trailhead, Clearwater County 39

◀ **Map 11**
**Clearwater County 39 Trailhead to Anchor Matson Road Trailhead**

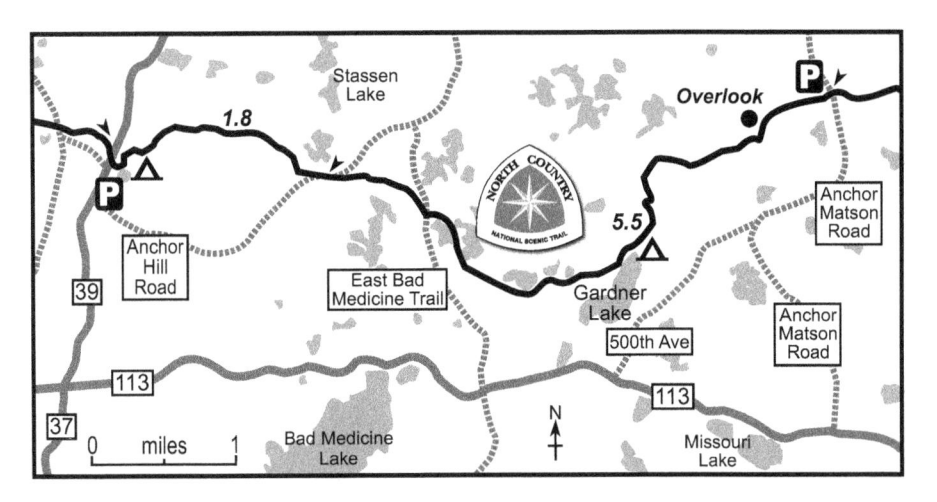

*Map 11. Clearwater County 39 Trailhead to Anchor Matson Road Trailhead*

**Distance**
- 7.3 miles Map 11.
- 47.6 cumulative miles west to east, beginning of Map 5 to end of Map 11.
- 123.0 reverse miles east to west, end of Map 29 to beginning of Map 11.

**Route:** The NCT passes through a wide variety of forest types, including old-growth pine and recently planted pine, birch, and aspen. It generally has gently sloping terrain, with occasional elevation changes that may challenge a less-experienced hiker, especially at Tim-Don-Del Overlook.

**Campsites**

See also "Camping along the Trail" in Accessing and Using the NCT in Minnesota in the front of this book, and Appendix B: Camping, Campsites, Campgrounds.
- Old Headquarters
- Gardner Lake

**Services**

See Appendix C for services and amenities available in these towns.
- Detroit Lakes
- Itasca State Park
- Park Rapids

### Winter Use

See Appendix E for winter parking at trailheads and groomed cross-country ski trails.

### Hunting Alerts

See Chapter 2: Safety on the Trail.

### Water Sources and Treatment

See Chapter 2: Safety on the Trail.

### Alerts

Confusing road names and numbers: Anchor Hill Road runs east-west, Anchor Matson Road runs north-south; a county road changes number just north of where it crosses Minnesota 113. Running south, it is Becker County 37; running north it is Clearwater County 39.

### Map 11 Mile-by-Mile

**0.0 (7.3) Miles**

Trailhead, Clearwater County 39
- GPS Coordinates: 47.166307, -95.415062
- Driving Directions: From Detroit Lakes, head east on Minnesota 34 for 15.7 miles; north on Becker County 37 for 21.6 miles. At the intersection with Minnesota 113, continue straight on Clearwater County 39 for 1.6 miles.
- Details: Parking for 8 to 10 vehicles; bench; kiosk; a short spur trail exits the parking area, crosses a puncheon, and joins NCT.

### The Trail

The NCT generally follows early 1900s logging railroad grade, which it eventually exits. It passes through a Norway pine plantation (planted in the 1990s) and alongside a marsh. Watch for raspberries in season.

**0.2 (7.1) Miles**

Campsite, Old Headquarters
- Four tent sites, fire ring, privy, bench

*In Itasca State Park, the Lake De Soto campsite is just a few steps from the water. Photo by Deane Johnson.*

### The Trail

Watch for the short campsite spur trail when the NCT heads northeast. The campsite is in a mature grove of white and Norway pine and has a nice view of a small lake. It is a good place to stop for lunch if not camping overnight.

### 1.8 (5.5) Miles

Access Point, Anchor Hill Road
- GPS Coordinates: 47.165501, -05.380640
- Driving Directions: From Detroit Lakes go east on Minnesota 34 for 15.7 miles; turn north onto Becker County 37 and go 22.1 miles; continue straight onto Clearwater County 39 for 0.8 mile; turn east onto Anchor Hill Road and go 2.2 miles.

### The Trail

The NCT enters and exits an old railroad grade and logging road. When on the old railroad bed, note that subtle bumps can be felt in the trail from the long-ago rotted away railroad ties. The trail goes off and onto an old railroad grade, then off and onto an old logging road. It runs alongside several sloughs. There are some changes in elevation. Puncheons span some low areas and there is evidence of beaver activity.

---

**Off-Trail Side Trip (brief)**

This area is referred to as "Old Headquarters." It was the headquarters of the Nichols-Chisholm Lumber Company. They took white pine from all around this area in the winter, hauled the logs via railroad, and stacked them on ice-covered Elbow Lake. In the spring, logs were floated down the Otter Tail River to the company's sawmills in Frazee. During the New Deal years in 1933, this became a CCC camp (CCC-569) known as Lake Camper Headquarters Camp. CCC activities included tree planting and fire protection. Today all that remains is a fieldstone fireplace and chimney. To visit, cross Clearwater County 39 to the west and look for the ruins in the pine grove south of Chimney Road. See if you can find the names of the stonemasons chipped into a rock in the fireplace! A large plaque details the history of the site.

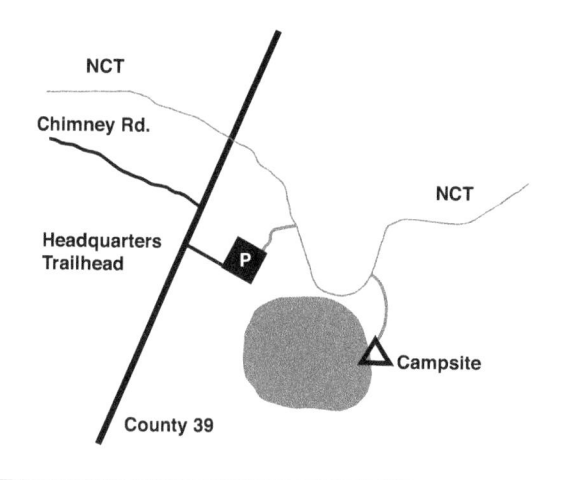

---

## 2.9 (4.4) Miles

Crossing: East Bad Medicine Lake Trail

**The Trail**

The NCT joins Old Bad Medicine Lake Trail. Turn south onto the road for 0.11 mile, then east onto the old logging road for 100 feet, then bear north off of the logging road. There is a puncheon over a small stream between a lake and a slough. The NCT then goes through some large birch trees along the lakeshore. A logging road crosses the trail. The NCT leaves the railroad grade and turns westerly onto a two-track hill. At the top of the hill the NCT turns east on a single-track trail, briefly enters hilly terrain, crosses below a large beaver dam, and enters a small grove of old-growth white pine.

### 4.5 (2.8) Miles

Crossing: West Gardner Lake Road

### The Trail

The NCT continues through mixed forest on mostly level terrain.

### 5.0 (2.3) Miles

Campsite, Gardner Lake
- Two tent sites, fire ring, privy, bench
- Campsite is 120 feet south of the NCT; privy is 75 feet north of the NCT

### History—NCT Adopter/Volunteer

"As you travel the trail, stay on the lookout for fire-scarred trees scattered throughout this forest. These trees date back to 1918, the last major forest fire in this area. Nineteen-eighteen was a bad year for fires across much of Minnesota, including the famous Hinckley fire."

### The Trail

The NCT continues through mixed forest on mostly level terrain. Eventually the trail drops down to Gardner Lake and follows along its shore, crossing a lake access trail just before the campsite. After the campsite, watch for jack pine stands as well as raspberries in season.

### 6.3 (1.0) Miles

Overlook, Tim-Don-Del Hill
Elevation: 1,750 feet

### The Trail

The trail up and down may be a challenge for less-experienced hikers. Sit on the bench in a stand of mature Norway pine and enjoy the view. The Smoky Hills can be seen 18 miles to the south. The overlook is named for volunteers who were instrumental in constructing the site.

**7.3 (0.0) Miles**

Trailhead, Anchor Matson Road

## ◀ Map 12
## Anchor Matson Road Trailhead to 540th Avenue Trailhead

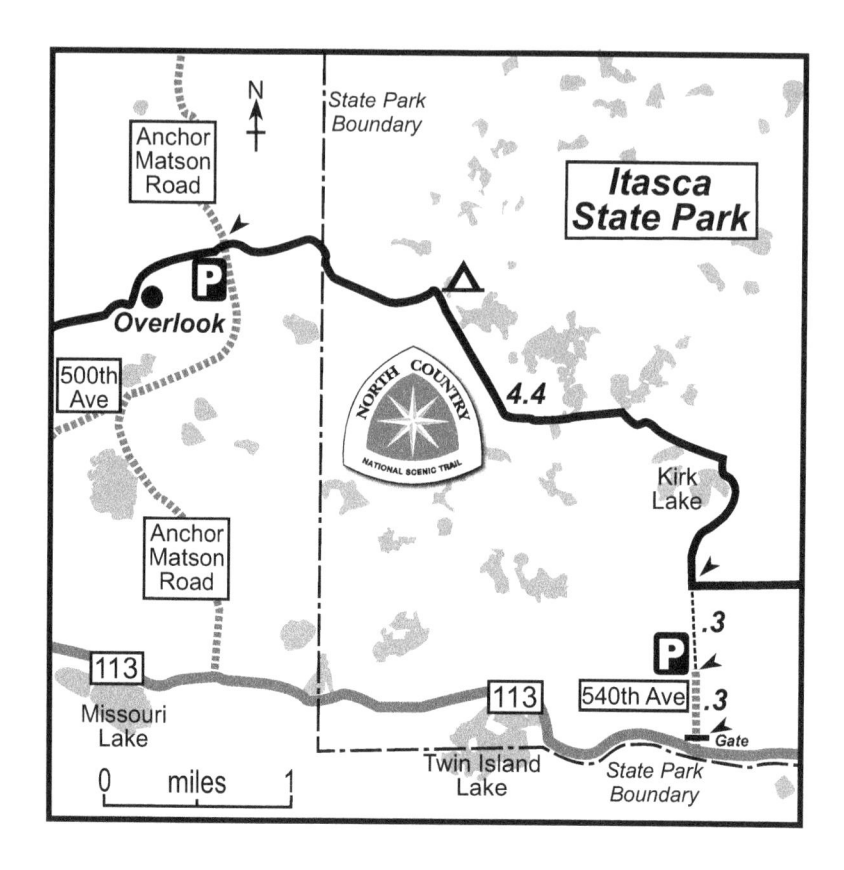

*Partially in Itasca State Park. See Appendix F: Restricted-Use Areas*

**Distance**
- 4.7 miles Map 12.
- 52.3 cumulative miles west to east, beginning of Map 5 to end of Map 12.
- 115.7 reverse miles east to west, end of Map 29 to beginning of Map 12.

**Route:** Continuing through rolling terrain with mixed forest, the NCT enters 33,000-acre Itasca State Park, sharing some old forest roads and park trails along the way. The park has mature forest, many lakes, and a large wetland complex. The remote section has evidence of wildlife and sightings (wolf, fisher, bear). Rescued from the loggers' saws in 1891 by citizens and legislators, the park is especially known as a sanctuary for old-growth pine. The headwaters of the Mississippi River is also here, at Lake Itasca.

## Campsites

See also "Camping along the Trail" in Accessing and Using the NCT in Minnesota in the front of this book, and Appendix B: Camping, Campsites, Campgrounds.
- West Itasca State Park
- Dispersed camping is not allowed in Itasca State Park.

## Services

See Appendix C for services and amenities available in these towns.
- Itasca State Park
- Park Rapids

## Winter Use

See Appendix E for winter parking at trailheads and groomed cross-country ski trails.

## Hunting Alerts

See Chapter 2: Safety on the Trail.

## Water Sources and Treatment

See Chapter 2: Safety on the Trail.

## Alerts

- Throughout Itasca State Park: Multiple trail/road crossings and sharings. Not all intersections or direction changes are marked with Carsonite posts. Rely on blue blazes for trail direction.
- There is a Y at the forest road intersection about 0.5 mile east of West Itasca State Park campsite. Hiking from west to east, the NCT takes the northerly angle.

**Note**

Lodging, camping, and food services are available in the park, which also features many trails (see Itasca Special Section in Chapter 3). Canoe, kayak, and bike rentals are available in the park as are selected camping and hiking supplies. Permit and camping reservations are required in the park.

*This trail-side campsite barely infringes on the forest. Photo by Matthew R. Davis.*

### Map 12 Mile-by-Mile

**0.0 (4.7) Miles**

Trailhead, Anchor Matson Road
- GPS Coordinates: 47.171161, -95.309658
- Driving Directions: From Detroit Lakes, head east on Minnesota 34 for 15.7 miles; north on Becker County 37 for 21.6 miles; east on Minnesota 113 for 5.7 miles; then north on Anchor Matson Road for 2.8 miles.
- Details: Parking for 5 vehicles; kiosk; regional information map; brochure box

## The Trail

Within a couple hundred feet of the trailhead, the NCT picks up an old logging rail grade. Rotted railroad ties are evident as depressions in the soil. For the next 0.3 mile, there is evidence of fill and cuts to level the rail grade. This was all done by hand or possibly with the aid of horses around 1915. At 0.6 mile, the NCT leaves the old rail grade and follows a single track.

## 0.7 (4.0) Miles

West Boundary, Itasca State Park (signed)

## The Trail

The NCT follows an old, over-grown forest road (park boundary), then returns for a short distance to single-track. At 1.5 miles, it turns south onto an old forest road.

### Accessibility—NCT Adopter/Volunteer

"Much of the NCT in Minnesota is comfortable for inexperienced hikers. One visitor commented, 'Is this the trail? I only know trails as asphalt.' Another hiker who was used to city pathways commented, 'Even I can use it!' He said it opened a world to him that he thought was inaccessible."

## 1.6 (3.1) Miles

Campsite, West Itasca State Park
- Spur trail to campsite, 270 feet, exits north from NCT
- Two tent sites, fire ring, privy

## Note

Camping permit and reservation are not required at this campsite within Itasca State Park.

## The Trail

The NCT continues on fairly level terrain through mixed forest and wetlands.

## 3.0 (1.7) Miles

Crossing: Small puncheon over wetland.

### The Trail

The NCT passes through a marshy wetland on a short puncheon with great views onto a wetland and open water to the north.

### 3.7 (1.0) Miles

Puncheon north of Kirk Lake

### The Trail

The NCT continues heading southeast, crosses over another short puncheon, then wraps around the east side of Kirk Lake.

### 4.4 (0.3) Miles

Spur trail to Gartner Farm Trailhead, 540th Street.

### The Trail

The NCT descends a gentle hill on the old road and reaches an intersection. It continues easterly on a spur trail (the same old road heading south), and continues south for 0.3 mile to reach the Gartner Farm Trailhead at the end of 540th Avenue. Minnesota 113 is 0.6 mile farther south.

### 4.7 (0.0) Miles

Trailhead, 540th Street

*In Itasca State Park. See Appendix F: Restricted-Use Areas. See also Map 13-A Itasca State Park Detail.*

## ◄ Map 13
### 540th Avenue Trailhead to Itasca State Park South Entrance Trailhead

### Distance

- 6.2 miles Map 13.
- 58.5 cumulative miles west to east, beginning of Map 5 to end of Map 13.
- 111.0 reverse miles east to west, end of Map 29 to beginning of Map 13.

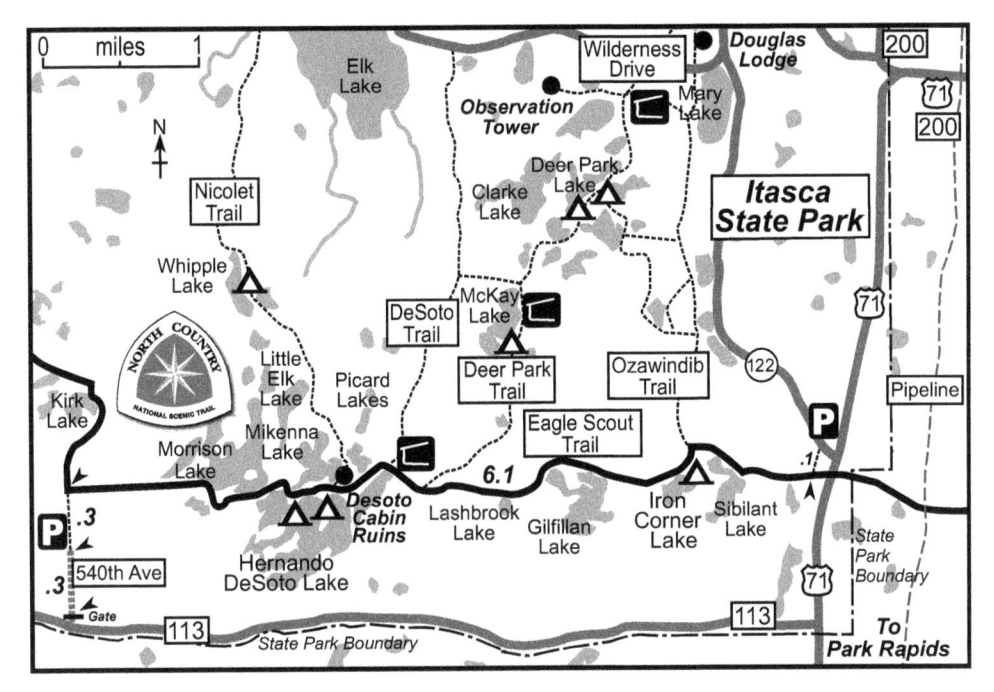

*Map 13. 540th Avenue Trailhead to Itasca State Park South Entrance Trailhead/Hubbard County 122*

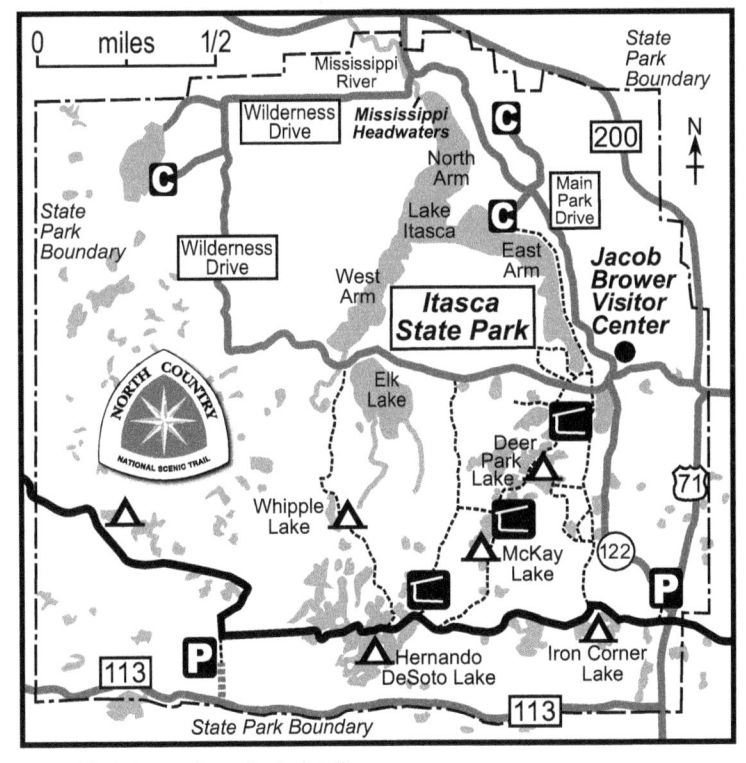

*Map 13-A. Itasca State Park detail.*

## Overview

The NCT continues through Itasca State Park, sometimes sharing old roads and wide park trails, and crossing well-used, unmarked portages. The trail undulates through old-growth and mixed forest, with some areas of magnificent mixed Norway and white pine and deciduous forest. Numerous historic sites. Access to Itasca State Park services. See Special Section in Chapter 3.

## Campsites (Permits and reservations are required.)

See also "Camping along the Trail" in Accessing and Using the NCT in Minnesota in the front of this book, and Appendix B: Camping, Campsites, Campgrounds.
- De Soto Lake
- Iron Corner
- Other Itasca State Park campsites and campgrounds.

## Services

See Appendix C for services and amenities available in these towns.
- Itasca State Park
- Park Rapids

## Winter Use

See Appendix E for winter parking at trailheads and groomed cross-country ski trails.

## Hunting Alerts

See Chapter 2: Safety on the Trail.

## Water Sources and Treatment

See Chapter 2: Safety on the Trail.

---

**Surprise—NCT Adopter/Volunteer**
"A deer and I surprised each other just a few feet apart on the trail. Our eyes met!"

---

### Alerts

The NCT shares two trails through Itasca and has junctures with others. To stay on the NCT, follow trail signs. Here's a brief breakdown on the trails and intersections:
- Mile 2.2: Juncture with Nicollet Trail terminus and the beginning of De Soto Trail. The NCT shares De Soto for a short distance, heading east.
- Mile 2.6: De Soto Trail turns north; Eagle Scout Trail begins; the NCT and Eagle Scout head east.
- Mile 2.9: Juncture with Deer Park Trail terminus.
- Mile 4.9: Juncture with Ozawindib Trail terminus; Eagle Scout Trail ends; Ozawindib and the NCT head due north, a 90-degree turn north away from Eagle Scout Trail.
- Mile 5.0: NCT exits Ozawindib after a short distance, heading due east as a single-track.
- Mile 6.2: US 71/Itasca State Park South Entrance Trailhead: the NCT bypasses trailhead.
- Only the Ozawindib Trail leads directly to park services. Park services can also be accessed via the South Entrance to the park (Hubbard County 122) and in more roundabout ways from the other trails. See Itasca State Park Map 13-A.

### Note

For more information about Itasca State Park see Chapter 3: Maplewood and Itasca State Parks.

### Map 13 Mile-by-Mile

**0.0 (6.2) Miles**

540th Avenue Trailhead
- GPS Coordinates: 7.144905, -95.254941
- Driving Directions: From Detroit Lakes, head east on Minnesota 34 for 15.7 miles; north on Becker County 37 for 21.6 miles; east on Minnesota 113 for 8.6 miles; then north on 540th Avenue (Kueber Road going south) for 0.6 mile. Access the NCT via a spur on a gated old road that heads due north 0.3 mile.
- Details: Parking for 6 vehicles

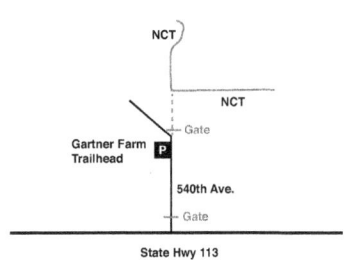

*Bench-tables like this one are placed at many campsites along the trail. Photograph by Matthew R. Davis.*

## Note

540th Avenue is locally called Gartner Farm Road, after a pioneer family. The trailhead is occasionally called Gartner Farm Trailhead. A few of the Gartner fields are still evident, but there are no farmstead remains.

## The Trail

The NCT winds eastward through a mix of old growth Norway and white pine and hardwood forest on an old park road.

### History

Hernando DeSoto Lake is near the southernmost point of the Mississippi Headwaters watershed. There is no noticeable stream flowing north from DeSoto Lake; the water drains through groundwater north toward Nicollet Lake or Elk Lake. To the south of DeSoto Lake, the land drains into the Crow Wing River, a Mississippi River tributary that enters much farther downstream. Some consider DeSoto Lake to be the true headwaters of the Mississippi River.

## 1.0 (5.2) Miles

NCT leaves old road

## The Trail

The NCT leaves the old road just before reaching Morrison Lake, turning south on single-track trail. Water can be easily obtained at the shore of the lake, but camping is not allowed there. The NCT crosses a narrow land bridge between Horn Lake and a bay of Morrison Lake, then follows along the south shore of Morrison Lake, passing through a majestic stand of old-growth Norway pine. Some up and down slopes, switchbacks, old-growth groves. There is also evidence of windfall from the 2010 storm.

**Alert**

Camping is not allowed on the shore of Morrison Lake.

**2.1 (4.1) Miles**

Campsites, Hernando De Soto Lake
- Two campsites, each with two tent sites and shared privy.
- Campsites B3 and B4 on park campground maps

**Note**

Nicollet Trail terminus/juncture with NCT.

**Reflection**
**Old Friends—NCT Adopter/Volunteer**

"While hiking on and maintaining this trail section, my wife and four young children and I have enjoyed the four Minnesota seasons. There are landmarks along the way that have become like old friends that we enjoy visiting each time we go out. These include the opening to Augusta Lake near the start of the single-track trail, the vista at the switchback overlooking the wetland west of DeSoto Lake—one day we *will* see a moose there—the large white and Norway pine, and the fabulous view of DeSoto Lake from the last stretch leading to the campsite."

**Winter Use**

Groomed cross-country ski trail from the intersection of Nicollet and Eagle Scout Trails to intersection of NCT and Ozawindib Trails.

**The Trail**

The NCT parallels DeSoto Lake to the south, with McKenna Lake to the north. It crosses up and down over small ridges, descends to the shore of DeSoto Lake and passes through the west DeSoto Lake campsite, sometimes skirting around a camper's tent. Spur trail descends via an elaborate wooden staircase to the lake from the campsite. Another spur trail leads straight

**Recommendation**

At the De Soto Lake campsite, the space on the NCT between the two tent sites is a great spot for a picnic, sitting on the ground on the pine needles overlooking the lake and Brower Island.

ahead to the east of De Soto Lake campsite. A third spur trail on the west side of the NCT leads 150 feet to a privy.

## 2.2 (4.0) Miles

Historic Site—De Soto Cabin Ruins
Nicollet Trail

### The Trail

Continuing through mixed old-growth and younger forest, the NCT passes the remains of historic DeSoto Cabin and intersects with the south terminus of Nicollet Trail. Continue east on Eagle Scout Trail to stay on the NCT through the park.

### Alert

The Nicollet Trail does not lead to park services. Stay on the NCT/Eagle Scout Trail to Deer Park Trail, Ozawindib Trail, or South Entrance Trailhead. Services can be accessed by heading north from any of these points. For distances, see Map 13-A.

---

**Itasca State Park Facts and Features**
See Chapter 3: Maplewood and Itasca State Parks.

---

## 2.6 (3.6) Miles

Juncture, DeSoto Trail, Eagle Scout Trail, Warming Shelter

### The Trail

The DeSoto Trail exits the NCT, turning north. The Eagle Scout Trail originates. The NCT and Eagle Scout Trail continue east through rolling terrain and old-growth pine and mixed hardwood forest.

## 2.9 (3.3) Miles

Juncture, Deer Park Trail and Eagle Scout Trail

### Defining "Headwaters"

Lake Itasca is the designated headwaters of the river we know as the Mississippi, which runs from Lake Itasca to the Gulf of Mexico and is the fourteenth longest river in the world. However, the lower Mississippi River carries the water of two other rivers: the Ohio, which contributes more than twice the volume of water as does the upper Mississippi, and the Missouri River. The Missouri-Mississippi is the fourth longest river in the world. For an excellent discussion of this issue, including watersheds, volume, and length, visit the displays at the Mary Gibbs Mississippi Headwaters Center at Itasca State Park.

## The Trail

Deer Park Trail terminus/juncture with NCT/Eagle Scout Trail. To stay on the NCT, continue east on Eagle Scout Trail. On the east side of Gilfillan Lake, watch for a concrete post to the south placed by CCC workers in the 1930s.

### 4.8 (1.4) Miles

Campsite, Iron Corner Lake
- One tent site, fire ring, privy

### Iron Corner

Three counties—Becker, Clearwater, and Hubbard—come together at this juncture. It is believed the name Iron Corner comes from an iron surveyor's post used to mark the location.

## The Trail

Forested throughout with aspen, birch, and other deciduous trees and scattered groups of mature Norway pine. In spring, look for wildflowers and nesting trumpeter swans.

### 4.9 (1.3) Miles

Ozawindib Trail Juncture with NCT

## Notes

- East terminus of Eagle Scout Trail.
- The NCT turns north, following Ozawindib Trail.
- After approximately 500 feet, the NCT exits the Ozawindib Trail, heads east on its own, and returns to single track.

### 6.2 (0.0) Miles

Trailhead, Itasca State Park South Entrance/Hubbard County 122. Spur trail between NCT and trailhead: 0.1 mile.

### ◀ Map 14
### Itasca State Park South Entrance Trailhead/Hubbard County 122 to Spider Lake Road Access Point

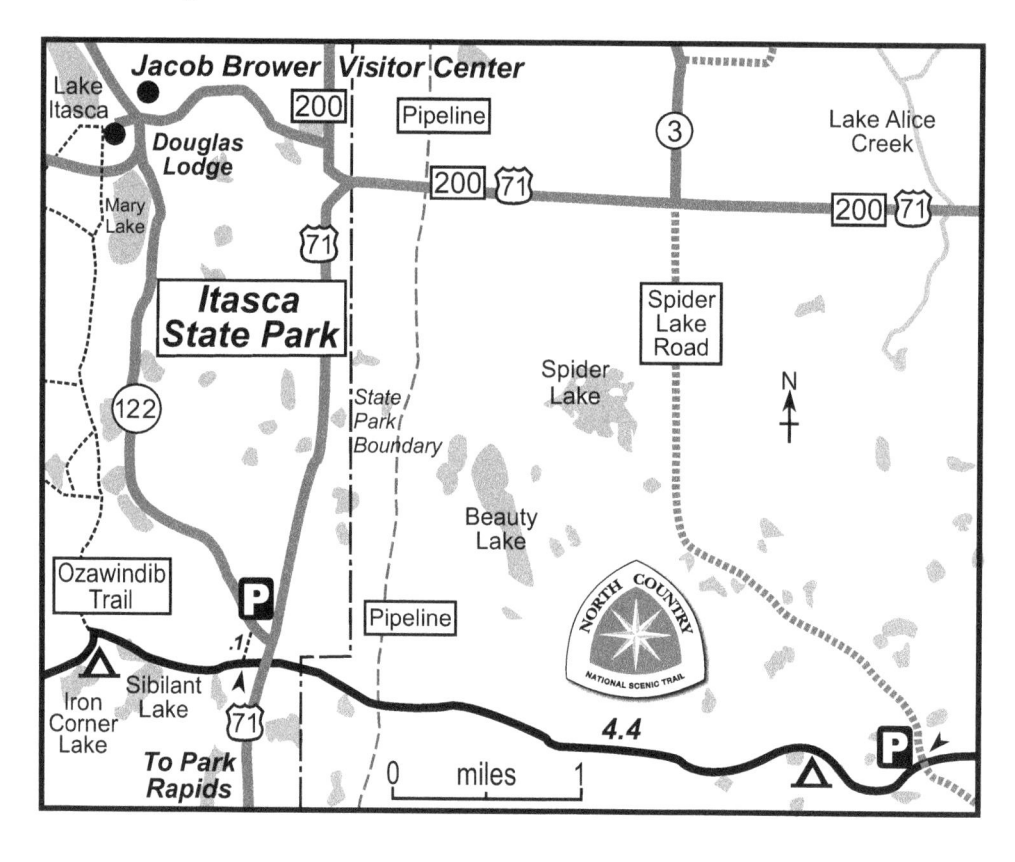

### Note

The NCT exits Itasca State Park shortly after the trail crosses US 71.

### Distance
- 4.4 miles Map 14.
- 62.9 cumulative miles west to east, beginning of Map 5 to end of Map 14.
- 104.8 reverse miles east to west, end of Map 29 to beginning of Map 14.

**Route:** The NCT leaves the wide, heavily intersected trails of Itasca State Park and returns to narrower tread and quiet forest. Gently rolling terrain, mostly deciduous forest with some passages through wetlands, typical up and down moraine topography.

### Campsites

See also "Camping along the Trail" in Accessing and Using the NCT in Minnesota in the front of this book, and Appendix B: Camping, Campsites, Campgrounds.
- Zingwaak *(means white pine in Ojibwe)*

### Services

See Appendix C for services and amenities available in these towns.
- Itasca State Park
- Park Rapids

### Winter Use

See Appendix E for winter parking at trailheads and groomed cross-country ski trails.

### Hunting Alerts

See Chapter 2: Safety on the Trail.

### Water Sources and Treatment

See Chapter 2: Safety on the Trail.

*Student Conservation Association volunteers help build trail on the NCT. Photo by Matthew R. Davis.*

## Map 14 Mile-by-Mile

**0.0 (4.4) Miles**

Trailhead, Itasca State Park South Entrance/Hubbard County 122
- GPS Coordinates: 47.153887, -95.151129

- Driving Directions: From Park Rapids, head north on US 71 for 18.4 miles. Turn west and go 0.1 mile to South Entrance of Itasca State Park.
- Details: Parking for 10 vehicles; from kiosk, follow spur trail, marked by Carsonite posts, southward across Park Entrance Road 900 feet to NCT.

**The Trail**

The NCT bypasses the State Park South Entrance Trailhead and crosses a snowmobile trail (old highway) before descending to cross US 71. When crossing, stay alert for speeding traffic. The NCT climbs up from the road cut and heads due east, soon crossing the east property boundary for Itasca State Park. It skirts the edge of an old field, swings south, then east through white birch forest and a recent logging site.

**0.8 (3.6) Miles**

Crossing, Pipeline

**The Trail**

The NCT crosses an underground oil pipeline, then a hunter walking trail. It enters a large clear-cut, then continues through mixed forest, skirting around several small wetlands and ponds.

**2.1 (2.3) Miles**

NCT enters clear-cut.

**The Trail**

The NCT enters a recent clear-cut regenerating to aspen and crosses it for the next 0.4 mile heading east.

**3.0 (1.4) Miles**

NCT passes by Three Pines Pond.

**The Trail**

The NCT reaches a view southeast across Three Pines Pond. Continue on for 0.5 mile to the next pond. The Zingwaak campsite is located on the far shore under the canopy of the pines.

### 3.5 (0.9) Miles

Spur trail to Campsite, Zingwaak
- West: Three tent sites, fire ring, privy shared with east side site; protective hardwood canopy.
- East: One tent site, table/bench, fire ring, privy shared with west side site; no protective canopy

### The Trail

The campsite is reached via a 0.2-mile spur trail on the south side of the NCT.

### 4.4 (0.0) Miles

Access Point, Spider Lake Road

### ◀ Map 15
### Spider Lake Road Access Point to Hubbard County 4 Trailhead

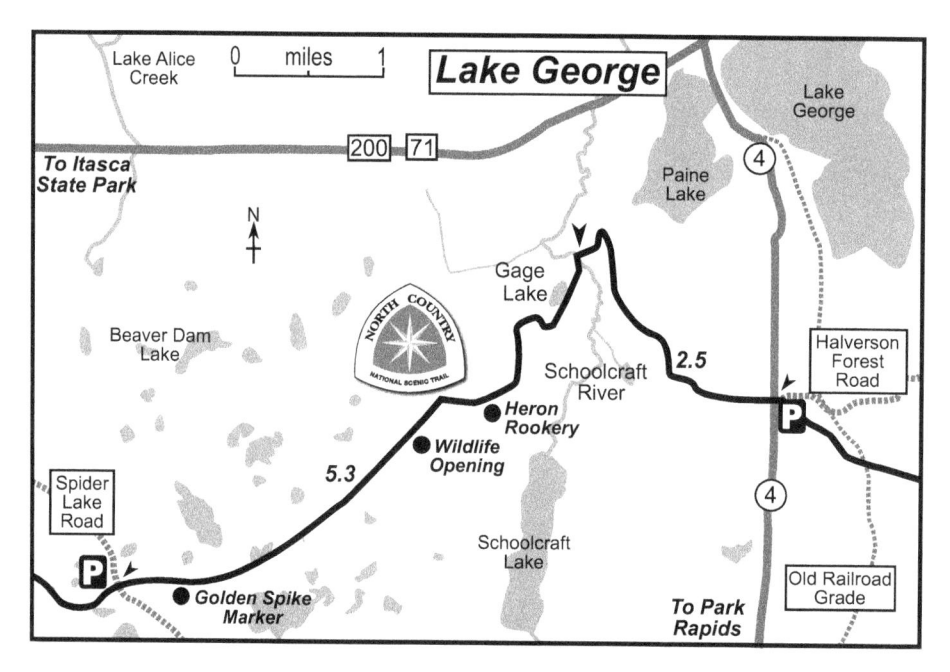

## Distance
- 7.8 miles Map 15.
- 70.7 cumulative miles west to east, beginning of Map 5 to end of Map 15.
- 100.4 reverse miles east to west, end of Map 29 to beginning of Map 15.

**Route:** The NCT crosses open fields with good views and majestic pine stands. It traverses the valley of the historic Schoolcraft River, crosses its flood plain, then the river, and back up again. Excellent vistas.

## Campsites

See also "Camping along the Trail" in Accessing and Using the NCT in Minnesota in the front of this book, and Appendix B: Camping, Campsites, Campgrounds.
- No designated campsites.

## Services

See Appendix C for services and amenities available in these towns.
- Bemidji
- Itasca State Park
- Lake George
- Park Rapids

## Winter Use

See Appendix E for winter parking at trailheads and groomed cross-country ski trails.

## Hunting Alerts

See Chapter 2: Safety on the Trail.

## Water Sources and Treatment

See Chapter 2: Safety on the Trail.

## Alerts

- The NCT crosses private land for a short distance. Please observe signs and stay on the trail.

*NCT trail adopters clear a fallen tree from the path after a major summer storm. Photo by Ray Vlasak.*

## Map 15 Mile-by-Mile
### 0.0 (7.8) Miles

Access Point, Spider Lake Road
- GPS Coordinates: 47.146123, -95.075254
- Driving Directions: From Lake George, go west on US 71 for 5.6 miles, then south onto Spider Lake Forest Road and go 3.6 miles.

## The Trail

The NCT passes through a young aspen forest, then white pine plantation. It continues through a hilly area with numerous kettle ponds emblematic of the Itasca Moraine landform and follows the north edge of a wildlife opening. There are numerous ponds and crossings of forest roads, including an old logging sprinkle road.

---

**Sprinkle Roads**

The NCT trail crosses over old "sprinkle roads." Early in the twentieth century, during the winter, water was sprinkled on logging roads. It froze, of course, making an ice road that made it easier for horse-drawn sleds to pull monstrous loads of pine logs out of the forest.

---

## 0.5 (7.3) Miles

Marker, Golden Spike Plaque

### The Trail

A plaque alongside the trail commemorates completion of the Itasca Moraine section of the trail in 2009. The NCT continues through Itasca Moraine landform and south of Gage Lake it crosses boggy wetland on a 180-foot puncheon. Look for a beaver lodge on the east shore of the lake. The NCT emerges from dark spruce and jack pine forest to follow a gravel logging road with a double culvert that crosses Schoolcraft River.

### Before the Trail

If you wonder what an area looked like before it was made into a trail, just look to the left or right—that's what you'd be trying to walk through if there were no trail. Volunteers tell about some sections taking two people half a day to clear a half-dozen feet of trail. It goes faster with the help of crews from Americorps and the Conservation Corps of Minnesota and Iowa!

## 2.4 (5.4) Miles

Wildlife opening

### The Trail

The NCT leaves the woods and enters a mowed field heading northeast for 0.1 mile before turning southeast onto a two-track road and re-entering the forest. The trail follows this road for a short way before turning north and then entering another clearing. The trail crosses the clearing directly toward an imposing deer stand on the other side.

## 3.1 (4.7) Miles

Natural Feature: Heron Rookery

### The Trail

On the south side of the trail, note the island-strewn wetland and extensive great blue heron rookery. Also look for osprey nests.

> **Stalked by a Bird!**
> Trail adopters reported that a Scarlet Tanager followed them down the trail for twenty minutes when they went out to work on the trail one spring. It was, they said, a truly amazing experience.

## 5.3 (2.5) Miles

Crossing, Schoolcraft River

### The Trail

The NCT crosses the Schoolcraft River on a forest road and then soon turns right entering a young Norway pine plantation under a sparse canopy of spruce, pine, and balsam. Upon crossing the Potlatch land, the trail changes direction abruptly, from heading north to heading south and passes through a mature spruce stand.

### Note

Crossing Private Land: Note the NCT sign, "You are now entering lands owned by the Potlatch Corporation. Thanks go to Potlatch for use of this dry passage. Please stay on the trail." This 100-yard section is the only place in Hubbard County where the NCT crosses private property.

## 6.0 (1.8) Miles

Enter forest /snowmobile trail (exit in 0.6 mile)

### The Trail

The NCT follows a forest /snowmobile trail for about 0.6 mile before exiting that trail and turning uphill to the east and starting to climb out of the valley on a single track. After another 0.5 mile, the NCT crosses

350th Street (unmarked), an unimproved road. Continue another 0.7 mile to Hubbard County 4 Trailhead.

### Schoolcraft River
In July, 1832, Ozawindib, a respected member of the Cass Lake Ojibwe community, led H. Schoolcraft and his party of European explorers from Lake Superior to the Mississippi River headwaters. They traveled across Cass Lake, Lake Bemidji, and Lake Irving, then took the Schoolcraft River and then a portage to Lake Itasca. From Cass Lake, their round trip took only five days, thanks to the knowledge and guidance of Ozawindib and the support of the Cass Lake Ojibwe community.

### 7.8 (0.0) Miles

Trailhead, Hubbard County 4/Halvorson Forest Road

### Map 16
### Hubbard County 4/Halvorson Forest Road Trailhead to Hubbard County 91 Trailhead

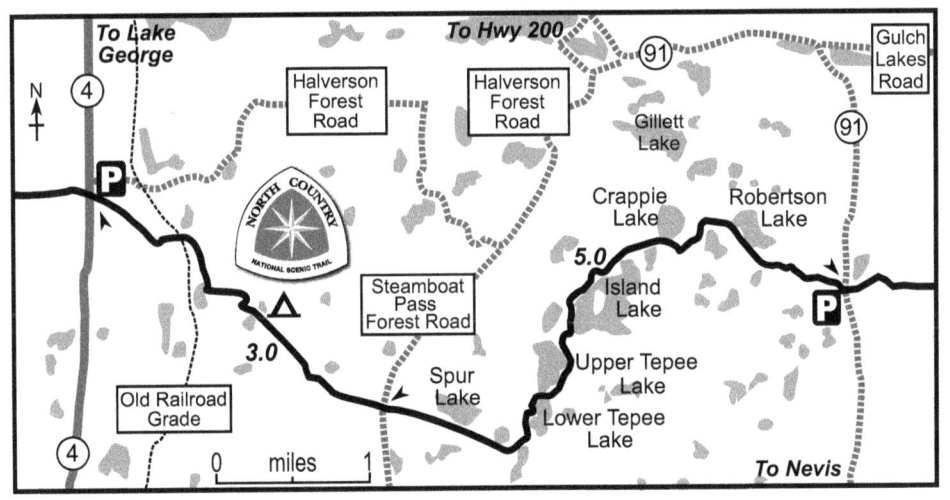

### Distance
- 8.0 miles Map 16.
- 78.7 cumulative miles west to east, beginning of Map 5 to end of Map 16.
- 92.6 reverse miles east to west, end of Map 29 to beginning of Map 16.

**Route:** The trail continues past lakes and through a variety of forest types with some moderate changes in elevation.

### Campsites

See also "Camping along the Trail" in Accessing and Using the NCT in Minnesota in the front of this book, and Appendix B: Camping, Campsites, Campgrounds.
- Amikwik Campsite (*Amikwik means beaver lodge in Ojibwe*)

### Services

*See Appendix C for services and amenities available in these towns.*
- Akeley
- Bemidji
- Lake George
- Park Rapids

### Winter Use

See Appendix E for winter parking at trailheads and groomed cross-country ski trails.

### Hunting Alerts

See Chapter 2: Safety on the Trail.

### Water Sources and Treatment

See Chapter 2: Safety on the Trail.

### Alerts

Confusing Road Names: Steamboat Pass Forest Trail is westerly on the NCT and crosses north-south. Steamboat Forest Road crosses farther east and is passable by cars.

### Map 16 Mile-by-Mile
### 0.0 (8.0) Miles

Trailhead, Hubbard County 4/Halvorson Forest Road

- GPS Coordinates: 47.166237, -94.980959
- Driving Directions: From Park Rapids, head east on Minnesota 34 for 2.1 miles; north on Hubbard County 4 for 17.4 miles; then east on Halverson Forest Road 100-feet to the trailhead.
- Details: Parking for 5 vehicles; kiosk.

*Wolf scat looks a lot like dog scat except it is grayer, more firm, and full of fur. It is fairly common on the NCT in Minnesota, though wolf sightings are rare. Photo by Matthew R. Davis.*

## The Trail

The NCT crosses Hubbard County 4 and heads east, sharing Halverson Forest Road for a while, then turns south to the Hubbard County 4 trailhead parking lot. The NCT enters a young aspen forest, then passes along the edge of a steep east-facing slope and down a hill. Watch for a pond with a large, active beaver lodge.

### 0.8 (7.2) Miles

Crossing, Old Railroad Grade

**Birdland**
A hiker/volunteer has seen flocks of yellow-shafted flickers—thousands of them—in the spring and fall.

## The Trail

The NCT crosses an old logging railroad bed, now a hunter walking trail. The forest segues from old-growth white pine to young aspen to mature deciduous forest. The trail ascends to a high point, then descends along a steep, north-facing slope that overlooks tamarack and black spruce bogs. Notice a magnificent stand of birch in the distance and tall white pines to the southeast. Elevations on this section may be a challenge for some hikers.

### 1.8 (6.2) Miles

Campsite, Amikwik
- Three tent sites, fire ring, privy, table/bench.

## The Trail

This campsite overlooks a pond with towering white pine along its west shore. A beaver lodge (*amikwik* in Ojibwe) is also in view. The NCT continues on through mature, mixed broadleaf/deciduous forest, including birch, oak, basswood, and poplar. At the perched drainage ponds, listen for peeper frogs in the spring. The trail proceeds to a cutover area where the corridor is walled off by shrubs in the summer. A stretch of young aspen dominates, then gives way to a lovely stretch of young birch.

### 3.0 (5.0) Miles

Crossing, Steamboat Pass Forest Road

### The Trail

Steamboat Pass Forest Road, an old logging railroad bed, has moderate changes in elevation from low wetland to high vista. The trail enters a small stand of mature Norway pine, then it's mostly mature, mixed hardwood, birch, oak, basswood, and poplar. There are perched drainage ponds on either side of the trail. Watch for a beaver lodge and, at a vista overlooking a wetland, look for a "pyramid" rock on the south side of the trail (how far does it go below ground?). The trail segues through mature hardwood forest, aspen re-growth and mature Norway pine. The NCT crosses other trails and roads.

### Alert

Steamboat Pass Forest Road is a minimum maintenance road; 4-wheel drive vehicles only; no parking.

### 4.3 (3.7) Miles

NCT switches directions several times on this section.

### The Trail

The NCT east of Steamboat Pass Forest Road generally travels in a southeast direction, passing Spur Lake and another small, round pond on the way. Just before reaching another small wetland, the NCT turns to the northeast and then comes close to Lower Teepee Lake before swinging southeast out onto a little point that juts into the lake and then curving back to the north before reaching a gravel road/snowmobile trail. The NCT follows this road east crossing the "land bridge" between Upper and Lower Teepee Lakes before leaving the road heading northeast.

## 5.0–7.0 (1.0–3.0) Miles

Elevations and Overlooks, Upper Tepee Lake and Robertson Lake

### The Trail

Forest transitions from younger deciduous into mature oak, aspen, and birch. Between Upper Tepee and Crappie (stocked with trout by the DNR), continual up-down-up-up elevation changes. In the Robertson Lake area, the NCT crosses a sprinkle road. Leaving Robertson Lake area, the NCT enters a mature forest of large oak with some young aspen. It crosses a hunter walking trail, then passes by a deep gully and crosses an old logging road. There is a 127-foot puncheon alongside a beaver pond. Multiple trail and road crossings.

**Recommendation—NCT Adopter/Volunteer**

"Great views from several overlooks along this stretch. Benches at Upper Tepee and Robertson Overlooks. From Upper Tepee, water can be seen for 180 degrees."

**Berries**

In mid- to late summer, there are many berries in the woods, including blackberries, blueberries, strawberries and raspberries. Some are safe to eat and are delicious. However, always identify a plant before eating its berries because there are poisonous berries in Minnesota's northern forest.

## 8.0 (0.0) Miles

Trailhead, Hubbard County 91

# Map 17
## Hubbard County 91 Trailhead to Steamboat Forest Road Access Point

### Distance
- 6.3 miles Map 17.
- 85.0 cumulative miles west to east, beginning of Map 5 to end of Map 17.
- 84.6 reverse miles east to west, end of Map 29 to beginning of Map 17.

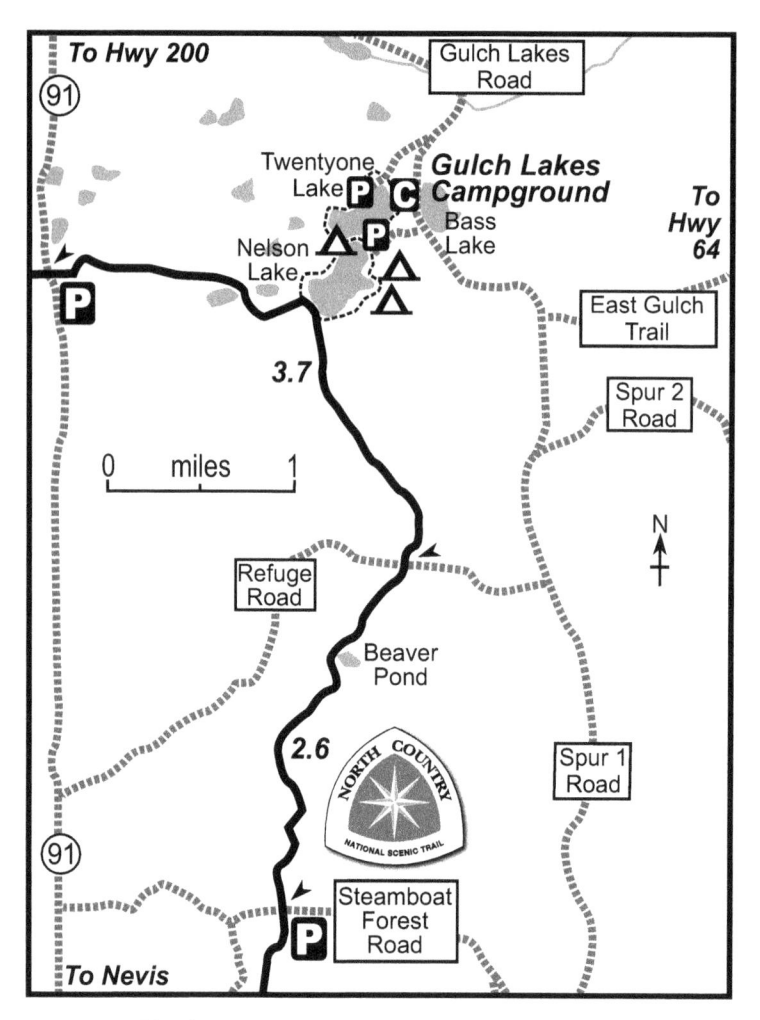

*Map 17. Hubbard County 91 Trailhead to Steamboat Forest Road Access Point*

**Route:** Typical Itasca Moraine topography of gently rolling hills and many ponds, with some excellent vistas. Passes through young birch, Norway pine, aspen. Game trails and beaver lodges around many small ponds. The NCT accesses Gulch Lakes Campground (DNR) with many tent sites.

## Campsites

See also "Camping along the Trail" in Accessing and Using the NCT in Minnesota in the front of this book, and Appendix B: Camping, Campsites, Campgrounds.

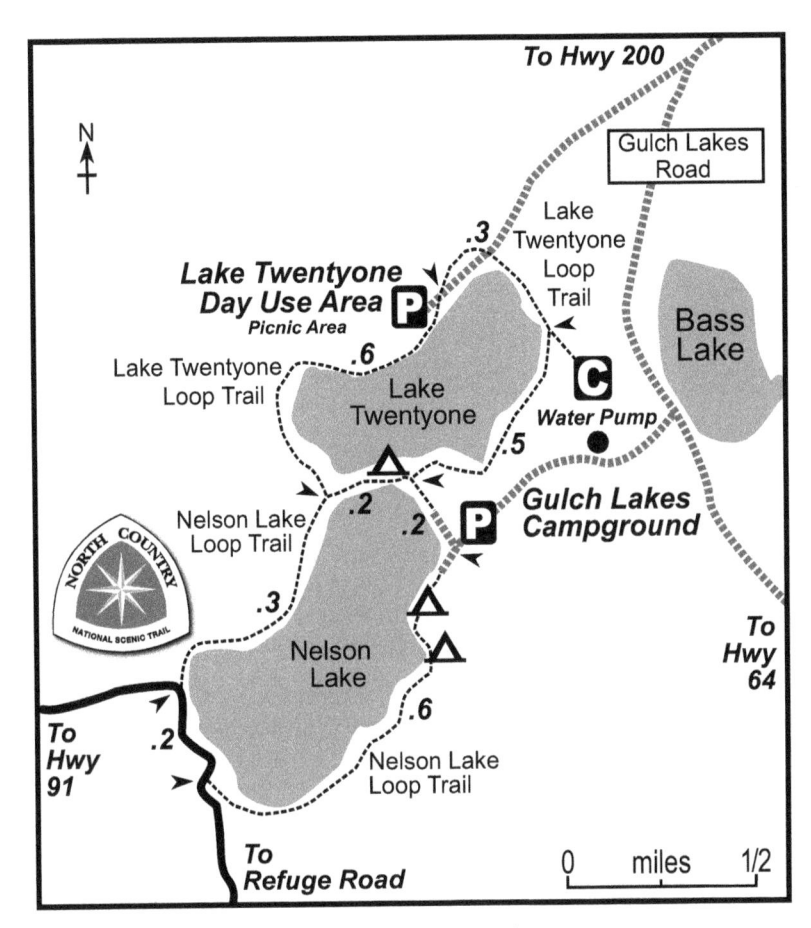

*Map 17-A. Gulch Lake Campground and Day-Use Area*

- Nelson Lake
- Gulch Lake Campground

**Services**

See Appendix C for services and amenities available in these towns.
- Akeley
- Laporte
- Nevis
- Walker

**Winter Use**

See Appendix E for winter parking at trailheads and groomed cross-country ski trails.

### Hunting Alerts

See Chapter 2: Safety on the Trail.

### Water Sources and Treatment

See Chapter 2: Safety on the Trail.

### Map 17 Mile-by-Mile
### 0.0 (6.3) Miles

Trailhead, Hubbard County 91
- GPS Coordinates: 47.156980, -94.877071
- Driving Directions: From Park Rapids, head east on Minnesota 34 for 5.2 miles; north on Minnesota 226 for 2.0 miles (town of Dorset). North of Dorset, Minnesota, 226 becomes Hubbard County 7. Continue north on County 7 for 8.7 miles where County 7 becomes Hubbard County 91. Stay on County 91 for 6.2 miles to trailhead. From Nevis, head west on Hubbard 18 for

*Beaver lodges, like this one, and beaver dams are often seen along the NCT from the Tamarac National Wildlife Refuge through the Chippewa National Forest. Note the pair of swans in the center of the photograph. Photo by Matthew R. Davis.*

2.1 miles; north to stay on 18 for additional 3.4 miles; east on Hubbard County 7 for 8.7 miles. County 7 becomes Hubbard County 91. Go 6.2 miles to trailhead.
- Details: Parking for 2 vehicles.

## The Trail

The NCT traverses both wetland and upslope terrain with ferns, blueberries, wildflowers, and mixed deciduous trees. Multiple logging road and ATV trail crossings.

---

**Bearly**

It is unusual to see a bear on the trail—bears have good hearing and a good sense of smell. They stay away when humans are around. It's a gift to see a bear on the trail. If one is nearby, you will know—they stink!

But bears have been sighted: a volunteer doing maintenance saw a sow and two cubs. Another time he saw a cinnamon-colored bear, a phase of the black bear. And recently he saw a bear loping along the trail. The bear was only 30 feet away but had not detected him. Other bear sightings: a bear and cubs playing, observed for ten minutes; a sow and three cubs going into a field; two cubs up in a tree.

---

## 1.8 (4.5) Miles

Juncture (westerly), Nelson Lake Loop Trail; Lake 21 Loop Trail Trailhead, Nelson Lake at Gulch Lake Campground and Day-Use Area. (DNR, managed by Lake Bemidji State Park) (Nelson Lake, Lake 21, Bass Lake). *See Map 17-A, Gulch Lake Campground for details.*
- GPS Coordinates: 47.157743, -94.840406
- Driving Directions: From Akeley, go east on Minnesota 34 for 0.6 mile; north on Minnesota 64 for 11.5 miles; west on Spur 2 Forest Road/Gulch Trail for 1.2 miles; north for 0.8 mile; sharp west onto Gulch Lakes Road and go 0.5 mile. From Laporte: Take Minnesota 200 west 2 miles to Minnesota 64; south 4.5 miles to East Gulch Forest Road; west 2 miles to campground entrance.
- Details: Parking for 10 or more vehicles; kiosk

## Campsites

Fee required. Contact Lake Bemidji State Park, 218-308-2300.

- Nelson Lake Loop: 3 tent sites, fire rings, picnic tables, privies, water well at campground.
- Gulch Lake Campground: 5 tent sites, fire rings, picnic tables, privies, water well.

**Loop Trails**

These two loops form a figure eight with some overlap.
- Nelson Lake: 1.4 miles, access from NCT or Recreation Area.
- Lake 21: 1.3 miles, access from Nelson Lake trail or Recreation Area.

**Alert**

Fee but no reservations; payment box on-site. Contact Lake Bemidji State Park, 218-308-2300.

**The Trail**

The figure-eight loop trails exit the NCT to the north and re-enter the NCT a short distance from the exit. There is a bench at Nelson Lake overlook. The NCT passes by the southwest end of this DNR recreation area and shares the Nelson Lake loop trail for a short distance.

**3.7 (2.6) Miles**

Crossing, Refuge Road

**The Trail**

The NCT continues along typical Itasca moraine topography, gentle up and down and up again, passing through some older clear-cuts with fifteen-year-old pine plantations.

**4.5 (1.8) Miles**

Natural Feature, Beaver Pond

**The Trail**

The NCT path goes around a large beaver pond that is on the east side of the trail.

**Step-by-Step Feature**
**Nelson Lake and Lake 21 Loop Trails**
**Gulch Lake Campground and Day-Use Area**
**Bruce M. Johnson**

The Nelson Lake loop (1.5 miles) and Lake 21 loop (1.6 miles) trails form a figure "8" that total 2.7 miles. They can be accessed from each of the lake's public access or from the Upper Gulch Lake campgrounds via a 200-yard spur trail near campsite 6. At the Nelson Lake public access there is a NCT kiosk and a "modern" outhouse. Three walk-in campsites on the lake are a part of the Gulch Lake campgrounds. There is a fee, and self-registration envelopes are available at the campgrounds. The area is a game refuge and for non-motorized use only.

To start the figure "8" hike from the kiosk at the Nelson Lake access parking lot, face the lake and go right. Continue past the boat landing and dock for 200 yards to a bridge that crosses the creek between Nelson and Lake 21 to arrive at a scenic campsite. Skirt the creek side of the campsite and continue along the north edge of Nelson Lake through the mixed hardwood deciduous forest. In about 150 yards the Lake 21 loop veers off to the north and the Nelson loop continues straight ahead overlooking pristine Nelson Lake.

On the west end of Nelson Lake the blue-blazed NCT goes off the loop trail in two places. The first heads west toward Hubbard County 91. The next leads to Refuge Road and beyond. Both T-junctions are signed so the loop trail is easy to follow. Just before finishing the Nelson loop, the trail passes two more lakeside campsites.

To complete the figure "8" retrace your start past the dock, bridge, campsite, and head west to the Lake 21 trail. Along Lake 21 on the peninsula between the two lakes there are two open stands of ironwood trees. At the west end of the Lake 21 loop one crosses near a beaver dam with views of a pond to the west and lake to the east. The trail meanders through a mature forest, past picnic areas with tables, an outhouse, boat landing, and shelter house. (Lake 21 picnic area is Day-Use only.)

The trail continues past the shelter house overlooking the lake, parallel to the entrance road. Then it crosses the road and continues along the east side of the lake to the Gulch Lake campgrounds overlook. Here there are steps leading to a dock along the lakeshore. A spur trail goes past a bench 200 yards to the campgrounds. The Lake 21 loop continues and descends, crossing a creek and gradually leading back up to a spectacular overlook of the lake. Then the trail leads back down to the bridge between the two lakes.

*Bruce M. Johnson is president of the Itasca Moraine Chapter of the NCTA.*

**6.3 (0.0) Miles**

Access Point, Steamboat Forest Road

◀ **Map 18**
**Steamboat Forest Road Access Point to Akeley Cutoff Road Trailhead Waboose Lake Loop Trail**

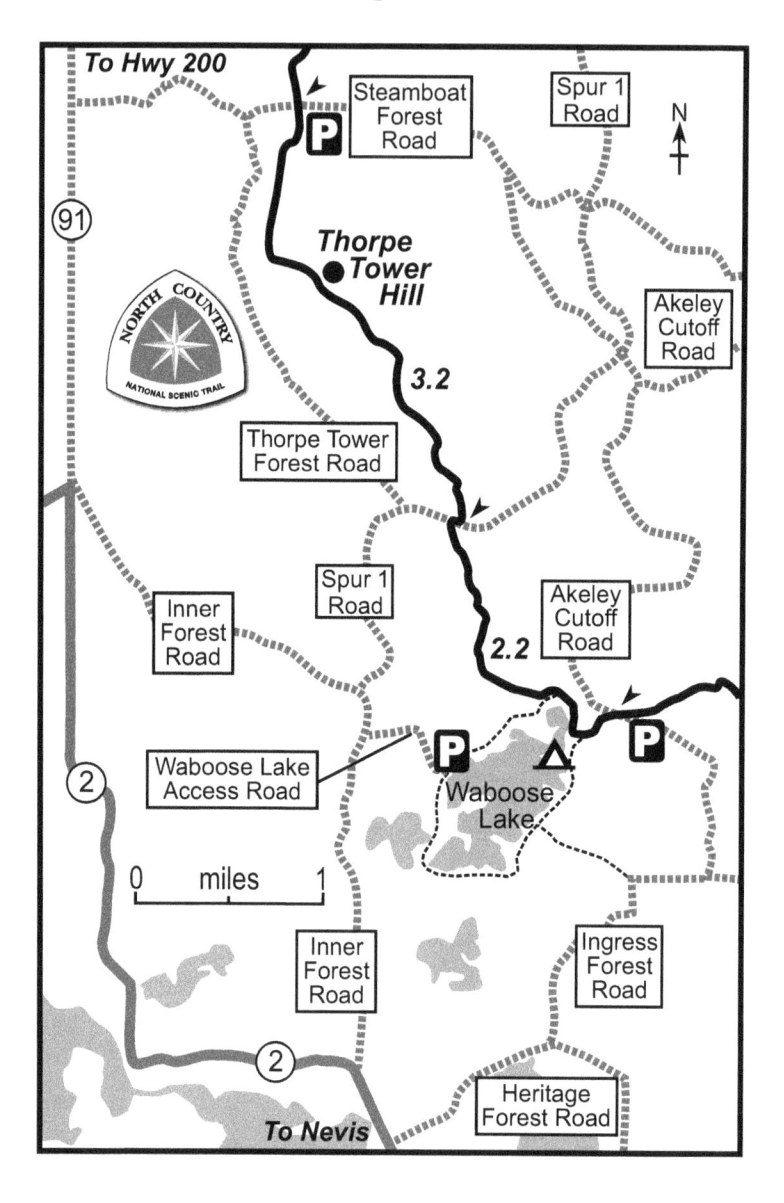

## Distance
- 5.4 miles Map 18.
- 90.4 cumulative miles west to east, beginning of Map 5 to end of Map 18.
- 78.3 reverse miles east to west, end of Map 29 to beginning of Map 18.

**Route:** Beautiful mixed forest with some up and down and occasional steeper elevation. This section includes the lovely Waboose Lake Loop Trail.

## Campsites

See also "Camping along the Trail" in Accessing and Using the NCT in Minnesota in the front of this book, and Appendix B: Camping, Campsites, Campgrounds.
- Waboose Lake

## Services

See Appendix C for services and amenities available in these towns.
- Akeley
- Laporte
- Nevis
- Walker

## Winter Use

See Appendix E for winter parking at trailheads and groomed cross-country ski trails.

## Hunting Alerts

See Chapter 2: Safety on the Trail.

## Water Sources and Treatment

See Chapter 2: Safety on the Trail.

*Hazel and other shrubs thrive in the undergrowth in younger forests such as this one. Photo by Matthew R. Davis.*

**Alert**

Confusing Road Names: Steamboat Pass Forest Trail is westerly on the NCT, crosses north-south and is a minimum maintenance road suitable only for four-wheel drive vehicles. Steamboat Forest Road is easterly, crosses west-east and is passable.

---

**Porcupine Outhouse**

On the Waboose Lake Loop Trail, there is a porcupine den in a tree with a large pile of dung around its base. The waste is four-feet high on the west side of the hollow tree. It might be the biggest porcupine scat pile in the western hemisphere.

---

*Children like to peer through the holey-oak, as this twinned tree on the Lake Waboose Loop Trail is known to NCT hikers. Photo by Ron Alden.*

## 🥾 Map 18 Mile-by-Mile

### 0.0 (5.4) Miles

Access Point, Steamboat Forest Road
- GPS Coordinates: 47.107873, -94.849863
- Driving Directions: From Dorset, head north on Hubbard 7 for 9.2 miles. Continue north on Hubbard County 91 for 2.8 miles, then east on Steamboat Forest Road for 1.4 miles.

**The Trail**

The NCT travels a north-south ridge through middle-aged aspen and continues over typical Itasca moraine topography—gentle up and down and up again. Enjoy west-facing vistas, especially in fall. Where a hunter walking trail crosses, the NCT enters a Norway pine plantation.

### 1.0 (4.4) Miles

Thorpe Tower Hill

**The Trail**

The NCT ascends to the top of Thorpe Tower Hill. At the top, notice the concrete corner foundations of an old fire tower. In 1983, fire towers were abandoned in favor of airplanes for fire detection and Thorpe Tower was dismantled. Through the trees, Mantrap Lake can be seen about 4 miles to the west. There are hunter walking trail crossings. Descent from Tower site—sometimes steep—continues through Norway pine, then enters mature stand of deciduous and pine trees. The NCT then passes through mixed forest, including a magnificent old-growth pine stand on the west-facing slope.

### 2.3 (3.1) Miles

Old growth pines

**The Trail**

The NCT enters and passes through a magnificent old-growth Norway and white pine stand on the west-facing slope before crossing a snowmobile trail and entering young aspen.

## 3.2 (2.2) Miles

Crossing, Spur 1 Road

### The Trail

The NCT ascends and descends while continuing in and out of clear-cuts and young aspen re-growth. It passes by two small ponds east of the trail. The second one, partway down a descending ridge by an old logging road, is a potential source for water. After this pond, the NCT enters older aspen and pine, then a mature mixed forest. There are snowmobile trail crossings.

## 4.5 (0.9) Miles

Waboose Lake Loop Trail, westerly juncture
Spur trail to Waboose Lake Public Water Access and Trailhead

### Notes

The Waboose Lake Loop Trail (white blazes) intersects twice with the NCT, about 0.4 mile apart. The quickest route to the campsite is from the next/easterly juncture.

### The Trail

For additional information and details see Map 18-A: Waboose Lake Loop Trail and Campsite and the Step-by-Step Feature for the Waboose Lake Loop Trail.

## 4.9 (0.5) Miles

Waboose Lake Loop Trail, easterly juncture
Campsite, Waboose Lake

### Campsite

- Trail access to campsite: Exit the NCT at second juncture of Waboose Lake Trail, following it south 0.1 mile. The spur trail to the campsite exit loops to the west. Follow 0.2 mile to campsite and lake.
- Three tent sites, fire grate, privy with privacy screen, table/bench.

*Hikers in a guided group take a break and enjoy a lake view. Photo by Matthew R. Davis.*

**5.4 (0.0) Miles**

Trailhead, Akeley Cutoff Road
Alternate Waboose Lake Loop Trail access

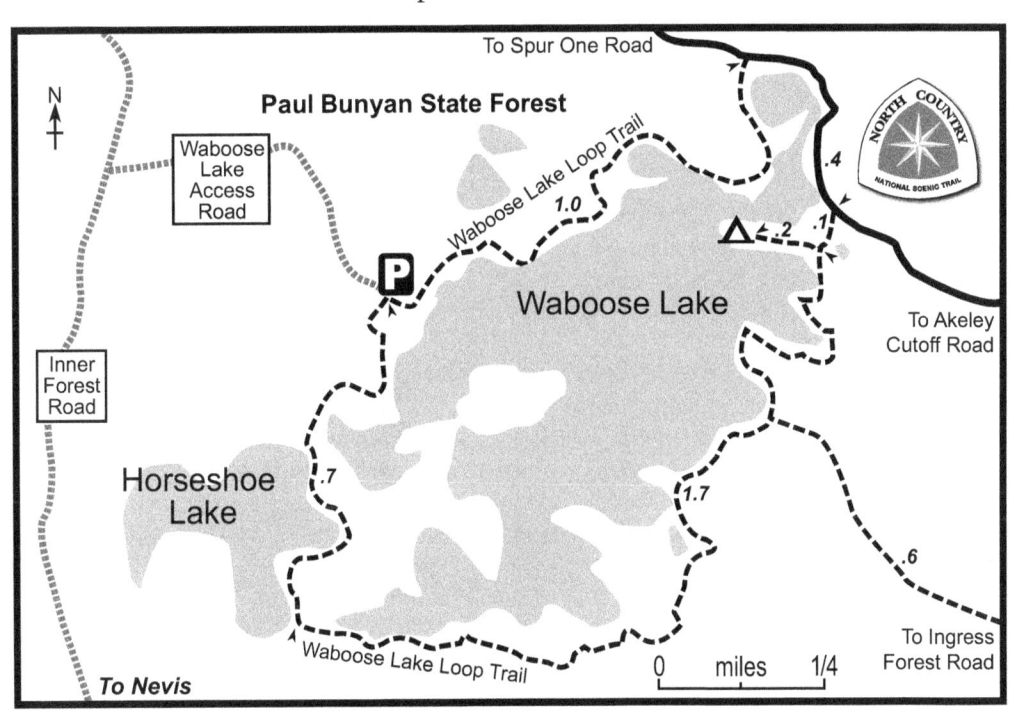

*Map 18-A. Waboose Lake Loop Trail and Campsite.*

Waboose Lake Loop Trail and Campsite
- 3.9 Mile Loop
- *Waboose* is the Ojibwe word for rabbit.
- Loop Trail blazes are white.

**Step-by-Step Feature**
**Waboose Lake Loop Trail**
**Bruce M. Johnson**
*Waboose means "rabbit" in Ojibwe*
*Loop Trail Blaze: White*

Walking north (clockwise) from the Waboose Lake public lake access/Trailhead on the west side of the lake, the loop trail enters a mature mixed pine/deciduous forest and follows along the pristine shoreline of crystal-clear Waboose Lake. The mix of trees is "as good as it gets." They include basswood, oak, maple, birch, poplar, and ironwood intermingled with white, Norway, balsam, spruce, and jack pine. Not too many places have such a rich variety of trees.

The loop trail meanders along the shore and veers off into the woods. It joins the NCT 1.0 mile from the public lake access. On the way it passes along a shallow bay where trumpeter swans are often spotted, then up a slope and through a stand of mature white and Norway pines. The next bay is home to a large, active beaver lodge. As the trail turns to the left and drops down a slope and into a brushy area, the north bay of the lake comes into view. Notice the beaver run crossing the trail.

Soon the trail ascends to the junction with the NCT where a sign indicates the NCT east and west. Follow the NCT east to stay on the loop trail. In 0.4 mile, the loop trail exits the NCT and heads back toward the lake. The spur to the Waboose Lake campsite is about 450 feet south of the NCT intersection. On the way there, look out into the bay on the right for another look at the beaver lodge. The loop drops down a hill to a short puncheon over a small ditch, then up hill where it meets the spur to the campsite. The spur goes straight ahead and the loop trail turns off to the left.

From the junction with the campsite spur, the loop trail heads south, crosses over a short puncheon and then turns to the right. Mature pines grace the path as it follows the lakeshore out onto another point. One white pine has been measured (chest high) with a 9-foot 1-inch circumference. The loop continues along the lakeshore to a beach. The public lake access can be seen straight across the lake from this point. Also notice a rough forest road leading uphill to the southeast. This unimproved road goes through a spectacular old-growth pine area and exits onto Ingress Forest Road in 0.6 mile. If you take a side trip on this road, remember to return by the same road back to the loop trail.

The loop trail continues south along the east shore of the lake for about a quarter of a mile before turning left and up onto a ridge where the trail winds between Norway and white pine and then between two mature jack pines. Most of the jack pine in Hubbard County died off in the 1980s from pine beetle infestation, so this is a precious spot. To see a cut-over area of regenerated twenty-year-old aspen, turn briefly off the ridge along the small bay.

The loop trail ascends a hill and turns to the right. Watch for the south bay of the lake from this vista. The trail then passes by some huge pine trees (they make great backrests for a lunch/rest stop), and arrives at an open lowland area to the left. A well-worn deer path parallels the hiking trail toward the lowland side. The trail continues, soon ascending a steep, north-facing slope. For 1,500 feet the trail is benched into the slope. Take a moment to stop and enjoy the scenic view of the south bay.

Continuing back toward the public lake access, the trail re-enters the woods for about 450 feet on its way to Horseshoe Lake. The trail turns right and follows along the east shore of Horseshoe Lake through mature mixed forest. About halfway along the shore the trail goes downhill and turns right. At the turn there is a unique tree: a "double" oak has turned around itself several times, grown together and created what looks like three holes in a single tree!

At the northeast corner of Horseshoe Lake the trail makes a 90-degree turn to the right and passes through an aspen re-growth. There is a marshy bay on the right and the open lake appears ahead as the trail turns to the left. It follows the shoreline about 600 feet back to the public lake access.

*Bruce M. Johnson is president of the Itasca Moraine Chapter of the NCTA.*

---

### Access to the Waboose Lake Loop Trail

**From the NCT:** Watch for loop trail white blazes. The Loop trail intersects twice with the NCT, about 0.4 mile apart. To access the loop from the NCT, hiking west to east, enter the loop at the first juncture (leaving NCT) and follow it counter-clockwise around the lake. The loop returns to the NCT 0.4 mile east of the exit onto the loop. For quickest access to the campsite, exit the NCT at the second/easterly juncture.

**From Waboose Lake public lake access** (GPS Coordinates: 47.058114, -94.832687): From Nevis, take Hubbard County 2 north for 4.8 miles to Inner Forest Road; keep going straight onto Inner Forest (County 2 veers west) for 1.8 miles to Waboose Lake Access Road/Waboose Forest Lane; go 0.6 mile to the parking area on the northwest side of lake. Follow the loop trail in either direction out of the parking area. The trail loops back to the public lake access. (Shares the NCT for 0.4 mile along the way.)

**From Akeley Cutoff Road Trailhead:** From Nevis, head north on Hubbard County 2 for 5 miles; east on Heritage Road for 1 mile to the 90-degree turn to the east; north-northeast on Ingress Forest Road for 1.1 miles; then west onto Akeley Cutoff Road for 1.3 miles. The NCT crosses the trailhead parking area. To access the loop, take the NCT west out of the parking area and follow it about 1 mile to the easterly juncture with the loop trail.

**From Access Point at Intersection of Akeley Cutoff Road and Ingress Forest Road** (GPS Coordinates: 47.050286, -94.812614): At the intersection of Ingress Forest Road and Akeley Cutoff Road look for a third road, an unnamed trail that goes off to the north-northwest. To access the Waboose Lake Loop, enter the woods on the unnamed road and walk 0.6 mile to the loop trail on the lakeshore.

### A Quick Trip into the Woods

From the road, follow directions to the access point at the intersection of Akeley Cutoff Road and Ingress Forest Road and walk into the woods on the unnamed forest road/trail, then walk back out to your vehicle. This road/trail passes through a spectacular old-growth forest that has the magical feel of ancient woods. For a longer hike, take the trail the 0.5 mile to the Waboose Lake Loop and keep going. The loop is 3.9 miles long.

From the Loop Trail, watch for the unimproved road/trail on the east side of the lake and follow it out to Ingress Forest Road. Remember to return to the loop trail (white blazes).

### Access to the Campsite

See above, 4.9 (0.5) Miles, Waboose Lake Loop Trail, easterly juncture.

### What to Watch for

The Waboose Lake Loop Trail passes through mature, mixed pine/deciduous forest. The water in Waboose Lake is crystal clear. Watch for bald eagles, trumpeter swans, other birds, and beaver activity. The loop meanders close to and away from the shoreline, passes through old-growth stands and mixed young forest, climbs and descends a steep slope where the trail is benched in (notice the view!), and skirts a lowland and the shore of Horseshoe Lake.

## Map 19
## Akeley Cutoff Road Trailhead to Minnestoa 64 Trailhead

### Distance
- 5.2 miles Map 19.
- 95.6 cumulative miles west to east, beginning of Map 5 to end of Map 19.
- 72.9 reverse miles east to west, end of Map 29 to beginning of Map 19.

**Route:** This section of the NCT is uninterrupted by roads or highways although there are several ATV trail crossings.

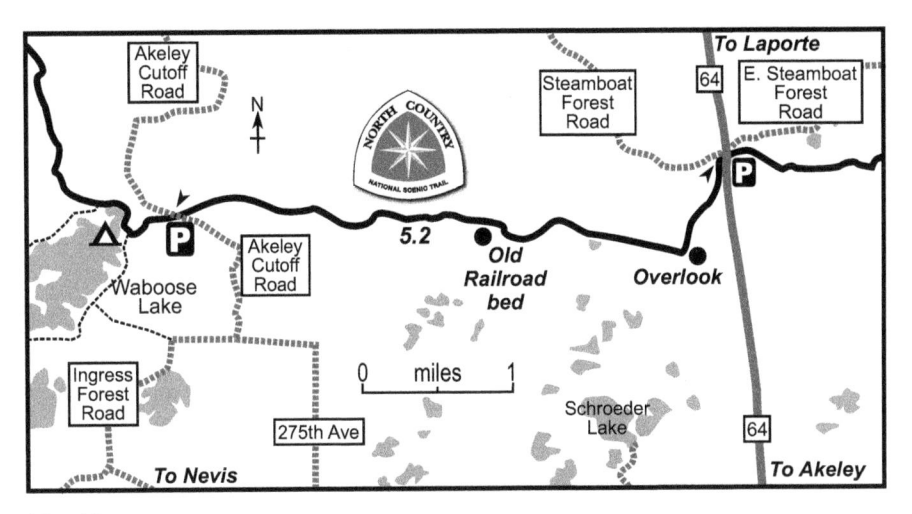

Map 19.

## Campsites

See also "Camping along the Trail" in Accessing and Using the NCT in Minnesota in the front of this book, and Appendix B: Camping, Campsites, Campgrounds.
- No designated campsites, although there is a campsite in the previous section at Waboose Lake.

## Services

See Appendix C for services and amenities available in these towns.
- Akeley
- Walker

## Winter Use

See Appendix E for winter parking at trailheads and groomed cross-country ski trails.

## Hunting Alerts

See Chapter 2: Safety on the Trail.

## Water Sources and Treatment

See Chapter 2: Safety on the Trail.

*Small lakes and ponds, and their wildlife, are abundant on the NCT from Tamarac National Wildlife Refuge through Chippewa National Forest. In spring, frog song is ubiquitous. Photo by Jerry Trout.*

## Map 19 Mile-by-Mile

**0.0 (5.2) Miles**

Trailhead, Akeley Cutoff Road
(Waboose Lake Loop Trail access)
- GPS Coordinates: 47.062112, -94.813643
- Driving Directions: From Nevis, head north on Hubbard County 2 for 5 miles; east on Heritage Road for 1.1 miles; north on Ingress Forest Road for 1.6 miles; then continue north on Akeley Cutoff Road for 1.3 miles.
- Details: Parking for 5 vehicles; the NCT crosses through the trailhead.

**Note**

Akeley Cutoff Road is a passable minimum maintenance road. It is not plowed in the winter.

> **Sighting**
> Between the Akeley Cutoff Road and Minnesota 64, a bull moose and a black bear were seen on the trail on the same day, although not at the same time.

## Alert

If using the Akeley Cutoff Road trailhead to access the Waboose Lake Loop Trail and campsite, follow the NCT west out of the trailhead. (This guide is written in the other direction, heading east.) It is about 1 mile to the first intersection with the loop. The next intersection is 0.4 mile farther west. The 0.4 mile is shared by the NCT and the loop. In addition to Map 19: Akeley Cutoff Road Trailhead to Minnesota 64 Trailhead, see Map 18-A: Waboose Lake Loop Trail and Campsite.

## The Trail

The NCT crosses through the trailhead and continues through mature, mixed forest. Watch for timber wolf signs and listen for roughed grouse drumming in spring and early summer. On windy days, be alert for falling branches from aging old-growth pines. There are multiple ATV trail crossings.

## 2.1 (3.1) Miles

Crossing old logging railroad grade/forest road

## The Trail

The NCT descends from a ridge heading northeast and crosses a forest road that was a logging railroad grade with high banks on the north that drop off to the south. The trail then heads east through mature mixed hardwoods.

## 4.2 (1.0) Miles

Overlook, Picnic Rock

## The Trail

The path passes through a beautiful white and Norway pine forest, with several beaver ponds. There is a moderate climb to a ridge with a short spur trail to a scenic overlook with bench. The overlook is especially beautiful during fall colors.

### 4.9 (0.3) Miles

Power line crossing

### The Trail

After a steep descent, the NCT crosses a power line right-of-way with an ATV trail. Notice the large boulder. Past the power line, the NCT parallels Minnesota 64 through a Norway pine plantation before reaching Spur 2 Forest Road, turning and crossing Minnesota 64 and following East Steamboat Forest Road for a short distance to the trailhead parking area.

### 5.2 (0.0) Miles

Trailhead, Minnesota 64/East Steamboat Forest Road

◀ **Map 20**
**Minnesota 64/East Steamboat Forest Road Trailhead to Minnesota 34/Shingobee Recreation Area Trailhead**

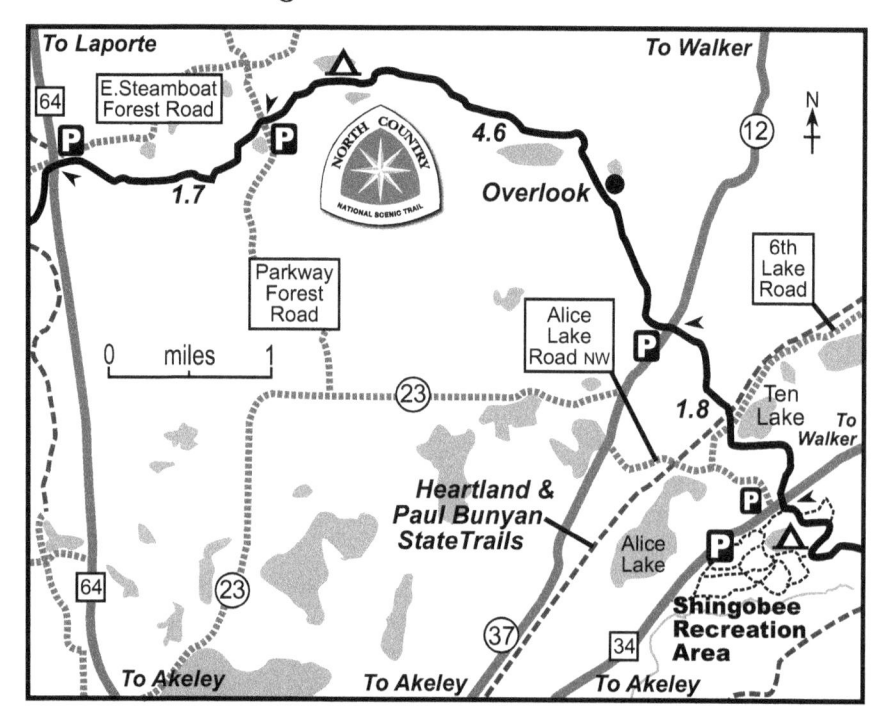

## Distance
- 8.1 miles
- 103.7 west to east, beginning of Map 5 to end of Map 20.
- 67.7 miles east to west, end of Map 29 to beginning of Map 20.

**Route:** The trail passes through mixed deciduous forest going by wetlands and a Norway pine plantation. After crossing Parkway Forest Road and beyond the campsite there is a sprinkle road between a pond and a wetland area. Continuing eastward the topography becomes hilly and the trail crosses re-growth areas. A sign marks where the NCT leaves the Paul Bunyan State Forest and enters the Chippewa National Forest. Watch for old-growth red and white pine in the predominantly mixed deciduous forest.

## Campsites

See also "Camping along the Trail" in Accessing and Using the NCT in Minnesota in the front of this book, and Appendix B: Camping, Campsites, Campgrounds.
- Sprinkle Road Lake

## Services

See Appendix C for services and amenities available in these towns.
- Akeley
- Walker

## Winter Use

See Appendix E for winter parking at trailheads and groomed cross-country ski trails.

## Hunting Alerts

See Chapter 2: Safety on the Trail.

## Water Sources and Treatment

See Chapter 2: Safety on the Trail.

**Alert**

- The NCT is in the Chippewa National Forest. Many forest roads cross the NCT in "the Chip" and sometimes the NCT shares a road for a short distance. Some of the roads are identified by number on the maps in this guide, some are not. All crossings and road walks are blue-blazed.

## Map 20 Mile-by-Mile

### 0.0 (8.1) Miles

Trailhead, Minnesota 64/East Steamboat Forest Road
- GPS Coordinates: 47.069029, -94.731867
- Driving Directions: From Akeley, go east on Minnesota 34 for 0.6 mile; north on Minnesota 64 for 4.4 miles; then east on East Steamboat Forest Road for 0.1 mile.
- Details: Parking for 5 vehicles; kiosk

---

**Magnificence**

It is one of the beauties of the trail that we sometimes see wildlife. There is no need to be afraid.

---

*Occasionally the NCT emerges from dappled-forest shadows into the sunlight of a field. Photo by Matthew R. Davis.*

### The Trail

The NCT continues through mixed forest with some up and down changes in elevation.

### 1.7 (6.4) Miles

Trailhead, Parkway Forest Road
- GPS Coordinates: 47.073863, -94.706354
- Driving Directions: From Akeley, go east on Minnesota 34 for 0.6 mile; north on Minnesota 64 for 4.4 miles; east on East Steamboat Forest Road for 1.5 miles; then south on Parkway Forest Road/Blue Trail Road for 0.4 mile.

### The Trail

The NCT meanders around hills and past ponds through mature deciduous forest.

### 2.1 (6.0) Miles

Spur Trail to Campsite, Sprinkle Road Lake
- 60 feet off NCT to the north
- Four tent sites, fire ring, privy, bench/table

### The Trail

The trail continues through mixed forest, gradually ascending to an overlook.

### 4.2 (2.1) Miles

NCT follows a logging road.

### The Trail

The trail leaves a recent timber harvest, re-enters a young aspen forest and then descends on an old skid trail to a logging road. It follows this road heading southeast, turning northeast at a fork where another road comes in from the southwest. The road and the NCT turn to the northeast, crossing into Cass County and the Chippewa National Forest before the NCT turns 90 degrees to the southeast and re-enters the woods.

### Chippewa National Forest's Many Roads

Just before "Aaron's Bench" (see below), the NCT enters the Chippewa National Forest. Many forest roads cross the NCT in "the Chip" and sometimes the NCT shares a road for a short distance. Some of the roads are identified by number on the maps in this guide, some are not. All crossings and road walks are blue-blazed.

### 4.6 (3.5) Miles

Overlook, Aaron's Bench

**The Trail**

Mixed forest and Norway pine plantations.

**Comment**

Just after entering the Chippewa National Forest, notice Aaron's Bench. It was an Eagle Scout project made for the "then" groomed cross-country ski trail. Notice how high off the ground it is to accommodate twenty inches of snow and a place for the skiers to sit and rest.

### 6.3 (1.8) Miles

Trailhead, Cass County 12
- GPS Coordinates: 47.054569, -94.651337
- Driving Directions: From Akeley, go east on Minnesota 34 for 3.3 miles; north on 73rd Avenue NW for 1.9 miles; slight turn to the east onto Cass County 12 NW and go 0.4 mile. From Walker, go west on Minnesota 200/Minnesota 371 for 0.2 mile; turn south on 10th Street South and go 0.4 mile; 10th Street becomes Cass County 12—continue on it for 4.5 miles.
- Details: Parking for 5 vehicles; kiosk

**Alert**

Crossing of Heartland and Paul Bunyan State Trails (paved for biking, hiking).

**The Trail**

The NCT meanders through pine and deciduous forests, especially Norway and white pine, birch, oak, and aspen along gentle, rolling hills.

### 7.1 (1.0) Miles

Crossing, Heartland and Paul Bunyan State Trails and 6th Lake Road

## The Trail

The NCT crosses the paved Heartland and Paul Bunyan State Trail and comes out to 6th Lake Road NW. The NCT turns south on the gravel road and re-enters the woods straight ahead as the road curves back to the west. The NCT then skirts the west side of Ten Lake past an inlet of marsh grasses. Look for trumpeter swans, Canada geese, and many ducks in spring, summer, and fall. Overall topography is gently rolling hills with many good scenic views. Traffic sounds can be heard as the NCT approaches Minnesota 34 crossing and trailhead.

---

### Side Trip to the city of Walker

The Heartland and Paul Bunyan State Trails and Shingobee Connection Trail, paved hiking/biking paths, provide a convenient detour into the city of Walker* and back to the NCT. When hiking the NCT west to east, exit the NCT on the Heartland/Paul Bunyan State Trail at the crossing of Alice Lake Road/6th Lake Road, Map 20. Take the Heartland/Paul Bunyan north to Walker, approximately 4.6 miles. At Walker, the Heartland crosses to the north side of Minnesota 200/US 371 and intersects with the Shingobee Connection Trail, which runs east and south through Walker, skirting Leech Lake and crossing 200/371 several times. It intersects with the NCT at the juncture with the Paul Bunyan State Trail near Cyphers Lake, Map 21. There is a warming shed at this intersection. From the warming shed, the Paul Bunyan Trail goes south to Brainerd (approximately 60 miles) and the NCT goes east. The Connection Trail is 6.1 miles from the Heartland Trail to the Paul Bunyan/NCT/warming shed.

The trip into Walker and back to the NCT is about **10.7** miles. It bypasses approximately 6 miles of NCT, including Shingobee Recreation Area and County Road 50 Trail System (hunter walking trail).

*For Walker details, see Appendix C: Service Towns.

---

## 8.1 (0.0) Miles

Trailhead, Minnesota 34/Shingobee Recreation Area
Additional 0.6 mile into Shingobee Recreation Area

## Map 21
## Minnesota 34/Shingobee Recreation Area Trailhead to Minnesota 371/Lake Erin Trailhead

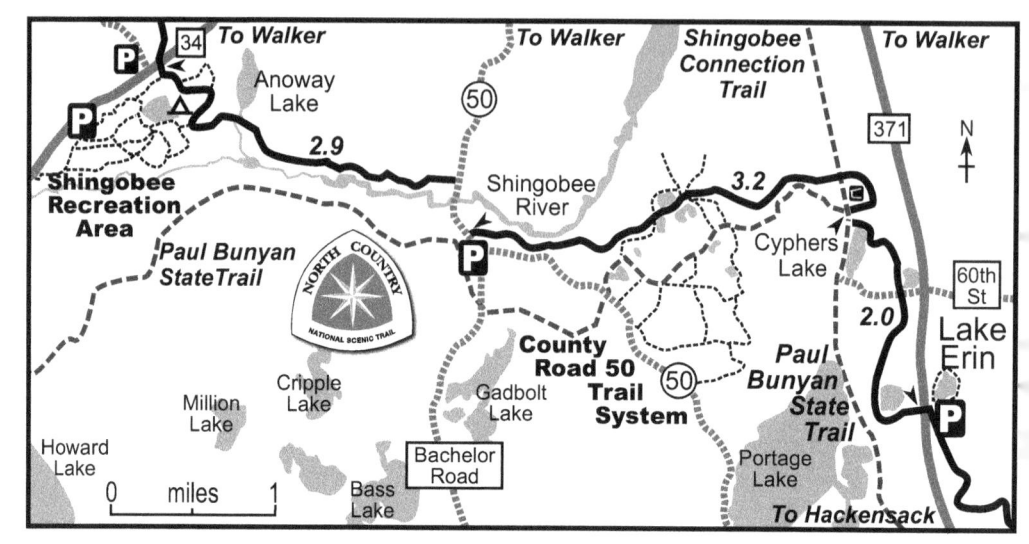

*Map 21. Minnesota 34/Shingobee Recreation Area Trailhead to Minnesota 371/Lake Erin Trailhead*

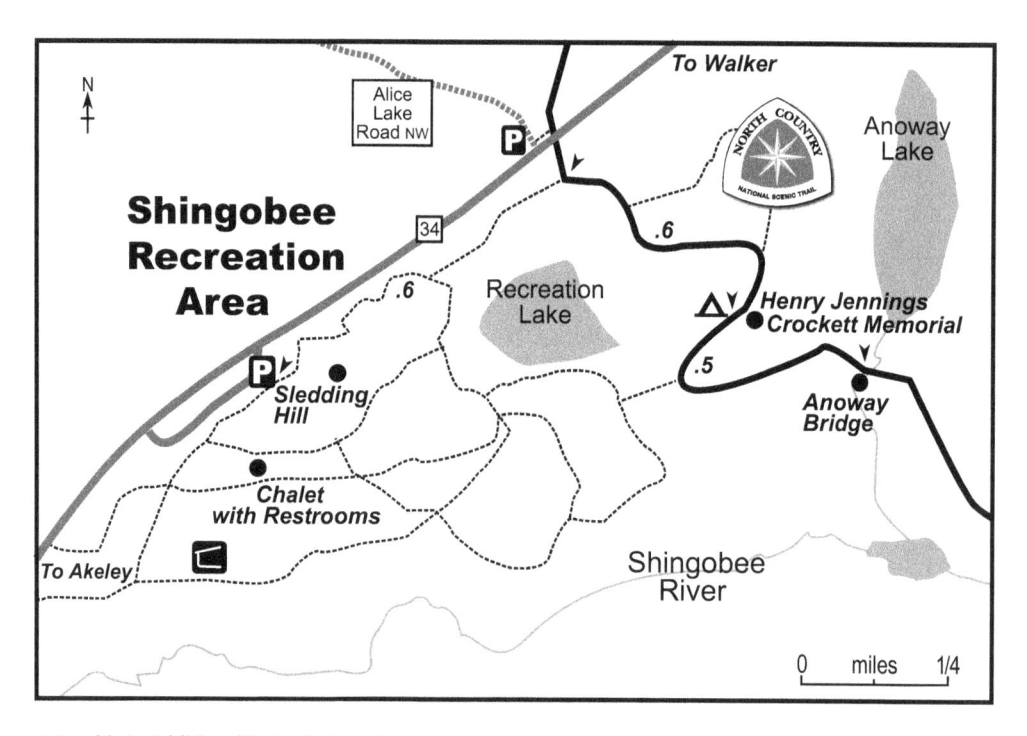

*Map 21-A. Additional 0.6 mile into Shingobee Recreation Area.*

**Distance**
- 8.1 miles Map 21.
- 111.8 cumulative miles west to east, beginning of Map 5 to end of Map 21.
- 59.6 reverse miles east to west, end of Map 29 to beginning of Map 21.

**Parking**
- Lake Alice Road NW, 200 feet northwest of Minnesota 34.
- Additional parking/trailhead in Shingobee Recreation Area, 0.6 mile west on Minnesota 34.

**Route:** Multiple trail crossings and switchbacks in the Recreation Area. One of the most hilly sections of the NCT in Chippewa National Forest. Leaving Shingobee Recreation Area, the NCT ascends, then turns south to an open meadow with a memorial to Harry Jennings Crockett on the south side and a campsite on the north. The NCT continues south with occasional sharp turns, crosses Anoway Stream on a bridge, then rises and descends on a ridge overlooking Shingobee River Valley, emerging out of forest at a large open bank that descends to Cass County 50. The NCT meanders through old-growth pine, fir, and hardwood forest, and a wealth of wildflowers. Some parts of the trail feel remote; expect traffic at Paul Bunyan Bicycle Trail intersections. Hilly terrain throughout.

**Campsites**

See also "Camping along the Trail" in Accessing and Using the NCT in Minnesota in the front of this book, and Appendix B: Camping, Campsites, Campgrounds.
- Shingobee Recreation Area Dispersed Camping
- Crockett Memorial Campsite

**Services**

See Appendix C for services and amenities available in these towns.
- Hackensack
- Walker

### Winter Use

See Appendix E for winter parking at trailheads and groomed cross-country ski trails.

### Hunting Alerts

See Chapter 2: Safety on the Trail.

### Water Sources and Treatment

See Chapter 2: Safety on the Trail.

*Backpackers enjoy a side trail to a vista overlook. The path is tended but does not disturb the forest. Photo by Matthew R. Davis.*

### 🥾 Map 21 Mile-by-Mile

### 0.0 (8.1) Miles

Trailhead, Minnesota 34/Shingobee Recreation Area

- GPS Coordinates: 47.037426, -94.643258
- Driving Directions: From Walker, head west on Minnesota 34 for 5.6 miles; the parking lot is to southeast. From Park Rapids, head east on Minnesota 34 for 22.6 miles.
- Details: Parking for 50 or more vehicles; kiosk, US Forest Service Map. Parking also available on Lake Alice Road NW off Minnesota 34.

### Note

Trailhead is 0.6 mile from the NCT. Follow the signs.

### Shingobee Recreation Area

"Nestled along the rolling hills of the Shingobee River Valley, the Shingobee Recreation Area provides a variety of summer and winter activities. The area offers 6 miles of trails for hiking, hunting, bird watching, camping, and cross-country skiing in the heart of Minnesota's northern forest. A sledding hill and a weekend warming chalet are also available for winter fun." (www.fs.usda.gov/recarea/chippewa) There are no public-use fees at Shingobee and it is open year-round. Chippewa National Forest, Walker Ranger District, 201 Minnesota Avenue East, Walker, MN 56484, 218-547-1044.
- Amenities: Warming chalet for events, gatherings; restrooms; winter sledding hill; hiking/cross-country ski trails.

### Campsites

See also "Camping along the Trail" in Accessing and Using the NCT in Minnesota in the front of this book, and Appendix B: Camping, Campsites, Campgrounds.
- Shingobee Camping: Dispersed camping within the Recreation Area.
- Crockett Memorial east of the Recreation Area: See 0.6 (7.5) Miles Shingobee Campsite, below.

### Winter Use

Groomed cross-country ski trail, just east of Minnesota 34 to just west of the Anoway Bridge.

### The Trail

Stop to enjoy beautiful views from Anoway Bridge, including wetlands, wild rice beds, and a tamarack swamp.

### 0.6 (7.5) Miles

Spur Trail to Shingobee Campsite

### The Trail

The NCT follows a couple of cross-country ski /hiking trails before entering a small open area with a memorial. Just past the memorial is the spur trail leading north to the Shingobee Campsite. The NCT parallels the Shingobee valley under a canopy of conifers.

**Evidence—NCT Adopter/Volunteer**

"While building a section of the trail, an Americorps volunteer found a bone of some kind. It was too thick and not long enough for a deer and too big for a beaver, so I took it to the DNR. They identified it as the femur of a wolf. They conjectured that it might have been an alpha or beta wolf that lost a struggle for dominance with another wolf."

### Campsites

Crockett Memorial east of the Recreation Area: 2 tent sites, fire ring, privy.

### Alert

Water is inconvenient to obtain at this campsite. It can be obtained at Ten Lake (west) or Anoway Stream (east).

### 2.6 (5.5) Miles

Cass County 50

### The Trail

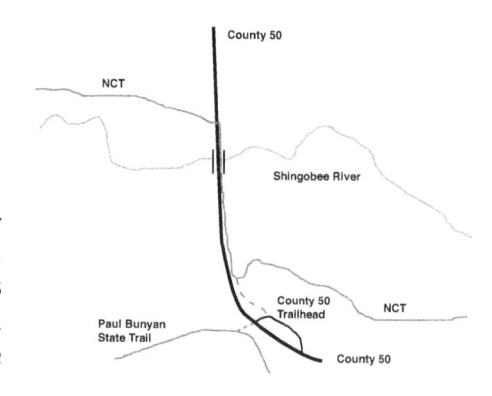

The NCT leaves the forest and descends a bank to reach County 50, turns, crosses Shingobee River, climbs a hill, then drops through the ditch and up the bank before entering the woods. Just before the forest, a short spur trail heads to the trailhead parking area.

## 2.8 (5.3) Miles

Trailhead, Cass County 50
- GPS Coordinates: 47.030238, -94.596062
- Driving Directions: From Walker, head west on Minnesota 34 for 2.8 miles, then east on Cass County 50 for 2.5 miles. From Hackensack, head north on Minnesota 371 for 4.6 miles; then west on Cass County 50 for 4.8 miles.
- Details: Parking for 20 or more vehicles; kiosk, US Forest Service Map; Paul Bunyan State Trail information; from parking area, follow signs on spur trail 0.1 mile to NCT.

## Alert

Multiple trail crossings of County Road 50 hunter walking trail system in the next 2 miles.

## The Trail

A short spur trail leads southeast to the trailhead parking area.

## 4.4 (3.7) Miles

Crossing, Hunter Walking Trail

## The Trail

The NCT crosses a wide hunter walking trail and then another after 0.3 mile.

**Shingobee River**
The river flows east then northeast into Shingobee Bay of Leech Lake east of Walker. Leech Lake is the third largest lake in Minnesota.

## 6.1 (2.0) Miles

Juncture, Shingobee Connection Trail, Warming Shelter
*The connector trail links the Paul Bunyan State Trail at Walker.*

## The Trail

The NCT intersects again with Paul Bunyan State Trail, crosses it, comes back to it, passing a warming shelter, and then shares it going south.

The shelter has a bench and a privy. To stay with the NCT, continue south for about 90 feet. Watch for the NCT to make a 90-degree turn east where it exits Paul Bunyan and re-enters the forest. Enjoy this excellent treadway by Cypher Lake.

### 6.7 (1.4) Miles

Crossing, 60th Street

### The Trail

The NCT meanders, crosses a small beaver run on a puncheon, and passes through wetlands. It turns east to cross Minnesota 371 and spur connector 0.1 mile to trailhead.

### 8.1 (0.0) Miles

Spur trail to trailhead, Minnesota 371/Lake Erin

## ◀ Map 22
### Minnesota 371/Lake Erin Trailhead to Forest Road 3790 Access Point

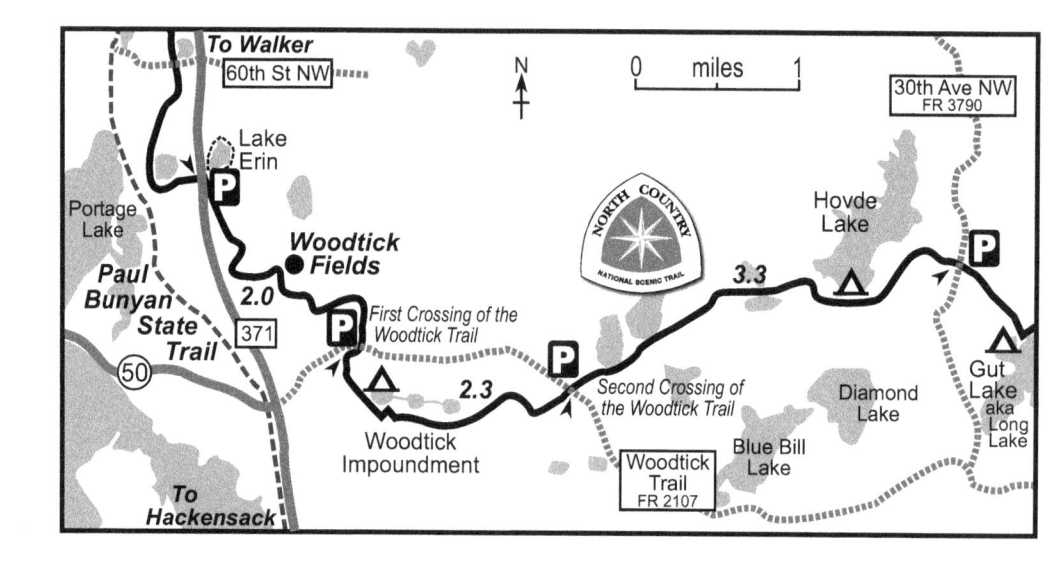

*Chippewa National Forest. See Appendix F: Restricted-Use Areas.*

## Distance
- 7.6 miles Map 22.
- 119.4 cumulative miles west to east, beginning of Map 5 to end of Map 22.
- 51.5 reverse miles east to west, end of Map 29 to beginning of Map 22.

**Route:** The NCT meanders through mostly level hardwood forest, with some ups and downs, typical of the Chippewa National Forest.

## Campsites

See also "Camping along the Trail" in Accessing and Using the NCT in Minnesota in the front of this book, and Appendix B: Camping, Campsites, Campgrounds.
- Woodtick Impoundment
- Hovde Lake

## Services

See Appendix C for services and amenities available in these towns.
- Hackensack
- Walker

## Winter Use

See Appendix E for winter parking at trailheads and groomed cross-country ski trails.

## Hunting Alerts

See Chapter 2: Safety on the Trail.

## Water Sources and Treatment

See Chapter 2: Safety on the Trail.

## Map 22 Mile-by-Mile

**0.0 (7.6) Miles**

Trailhead, Minnesota 371/ Lake Erin
Lake Erin Loop Trail
- GPS Coordinates: 47.015932, -94.535626
- Driving Directions: From Walker, head east then south on Minnesota 371 for 7.2 miles. From Hackensack, head north on Minnesota 371 for 6.1 miles.
- Details: Parking for 20 or more vehicles; kiosk, US Forest Service map; picnic tables; Lake Erin Loop Trail

*Wetlands are common along the middle passage of the NCT in Minnesota. The tamaracks in the center of this photo have turned golden and will soon lose their needles for the winter. Photo by Deane Johnson.*

### Engineers

The beaver dam one-half mile north of the first crossing of the Woodtick Trail is a master of beaver engineering. It is a gorgeous and functional dam, backing up a tremendous amount of water. The NCT used to be above the dam. Look for an old blue diamond trail marker on a dead tree in the pond above the dam.

## Lake Erin Loop Trail

0.6 mile. See alert below for intersections with NCT.

## Alerts

- From the trailhead, access the NCT via a spur trail to the southeast. This spur passes by the Lake Erin Loop Trail. Unless you want to walk around the lake, keep going straight until you get to the blue blazes.
- From the NCT to the trailhead, a connector spur goes north while the NCT continues east. Go straight past Lake Erin Loop Trail, which goes off to the east.

## The Trail

Forest is mixed hardwood; the trail sometimes meanders, crosses a stream on a wooded puncheon directly beneath a classic beaver dam.

## 0.7 (6.9) Miles

Woodtick Fields

## The Trail

The fields on both sides of the NCT were used by homesteaders in the early to mid 1900s. After the fields, the trail crosses a stream on a wooden puncheon directly beneath a classic ancient beaver dam. Below the dam is a fertile area with lots of moisture and it is difficult to keep vegetation from overwhelming the puncheon. If the path looks like a sea of green below the dam, probe with your walking stick to find the puncheon. It is nearly three feet wide and runs the entire distance of the dam, following the arc of the structure.

> **History**
>
> A large meadow east of the first crossing of the Woodtick Trail is known as Woodtick Fields. This land was cleared for sheep grazing early in the twentieth century and the Forest Service has kept it cleared for the benefit of wildlife.

## 2.0 (5.6) Miles

Trailhead, Woodtick Trail/Forest Road 2107, First Crossing (from Minnesota 371)
- GPS Coordinates: 47.000041, -94.513879
- Driving Directions: From Walker, head east on Minnesota 200/Minnesota 371 for 4.5 miles; follow 371 south onto Minnesota 371 for 4.0 miles; turn east onto Woodtick Trail for 0.7 mile.
- Details: Parking for 10 vehicles.

## The Trail

The NCT makes its first crossing of the Woodtick Trail/Forest Road 2107. The forest is mostly mixed hardwood with some noticeable wetlands.

> **Information**
>
> The Woodtick Trail/Forest Road 2107 was originally a logging railroad grade. It is generally open year round and is restricted to street-legal vehicles only. It is 14 miles long and can be accessed at its west end from Minnesota 371 about 3 miles north of Hackensack and at its east end from Cass County 5, about 5 miles west of Longville. The NCT crosses the Woodtick Trail four times. The first, second, and fourth crossings are trailheads and have cleared parking areas. The third crossing is an access point that accommodates roadside parking. Parking is not generally available at any of the Woodtick crossings in winter.

### 2.6 (5.0) Miles

Campsite, Woodtick Impoundment.
- Two tent sites, fire ring, privy (for location see below).

The impoundment wetland is north of the NCT. As the trail begins to descend to the base of the pond, watch the west side of the hill for a trail that goes up to a ridge. A wilderness privy (no screen) is at the top of the hill just past a previous campsite and fire ring. Continuing straight on the NCT, the trail quickly comes to the current campsite on the north side of the trail and near the shore of the pond. Just past the campsite is a small creek where water exits the pond. A constructed rock crossing allows passage across the creek but it can also be stepped across a few feet farther downstream. From the stream crossing, the NCT enters an open area and ascends a slope back into the forest. At the top of a hill, watch for an old-growth pine grove to the east. Take a minute to enter the grove, to step back in time. Notice the cooler temperature in the grove and the sweet silence of an old forest.

**Woodtick Impoundment**
Created in 1976 by the Forest Service, the impoundment discouraged water flow out of a wetland and was designed to provide shallow water for waterfowl feeding and nesting. It has been restored to its natural state.

### 4.3 (3.3) Miles

Trailhead, Woodtick Trail/Forest Road 2107, Second Crossing (heading east from Minnesota 371)
- GPS Coordinates: 46.996529, -94.486885
- Driving Directions: From Walker, head east on Minnesota 200/Minnesota 371 for 4.5 miles; follow 371 south for 4.0 miles; then east on Woodtick Trail for 2.1 miles. From Hackensack, head north on Minnesota 371 for 4.3 miles, then east on Woodtick Trail for 2.1 miles.
- Details: Parking for 5 vehicles

### The Trail

Glacial moraine ascends and descends in rolling hills and occasionally runs along the top of a long ridge with views down each side. Mature deciduous forest with lots of giant oaks, some maple and birch, and a few Norway and white pine. Most of the trail is shady or dappled shade.

Numerous small ponds, filled with water lilies, are visible on both sides of the trail. Multiple trail and road crossings.

### 6.6 (1.0) Miles

Spur trail to campsite, Hovde Lake
- North of the NCT at end of 35-foot spur trail.
- One tent site, fire ring, bench, privy (on south side of NCT). Campsite and privy trails are blazed where they intersect the NCT.

### The Trail

The trail continues through typical glacial moraine typography. Wildflowers include large trillium, bellwort, anemone, blue bead, hepatica, violets, and wild strawberries.

### 7.6 (0.0) Miles

Access Point, Forest Road 3790

### ◀ Map 23
**Forest Road 3790 Access Point to Woodtick Trail/Forest Road 2107 Access Point, Third Crossing (heading east from Minnesota 371)**

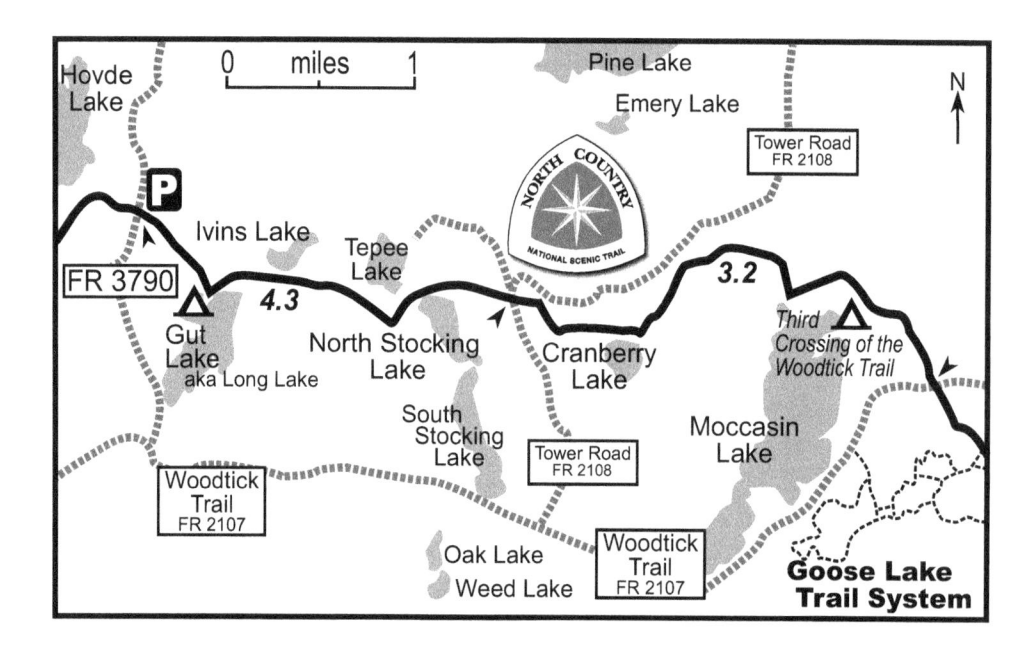

*Chippewa National Forest. See Appendix F: Restricted-Use Areas.*

## Distance
- 7.5 miles Map 23.
- 126.9 cumulative miles west to east, beginning of Map 5 to end of Map 23.
- 43.9 reverse miles east to west, end of Map 29 to beginning of Map 23.

**Route:** The trail passes by five named lakes as well as several unnamed ponds and wetlands. The trail is quite level with some gradual ups and downs. Vegetation is a mosaic of mixed pine and deciduous forests with some pine plantations. Wildflowers on the forest floor include trillium, bellwort, anemone, bluebeard, hepatica, violets, and wild strawberries.

## Campsites

See also "Camping along the Trail" in Accessing and Using the NCT in Minnesota in the front of this book, and Appendix B: Camping, Campsites, Campgrounds.
- Gut Lake

## Services

See Appendix C for services and amenities available in these towns.
- Hackensack
- Longville
- Walker

## Winter Use

See Appendix E for winter parking at trailheads and groomed cross-country ski trails.

## Hunting Alerts

See Chapter 2: Safety on the Trail.

## Water Sources and Treatment

See Chapter 2: Safety on the Trail.

*Fungi are common along the NCT, both on the path and in the woods. This one is probably a form of Laetiporus sulphureus, sulpher shelf, also called chicken of the woods.*

## Map 23 Mile-by-Mile

### 0.0 (7.5) Miles

Access Point, Forest Road 3790
- GPS Coordinates: 47.006275, -94.435859
- Driving Directions: From Hackensack, head north on Minnesota 371 for 4.3 miles; east on Woodtick Trail for 5 miles; north on Forest Road 3790 for 1.2 miles to NCT.

### The Trail

The NCT continues through gently undulating, mature pine forest with some wetlands.

### 0.5 (7.0) Miles

Campsite, Gut Lake (aka Long Lake)
Three tent sites, fire ring, privy; south side of NCT.

### Alert

Gut Lake was previously known as Long Lake and is still so identified on some older NCT maps.

### The Trail

The NCT continues past several larger lakes and a varied forest including a pine plantation and deciduous trees. The trail briefly utilizes an old forest road, then returns to a single track through a pine and deciduous forest. Several undeveloped lakes—Gut, Ivins, North Stocking, Cranberry (surrounded by county land) and Moccasin (some private land on east, south, and west).

## 4.3 (3.2) Miles

Crossing, Tower Road/Forest Road 2108

### Alert

The Tepee Lake campsite, still on some older NCT maps, has been dismantled. Use the campsite at Gut Lake, west of Stocking Lake.

### The Trail

The NCT continues through mixed forest, occasionally utilizing an old logging railroad grade, and passes by a wetland. A low ridge above Cranberry Lake offers scenic views. The trail passes through a majestic white pine plantation and skirts the north end of Moccasin Lake.

## 7.5 (0.0) Miles

Woodtick Trail/Forest Road 2107 Access Point, Third Crossing (heading east from Minnesota 371)

*Chippewa National Forest. See Appendix F: Restricted-Use Areas.*

◀ **Map 24**
## Woodtick Trail/Forest Road 2107 Access Point, Third Crossing (heading east from Minnesota 371) to Forest Road 2100 Access Point

### Distance
- 5.1 miles, Map 24.
- 132.0 cumulative miles west to east, beginning of Map 5 to end of Map 24.
- 36.4 reverse miles east to west, end of Map 29 to beginning of Map 24.

**Route:** The Goose Lake area is gently undulating terrain through mostly mixed hardwood forest.

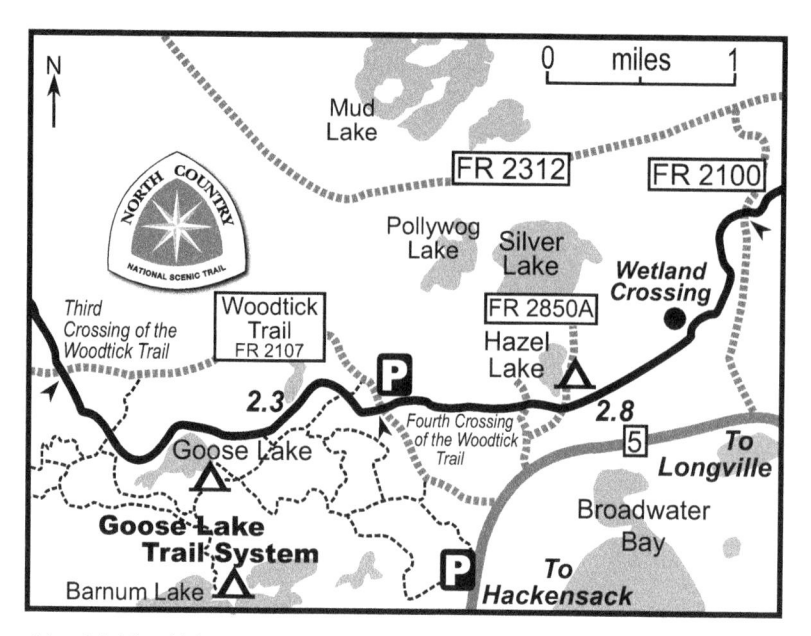

*Map 24. Woodtick Trail/Forest Road 2107 Access Point, Third Crossing (heading east from Minnesota 371) to Forest Road 2100 Access Point*

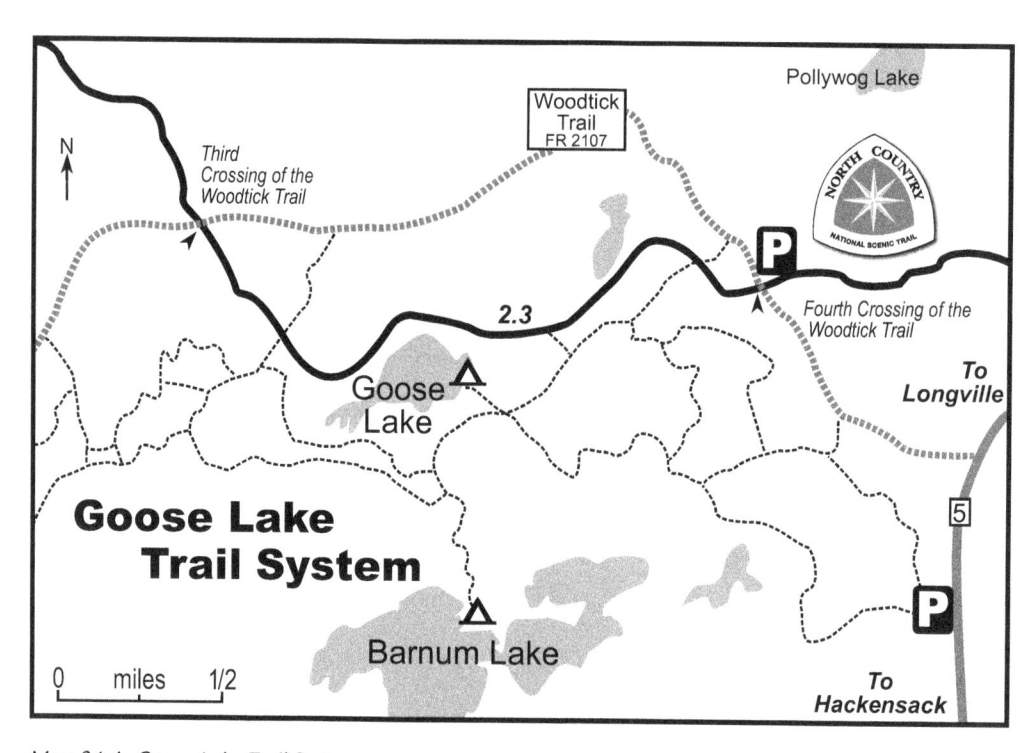

*Map 24-A. Goose Lake Trail System*

**Nature's Pantry—NCT Adopter/Volunteer**
"While flagging a new section of trail, I noticed several old bird nests four to six feet up in trees, that were full of mushrooms. The mushrooms were not growing there—they had been 'picked' and placed there. I asked the DNR folks about it and they did some research. Turns out that red squirrels will cache mushrooms in bird nests during the fall and then retrieve them in late winter or early spring!"

## Campsites

See also "Camping along the Trail" in Accessing and Using the NCT in Minnesota in the front of this book, and Appendix B: Camping, Campsites, Campgrounds.
- Off-trail: Goose Lake
- Hazel Lake

## Services

See Appendix C for services and amenities available in these towns.
- Hackensack
- Longville
- Walker

## Winter Use

See Appendix E for winter parking at trailheads and groomed cross-country ski trails.

## Hunting Alerts

See Chapter 2: Safety on the Trail.

## Water Sources and Treatment

See Chapter 2: Safety on the Trail.

## Alerts

- Goose Lake cross-country ski trails require a Minnesota Ski Pass, available where hunting and fishing licenses are sold.
- The Goose Lake Trail System is extensive—use a map. There is one in this guide and there are kiosks at some trail intersections.

*A day-hiker strolls through the welcoming forest on the Milton Lake esker. Photo by Matthew R. Davis.*

### Map 24 Mile-by-Mile

**0.0 (5.1) Miles**

Access Point, Woodtick Trail/Forest Road 2107, Third Crossing
- GPS Coordinates: 46.997466, -94.346166
- Driving Directions: From Hackensack, head north on Minnesota 371 for 0.4 mile; east on Cass County 5 NW for 7.0 miles; north on Interlachen Drive NW for 1.0 mile; continue on Evergreen Drive NW for 1.3 miles. Continue briefly on Rotter Trail NW, then east on Woodtick Trail NW for 1.3 miles.

## The Trail

The NCT continues east, relatively level with some gradual ups and downs.

**Trail Help—NCT Adopter/Volunteer**
"Deer love the trail and use it often. In winter, they sometimes break trail for snowshoers!"

## 0.4 (4.7) Miles

Crossings, Goose Lake Trail System (cross-country skiing and hunter walking)
    Off-trail campsite (0.6 mile from NCT)
    *See Map 24-A: Goose Lake Trail System for trail details.*

## Alert

Goose Lake is generally surrounded by wet bog and is not directly approachable. Use binoculars to observe from trails. The lake is typically populated with swans and other waterfowl.

## Campsite

The Goose Lake Campsite is off the NCT. To get to it, follow the NCT past Goose Lake to the first trail to the south. Take it 0.1 mile to the next crossing trail and take that one southwest for 0.3 mile. At the next crossing trail, turn northwest 0.2 mile to Goose Lake and the campsite. The Barnum Lake campsite toward the bottom of the map can also be used. Follow the map to get to it.

## Notes

On the NCT, watch for wolf and bear sign as well as whitetail deer, ruffed grouse (including males drumming in the spring), beaver in the many small pond/marshy areas on both sides of the NCT, song birds (especially in the spring and fall migrations). To the east of Goose Lake, the NCT runs on top of an esker with dramatic drops on either side.

## The Trail

The NCT has several junctures with the Goose Lake Trail system—see Map 24-A. The forest is mixed northern hardwood and pine plantations.

### 2.3 (2.8) Miles

Trailhead, Woodtick Trail/Forest Road 2107, Fourth Crossing (heading east from Minnesota 371)
- GPS Coordinates: 46.995827, -94.308701
- Driving Directions: From Longville, head northwest on Cass County 5 for 4.6 miles, then west on Woodtick Trail for 1.0 mile. From Hackensack, head north on Minnesota 371 for 0.4 mile; north on Cass County 5 for 13.8 miles; west on Woodtick Trail/2107 for 1.0 mile.
- Details: Parking for 10 or more vehicles.

### The Trail

The NCT enters a plantation of tall pine trees, then past a large marshy area and pond to the north, then into mixed forest, crossing a two-track forest road. Hazel Lake, north of the NCT, is stocked with rainbow trout by Minnesota DNR.

### 3.2 (1.9) Miles

Crossing, Forest Road 2850A
Off-trail campsite, Hazel Lake

### Sign—NCT Adopter/Volunteer

"Walking on the trail in summer, I saw wolf scat about every five feet for a quarter of a mile. Wolf scat is common on the trail but I had never seen that much before."

### Campsite

To access the campsite exit the NCT on Forest road 2850A and follow it to the public lake access on Hazel Lake, approximately 600 feet. The campsite has two tent sites and a privy. Fishermen often use the public lake access and campsite. This campsite is road accessible.

### Alert

There is a target range north of the NCT near Forest Road 2312. Gunshots can be heard from the range.

### The Trail

Continuing east from the 2850A juncture, the NCT passes through mixed forest with some planted young pines. Observe the protective cages for the seedlings, to keep deer from eating the buds. The NCT then passes through a large marshy area.

### 4.3 (0.8 ) Miles
Crossing, Wetland Area

### The Trail
The NCT leaves the Norway pine plantation and crosses a 300-foot marshy wetland on a narrow causeway of high ground with scattered clumps of birch trees. This is a rather unique area on the NCT.

### 5.1 (0.0) Miles
Access Point, Forest Road 2100
*Chippewa National Forest. See Appendix F: Restricted-Use Areas.*

## ◀ Map 25
## Forest Road 2100 Access Point to Minnesota 84 Trailhead
### Distance
- 4.7 miles Map 25.
- 136.7 cumulative miles west to east, beginning of Map 5 to end of Map 25.
- 31.3 reverse miles east to west, end of Map 29 to beginning of Map 25.

**Route:** The trail meanders through extensive pine plantations of multiple ages.

### Campsites
See also "Camping along the Trail" in Accessing and Using the NCT in Minnesota in the front of this book, and Appendix B: Camping, Campsites, Campgrounds.
- No designated campsites.

### Services
See Appendix C for services and amenities available in these towns.
- Longville
- Remer
- Walker

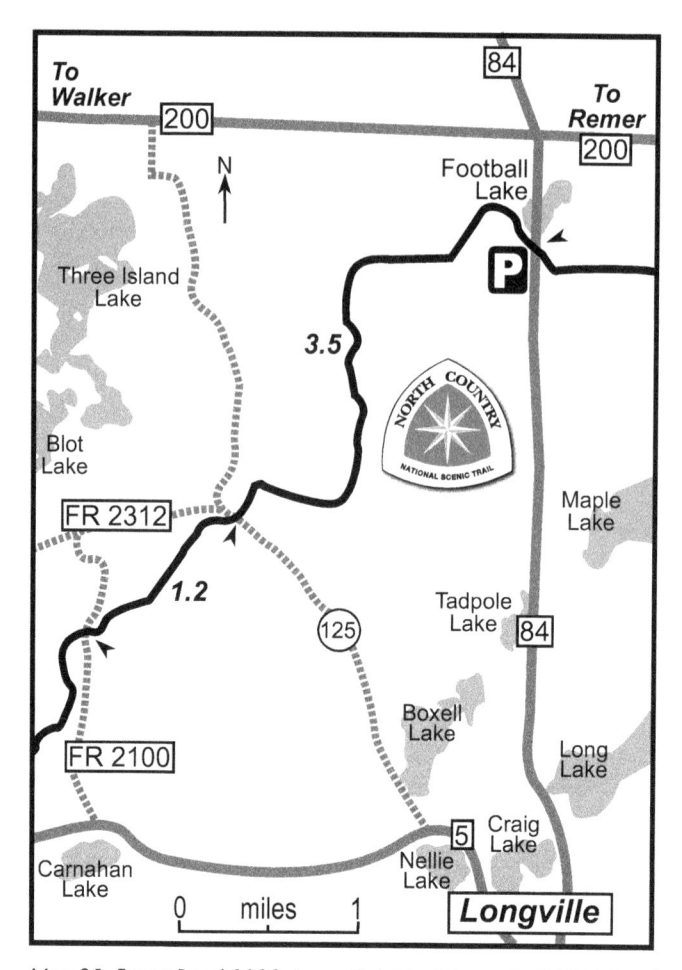

*Map 25. Forest Road 2100 Access Point to Minnesota 84 Trailhead*

**Winter Use**

See Appendix E for winter parking at trailheads and groomed cross-country ski trails.

**Hunting Alerts**

See Chapter 2: Safety on the Trail.

**Water Sources and Treatment**

See Chapter 2: Safety on the Trail.

*Porcupines are tidy. "Poop trees" can be found along the NCT. The porcupine is still in this one! Notice its quills in the tree hollow. Photo by Matthew R. Davis.*

## Map 25 Mile-by-Mile

**0.0 (4.7) Miles**

Access Point, Forest Road 2100
- GPS Coordinates: 47.011886, -94.267566
- Driving Directions: From Longville, go west on Cass County 5 NE/Woman Lake Road for 3.0 miles, then north on Forest Road 2100 for 1.2 miles. Off-road parking.

### The Trail

The NCT passes by a large marshy area with a small lake, enters a grove of tall pine, then crosses an electric line right-of-way/snowmobile trail.

### 1.2 (3.5) Miles

Crossing, Cass County 125

### Alert

The NCT occasionally crosses or shares forest and farm roads for short distances, and sometimes skirts private land. Please stay on the NCT.

### The Trail

The NCT slowly rises and falls, meandering over rolling hills. There is a variety of tree types, mostly hardwood and some distinctive stands of birch. It also passes by several pothole swamps and ponds and goes past a natural mineral lick (shallow round hole about 4-foot diameter). Watch for beaver activity and dam in wetland areas. The NCT shares an old forest road for a short distance, then re-renters the forest into mature hardwood forest. It enters a grove of tall pines with an old farm field on the south, also private land, then enters a stretch of hardwood forest.

---

**Wolf Stories**

I was walking on the trail in winter near a bog. Seems a wolf had taken the same path earlier: it left urine markings on trees along the path.

One day several of us were walking on the trail on our way to a work site when a huge wolf crossed the trail right in front of us.

---

### 3.5 (1.2) Miles

Crossing, Forest Road

### The Trail

The NCT leaves the Norway pine plantation and comes out to Forest Road 2872, which it follows for 0.1 mile before re-entering the forest.

### 4.0 (0.7) Miles

Farm field to the north

## The Trail

The NCT heads due east across private lands in a young hardwood forest and crosses a farm road connecting large farm fields to the north and south. Heading east, the NCT re-enters a Norway pine plantation.

### 4.7 (0.0) Miles

Trailhead, Minnesota 84

◄ **Map 26**
**Minnesota 84 Trailhead to Minnesota 200 Trailhead**

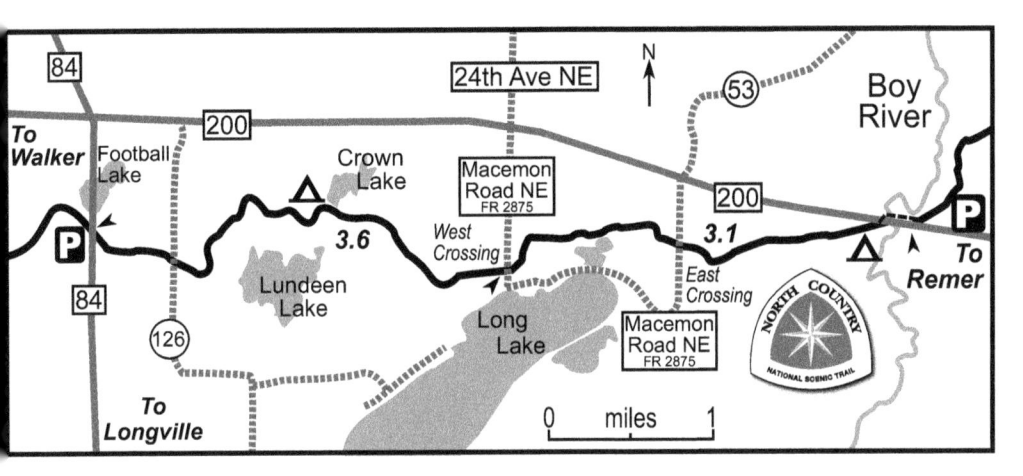

*Chippewa National Forest. See Appendix F: Restricted-Use Areas.*

### Distance
- 6.7 miles Map 26.
- 143.4 cumulative miles west to east, beginning of Map 5 to end of Map 26.
- 26.6 reverse miles east to west, end of Map 29 to beginning of Map 26.

**Route:** Generally flat with short climbs, mostly old road feel that is slowly growing in. Trail can be wet in spots. Norway pine plantation planted in the 1960s and the rest is mixed hardwood forest.

## Campsites

See also "Camping along the Trail" in Accessing and Using the NCT in Minnesota in the front of this book, and Appendix B: Camping, Campsites, Campgrounds.
- Crown Lake

## Services

See Appendix C for services and amenities available in these towns.
- Longville
- Remer

## Winter Use

See Appendix E for winter parking at trailheads and groomed cross-country ski trails.

## Hunting Alerts

See Chapter 2: Safety on the Trail.

---

**Thru-Hiker "Strider"**

*From March 27 through October 13, 2013, Luke Jordan, trail name "Strider," thru-hiked the North Country Trail from North Dakota to New York, from the west terminus to the east terminus, 4,600 miles. He tells his story at www.stridernct.com/. The following excerpt from his journal is about his hike through the Chippewa National Forest. Printed with permission from "Strider."*

**Sun. April 28**
**Trail Day 033**
**Miles hiked: 21**
**Crown Lake Campsite—Chippewa National Forest**

As I am hiking it is apparent that the snow is melting rapidly, many more puddles to cross today. Eventually I come to a spot with no snow, the trail is completely clear and dry. I take off the snowshoes to give my feet a break and continue hiking. I am amazed to find that the next half-mile of trail is completely clear. When it appears again the snow is only about three inches deep, so I decide to leave the snowshoes off. What a welcome change.

## Water Sources and Treatment

See Chapter 2: Safety on the Trail.

## Alert

Confusing Road Names: There are two crossings of Macemon Road NE/Forest Road 2875, which goes south then east/southeast (along the northeast side of Long Lake), then north, forming a horseshoe. North of Minnesota 200, Macemon west becomes 24th Avenue NE. North of Minnesota 200, Macemon east becomes Minnesota 53/Tobique Road NE.

## Map 26 Mile-by-Mile

### 0.0 (6.7) Miles

Trailhead, Minnesota 84
- GPS Coordinates: 47.043692, -94.214888

*Family time on the NCT. The grey swatch on the tree in the foreground is a blue blaze, the NCT's trail marker. Photo by Matthew R. Davis.*

- Driving Directions: From Walker, head east on Minnesota 200 for 20.3 miles, then south on Minnesota 84 for 0.6 mile. From Longville, head north on Minnesota 84 for 4.0 miles.
- Details: Parking for 10 vehicles; kiosk; US Forest Service map

## The Trail

The NCT passes through logged areas, and pine and spruce plantations with some young aspen.

---

### Gratitude

A trail volunteer helped a long distance-hiker (trail name "Mother Goose") bushwhack through a section of the trail still in development. It was spring and they were breaking through thick brush. The hiker was grateful when they arrived at a puncheon and the trail opened up again. She said to the volunteer, "I never appreciated how much work you do to get from what we walked through to real trail."

---

## 0.7 (6.0) Miles

Crossing, Cass County 126

## The Trail

After a short walk from Minnesota 84 through a mixed-conifer plantation and young aspen, the trail crosses Cass County 126 and continues through the mixed hardwood forest.

## 2.2 (4.5) Miles

Campsite, Crown Lake
Four tent sites, fire ring, privy.

## The Trail

The NCT continues through a variety of habitats. Some low areas have puncheons.

## 3.6 (3.1) Miles

Crossing, Macemon Road NE (west end)

## The Trail

The NCT traverses a variety of habitats between the west and east Macemon crossings, including Norway pine plantation, wetlands, and some changes in elevation in a mixed deciduous and pine forest. Look for beaver lodges where the NCT crosses a wetland with alders.

## 5.0 (1.7) Miles

Crossing Macemon Road NE (east end)

## The Trail

After the second Macemon crossing (east), the NCT enters a section of birch, brush, and mixed forest, then segues into aspen. The trail skirts a large stable wetland to the south where outbuildings can be seen on the far side. Past the wetland, the NCT re-enters pine forest. Forest segues into pine and mixed hardwood forest followed by brush and wetlands, then back into tall trees. Elevation increases with a slow climb to Boy River and the Minnesota 200 NCT trailhead. Approaching 200, note the numerous jack pine trees twisted and toppled from a strong wind.

**Recommendation—NCT Adopter/Volunteer**

"Watch for beaver dams and activity in low areas near the NCT culverts. Also watch for wolf sign, bald eagles, deer, grouse and wildflowers. The wetlands are especially beautiful and lively in spring and fall."

## 6.4 (0.3) Miles

Access Point, Minnesota 200

## The Trail

The NCT crosses an old road that heads south paralleling the Boy River to an informal campsite. The NCT angles to the northeast through jack pines to reach Minnesota 200. There is room for 1–2 cars to park in the road approach. From here, the NCT crosses the highway and follows Minnesota 200 east over the Boy River bridge before re-entering the forest and going to the trailhead.

## 6.7 (0.0) Miles

Trailhead, Minnesota 200

# Map 27
## Minnesota 200 Trailhead to Forest Road 2117 Access Point

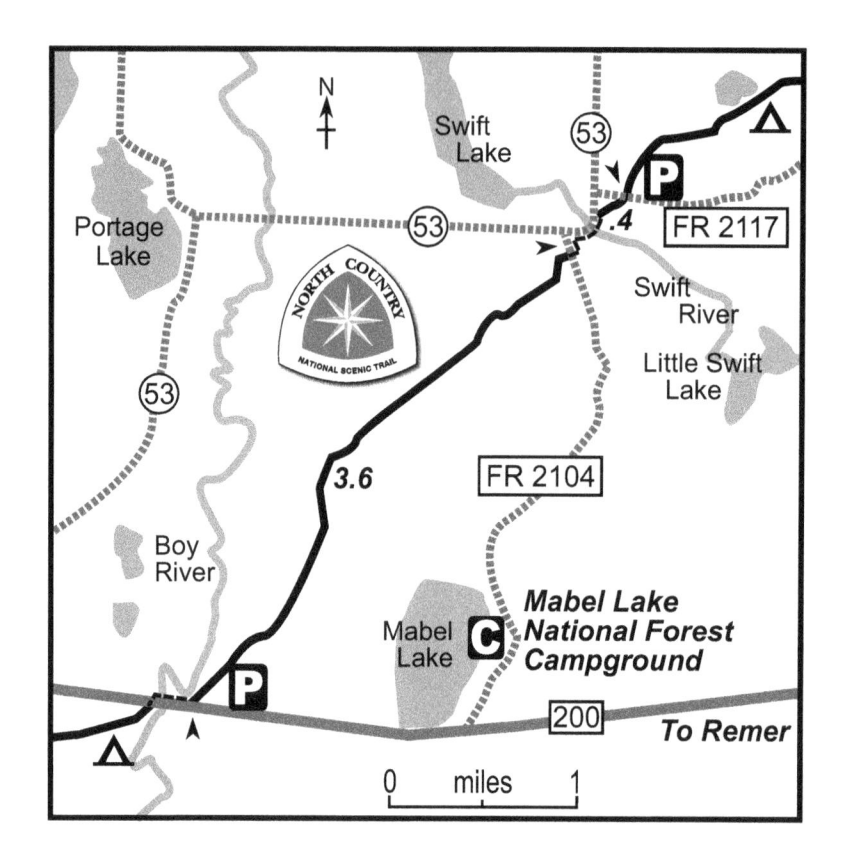

*Chippewa National Forest. See Appendix F: Restricted-Use Areas.*

**Distance**
- 4.0 miles Map 27.
- 147.4 cumulative miles west to east, beginning of Map 5 to end of Map 27.
- 19.9 reverse miles east to west, end of Map 29 to beginning of Map 27.

**Route:** The trail crosses the Boy River and Swift River and undulates gently through mixed forest.

**Campsites**

See also "Camping along the Trail" in Accessing and Using the NCT in

Minnesota in the front of this book, and Appendix B: Camping, Campsites, Campgrounds.
- Off-trail: Mabel Lake National Forest Campground is about 2.5 miles south of the NCT on Forest Road 2104, 21 campsites, fee required. Chippewa National Forest Supervisor's Office, 218.335.8600. www.fs.usda.gov/recarea/chippewa/recreation/hiking/recarea.

## Services

See Appendix C for services and amenities available in these towns.
- Longville
- Remer

## Winter Use

See Appendix E for winter parking at trailheads and groomed cross-country ski trails.

## Hunting Alerts

See Chapter 2: Safety on the Trail.

## Water Sources and Treatment

See Chapter 2: Safety on the Trail.

## Map 27 Mile-by-Mile

**0.0 (4.0) Miles**

Trailhead, Minnesota 200
- GPS Coordinates: 47.044686, -94.109402
- Driving Directions: From Walker, head east on Minnesota 200 for 25.3 miles. From Remer, head west on Minnesota 200 for 9.1 miles
- Details: Parking for 10 vehicles; kiosk; US Forest Service map

## The Trail

The NCT leaves the shoulder of Minnesota 200 and enters the forest

*NCT chapters sponsor group events all year, including snowshoe hikes in winter. Photo by Deane Johnson.*

heading north (watch for the large wooden NCT sign). Look for a short spur trail leading south to the trailhead parking area.

## 1.6 (2.4) Miles

Crossing, Forest Road 2561

---
**Trail Maintenance—NCT Adopter/Volunteer**
"Birds, animals and people like paths. Unlike paved paths, the hand-hewn natural footpath of the NCT has to be used or it is reclaimed by nature."

---

## The Trail

The NCT crosses Forest Road 2561 for the second time, descends around a slope, turns to the left, then crosses a grassy road. The NCT passes a marsh on the south, then passes through mixed forest and pine grove and crosses forest roads. The trail travels along a small ridge with lowlands north of the trail. There are occasional tall pines prior to Mabel Lake Road.

### 3.6 (0.4) Miles

Convergence, Forest Road 2104/Mabel Lake Road, Cass County 53

### The Trail

The NCT intersects with Forest Road 2104/Mabel Lake Road and takes it north for a short distance to the intersection with gravel Cass County 53. The road walk continues east on 53, which makes a 90-degree turn north just before the Swift River crossing.

### 3.8 (0.2) Miles

NCT leaves County 53

### The Trail

Almost immediately after County 53 turns north, the NCT leaves 53 and re-enters the forest to the east. In 0.2 mile, the NCT crosses Forest Road 2117 at the Access Point.

### 4.0 (0.0) Miles

Access Point, Forest Road 2117
*Chippewa National Forest. See Appendix F: Restricted-Use Areas.*

## ◄ Map 28
## Forest Road 2117 Access Point to Milton Lake Drive/Forest Road 2324 Trailhead

### Distance
- 9.2 miles Map 28.
- 156.6 cumulative miles west to east, beginning of Map 5 to end of Map 28.
- 15.9 reverse miles east to west, end of Map 29 to beginning of Map 28.

**Route:** The NCT crosses through a low area with extensive wetlands before crossing a higher area with rolling low hills and crossing numerous forest roads and trails. It passes through a mixture of Norway pine plantations, aspen, mixed hardwood and coniferous forest, and has some large pines scattered along it.

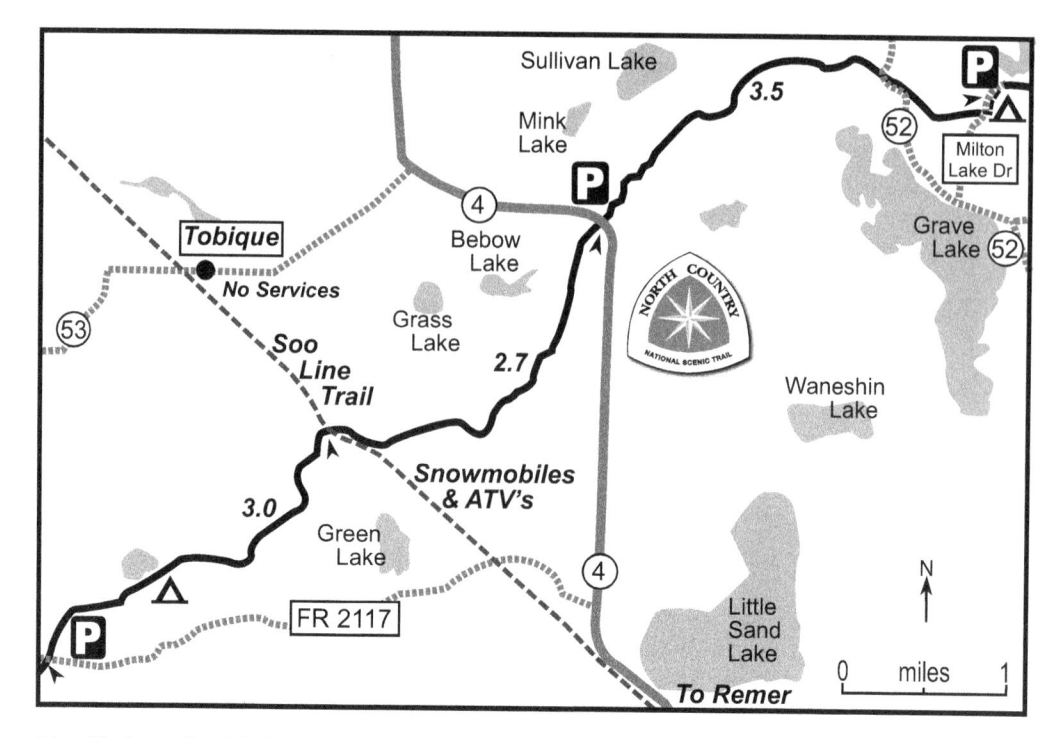

*Map 28. Forest Road 2117 Access Point to Milton Lake Drive/Forest Road 2324 Trailhead*

## Campsites

See also "Camping along the Trail" in Accessing and Using the NCT in Minnesota in the front of this book, and Appendix B: Camping, Campsites, Campgrounds.
- Old Pines Lake

## Services

See Appendix C for services and amenities available in these towns.
- Longville
- Remer

## Winter Use

See Appendix E for winter parking at trailheads and groomed cross-country ski trails.

## Hunting Alerts

See Chapter 2: Safety on the Trail.

## Water Sources and Treatment

See Chapter 2: Safety on the Trail.

## Map 28 Mile-by-Mile

### 0.0 (9.2) Miles

Access Point Forest Road 2117
- GPS Coordinates: 447.082850, -94.060264
- Driving Directions: From Remer, go west on Minnesota 200 for 7.5 miles; north on Mabel Lake Road NE/Forest Road 2104 for 3.0 miles; east on Tobique Road NE/County Road 53 for 0.3 mile; take the first right onto Forest Road 2117 and go 0.1 mile.

*Winter campers enjoy brisk sub-zero temperatures near the Milton Lake Esker. Photo by Bruce M. Johnson.*

### The Trail

The NCT crosses Forest Road 2117 at the access point (2117 was a railroad grade known as the Speakers Truck Trail) then through mixed forest to Old Pines Lake.

---

**Sharing the Path—NCT Adopter/Volunteer**
"It is the best gratification at the end of a day on the trail to see recent deer tracks on the path. They often go in both directions. Deer love the trail!"

---

### 1.0 (8.2) Miles

Campsite, Old Pines Lake
- Four tent sites, fire ring, privy, table/bench.

### The Trail

Old Pines Lake campsite, directly off the NCT, enjoys a grassy shoreline on the lake and is a good spot for a break. Continuing eastward, utilizing puncheons, the trail skirts a large beaver pond complex with good wildlife-watching opportunities, then enters a mixed forest.

### 3.0 (6.2) Miles

Crossing, Soo Line Trail

### Note

The Soo Line Trail is a former railroad grade used by ATVs and snowmobiles.

### The Trail

The NCT parallels the Soo Line trail on an older railroad bed for approximately 900 feet, then continues east back into the forest. Walk west on the old railroad grade to see the remains of a trestle that crossed a small pond. The NCT enters a young, mixed forest and eventually crosses two forest roads and skirts extensive wetlands and old fields.

## 5.7 (3.5) Miles

Trailhead, Cass County 4
- GPS Coordinates: 47.121658, -93.989239
- Driving Directions: From Remer, head northwest on Cass County 4 for 7.3 miles. Turn right onto Forest Road 2792.
- Details: Parking for 5 vehicles; kiosk

## Alert

Confusing routing. See map below.

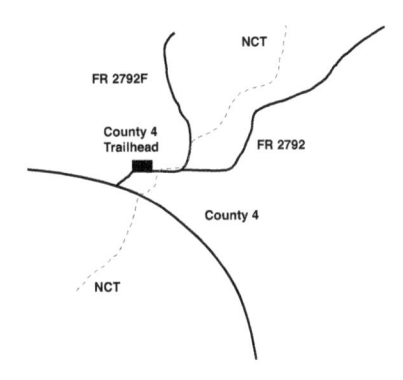

## The Trail

The land here begins to rise along several ridges and offers many good views of distant lakes.

## 6.8 (2.4) Miles

NCT follows forest road.

---

### Winter Delight—NCT Adopter/Volunteer
"Out on the trail in the middle of winter, bitter cold, beautiful sky, lots of snow, all day thing. Took lunch, sat on a snowbank on the south shore of a lake and ate our lunches."

---

### The Trail

The NCT leaves a mixed hardwood forest, comes out to Forest Road 2792, follows it for about 80 feet, and then re-enters the woods in a Norway pine plantation.

### 8.1 (1.1) Miles

Crossing, Cass County 52

### The Trail

The NCT crosses Cass County 52, turns southwest and follows a power line, then climbs to a knob heading southeast. After following a flat ridge with mixed hardwoods, the NCT crosses a wide power line access before descending.

### 8.9 (0.3) Miles

NCT reaches Milton Lake Drive/Forest Road 2324

### The Trail

The NCT reaches Milton Lake Drive/Forest Road 2324, turns left and follows it for 0.3 mile, passing by several rustic cabins. The NCT/road crosses a low wet spot with a hard cobble bottom. Water levels fluctuate greatly here. Inquire at Chippewa National Forest for more information.

### 9.2 (0.0) Miles

Trailhead, Milton Lake Drive
Campsite, Milton Lake Campsite
Natural Feature, Milton Lake Esker

*Chippewa National Forest. See Appendix F: Restricted-Use Areas.*

## ◀ Map 29
## Milton Lake Drive/Forest Road 2324 Trailhead to Forest Road 2101 Trailhead at Minnesota 6

### Distance
- 6.7 miles Map 29.

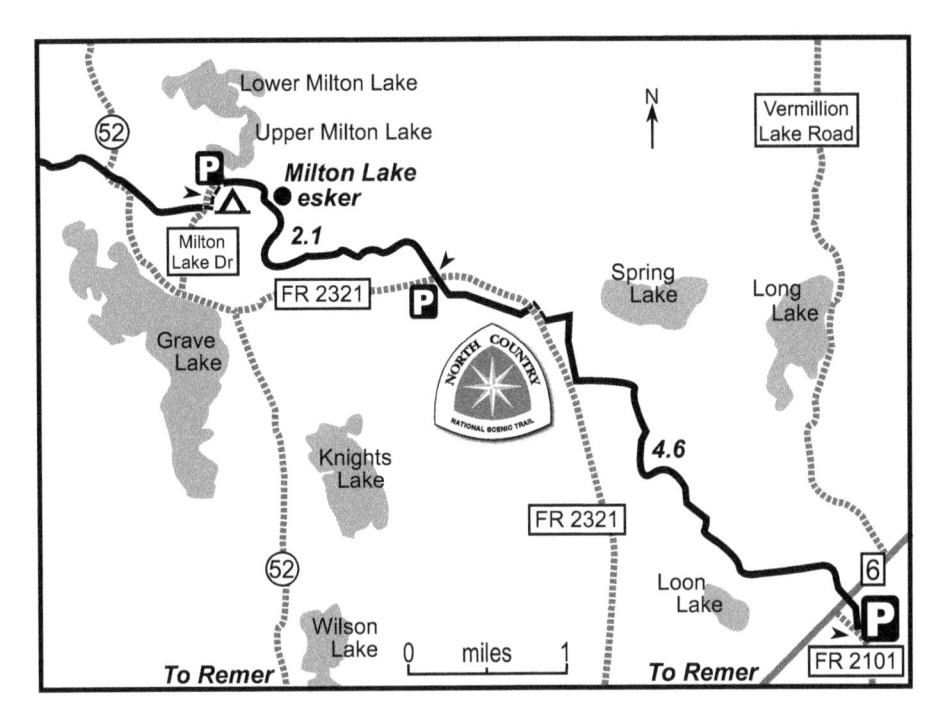

*Map 29. Milton Lake Drive/Forest Road 2324 Trailhead to Forest Road 2101 Trailhead at Minnesota 6*

- 163.3 cumulative miles west to east, beginning of Map 5 to end of Map 29.
- 6.7 reverse miles east to west, end of Map 29 to beginning of this map.

**Route:** This section is challenging because of ups, downs, and elevations, which are sometimes steep. It includes a 1,732-foot long esker, a spectacular hiking feature.

## Campsites

See also "Camping along the Trail" in Accessing and Using the NCT in Minnesota in the front of this book, and Appendix B: Camping, Campsites, Campgrounds.
- Milton Lake

## Services

See Appendix C for services and amenities available in these towns.
- Remer

## Winter Use

See Appendix E for winter parking at trailheads and groomed cross-country ski trails.

## Hunting Alerts

See Chapter 2: Safety on the Trail.

## Water Sources and Treatment

See Chapter 2: Safety on the Trail.

## Map 29 Mile-by-Mile

### 0.0 (6.7) Miles

Trailhead, Milton Lake Drive
Campsite, Milton Lake Campsite
Natural Feature, Milton Lake Esker

### Trailhead

- GPS Coordinates: 47.134476, -93.934264
- Driving Directions: From Remer, head northwest on Cass County 4 for 1.6 miles; north on Cass County 52 for 3.7 miles; then north on Milton Lake Drive NE for 0.9 mile.
- Details: Parking for 5 vehicles.

### Campsite

- Approximately 225 feet east of the trailhead (signed).
- South side of trail: tent site, fire ring, wood rack, bench.
- North side of trail: privy.

### Natural Feature, Esker, 1,732 feet long

The NCT progresses from the campsite along a spectacular esker with up and down elevations, including a high point at 1,394 feet, and drops up to 100 feet on both sides. Forest includes towering Norway pine, spruce, and fir, with a few cedar and birch trees mingled in. The NCT descends steeply from esker to gently rolling terrain with mixed hardwood forest, occasional low spots (note culverts), and a small stand of balsam fir.

*Take only memories, leave only footprints. Photo by Matthew R. Davis.*

---

### Esker!

From the Milton Lake Trailhead, the NCT goes up a sharp hill. It passes a campsite while continuing straight up, then turns flat. The land drops away more than 100 feet on both sides and the trail narrows to six to eight feet. The esker is populated with large Norway pine with an other-worldly feel. After about one-third of a mile, it sharply drops back down. In spring and summer, look for the lavender colors of wild clematis and virgin's bower.

## The Trail

Continuing on the NCT past Milton Lake area, a large wetland is visible to the north followed by a clearing, with balsam fir, spruce, and hardwood forest dominating the south side. Observing again to the north, watch for huge cedar trees on the north side of the trail just before you enter a spruce tunnel. The tunnel ends at a cedar wetland to the south and segues into mixed hardwood forest with culverts under some low spots. As spruce and large Norway pine appear, watch for large, tall, old trees. The NCT continues through shrubs and a young hardwood forest with a few large pine, spruce, and balsam fir and large wetlands on both sides of the trail.

## 2.1 (4.6) Miles

Crossing (westerly), Forest Road 2321

## Note

There is off-road parking at this crossing.

## Alert

Forest Road 2321 crosses the NCT twice and brushes close to it a third time.

## The Trail

The NCT crosses Forest Road 2321 north to south, continues through shrubs and mixed hardwood forest with Norway pine and balsam fir scattered throughout, then predominantly spruce and balsam fir, with occasional cedar and wetlands on both side of the trail.

## 2.7 (4.0) Miles

Crossing (easterly), Forest Road 2321

## The Trail

The NCT meets 2321 from west to east, utilizing the road for about 50 feet. It crosses over a flowage before re-entering the forest on the north side of 2321. The trail passes a cedar grove, red and white pine, some balsam fir and mixed hardwood forest with some mild elevation changes; seasonal wet spots.

## 4.3 (2.4) Miles

Crossing, Forest Road 2321D

**Fawn—NCT Adopter/Volunteer**

"A whole group of hikers walked right past a fawn lying next to the trail. The last hiker in the group was the first to spot it."

## The Trail

The NCT crosses Forest Road 2321D heading south within a large Norway pine plantation. The NCT curves around the north side of a wetland, crosses a small puncheon heading northeast, then curves back to head southeast.

## 5.6 (1.1) Miles

Crossing, Forest Road 3705

## The Trail

The NCT crosses Forest Road 3705 heading south still within the large Norway pine plantation. The NCT turns heading east and climbs up a ridge before descending, entering a young aspen stand, and then reaching Minnesota 6.

## 6.7 (0.0) Miles

Trailhead, Forest Road 2101 at Minnesota 6
(known as the Remer terminus)
- GPS Coordinates: 47.094552, -93.854485
- Driving Directions: From Remer, head northeast on Minnesota 6 for 4 miles, then east on Forest Road 2101/Boundary Road NE for 0.1 mile.
- Details: Parking for 5 vehicles.

## The Trail

The NCT crosses Minnesota 6 and continues through the forest to the trailhead at Forest Road 2101.

## Road walk to Remer

To reach Remer from FR 2101/Minnesota 6 trailhead, walk northwest on FR 2101 for 0.2 mile, turn left on Minnesota 6 and follow it 4.1 miles into Remer.

---

### Thru-Hiker "Strider"

*From March 27 through October 13, 2013, Luke Jordan, trail name "Strider," thru-hiked the North Country Trail from North Dakota to New York, from the west terminus to the east terminus, 4,600 miles. He tells his story at www.stridernct.com/. The following excerpt is from his journal. Printed with permission from "Strider."*

**Tue. April 30**
**Trail Day 035**
**Miles hiked: 27**
**Itasca County Fairgrounds—Grand Rapids, MN**

It's a four-mile road walk along MN-6 to the point where the NCT crosses the road. Later in the day I am walking along the Tioga Trail, a paved bike trail that parallels the road for much of its route. ... I make it to the town of Grand Rapids where I plan to spend the night at the county fairgrounds. This is where the Mesabi Trail begins, a paved bike trail that is completed in segments between Grand Rapids and Ely. I will be hiking this trail over the next several days as the first of four trails that make up the Arrowhead Re-route. [Editor: Originally, the NCT was mapped from Grand Rapids due east to Duluth. The "re-route" takes the NCT on the Kekekabic, Border Route, and Superior Hiking Trails.] I arrive at the fairgrounds just before dark and pitch for the night beneath a row of pine trees.

---

**Continuing on ...**
After the NCT leaves the Chippewa National Forest near Remer, it takes what is called the Arrowhead Re-route heading northeast through Grand Rapids, on to Ely, then east over to Lake Superior and south to Duluth. This area in Minnesota is known as the Arrowhead because of its shape on the map.

The re-route was developed to address the difficulty of creating trail in the original route from Remer due east to Duluth, which is rife with wetlands, and to offer more challenging terrain for hikers, with a bonus of stunning vistas. The re-route requires the approval of Congress, and that legislation is in progress.

The re-route has orphaned an original 9.2-mile trail segment from Forest Road 2101 to the Chippewa National Forest's boundary east of Sailor Lake at the Cass County-Aitken County line. This segment will not be maintained.

For more information about the Arrowhead Re-route and updates on its status, visit northcountrytrail.org/get-involved/advocacy/arrowhead-re-route/.

*Wild rice lines the shore of this river on the NCT. Photo by Matthew R. Davis.*

# Chapter 6
# Chippewa National Forest near Remer to Jay Cooke State Park

**Distance: 558.3 Miles**

**Route: Remer to Ely:** Paved bicycle trail and road walking.
**Ely to Jay Cooke State Park:** Contiguous rugged footpaths, some traversing remote wilderness.

*For alerts, corrections, updated maps, and additional map resources:* northcountrytrail.org/mnguidebook/. Jay Cooke State Park: www.dnr.state.mn.us/state_parks/jay_cooke. Less than 20 miles from the Wisconsin border.

*The Mesabi Trail offers NCT hikers a rich alternative route from Grand Rapids to Ely. Photo by Doug "Windigo" Boulee.*

NCT hikers share with cyclists the bedrock and tall pine views of the Mesabi Trail. Photo by Doug "Windigo" Boulee.

◀ **Map 30**
**Chippewa National Forest near Remer to Ely via Grand Rapids and the Mesabi Trail (recommended route). Visit www.mesabitrail.com/**

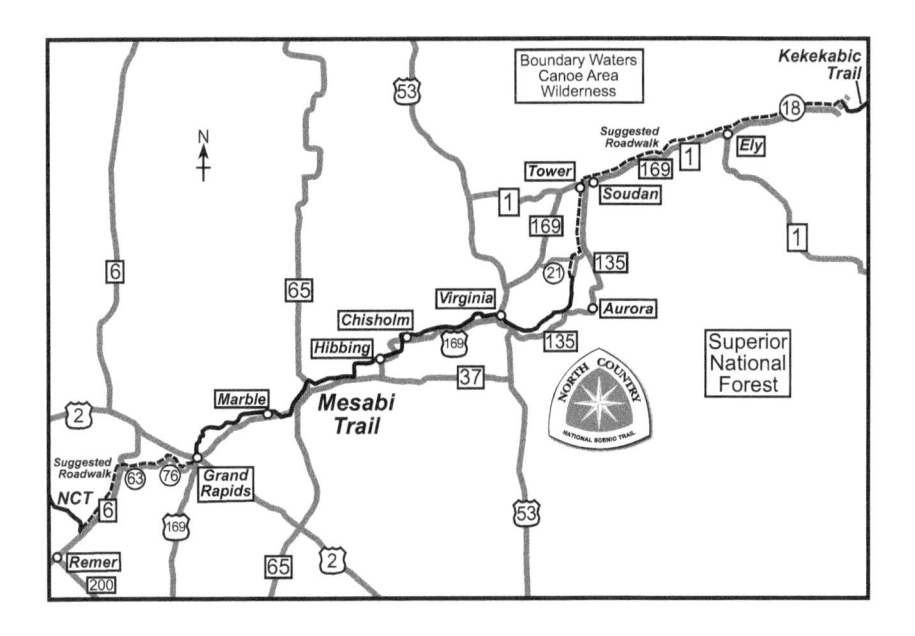

### 🚶 Map 30 Remer to Grand Rapids by trails and road walks

**Distance:** Approximately 23 miles.

Take Minnesota 6 out of Remer, heading north (toward Cohasset) 10.5 miles to Itasca County 63; head east on County 63 for 9.7 miles toward Grand Rapids. Just before a bridge crosses over a narrow channel of Pokegama Lake, watch for the paved Tioga Trail coming from the south (GPS: 47.235349, -93.611596). This trail can be walked for the next 1.5 miles instead of the highway shoulder.

Follow the Tioga Trail to its terminus at County 63's junction with County 76. From there, walk 1.6 miles on 76 to the Forest History Center entrance (GPS: 47.224337, -93.56846). This provides a detour into Grand Rapids that avoids walking heavily traveled US 2.

View a map of the non-motorized trails in the Grand Rapids area at getfititasca.org/grtrails.pdf

After a short walk north on the Forest History Center's entrance road (GPS: 47.225714, -93.566008), follow a paved trail for .9 mile heading east through the Forest History Center property, across UPM-Blandin forest land, and behind the Grand Itasca Clinic & Hospital property to the edge of downtown Grand Rapids and the city's Sylvan Point trailhead (GPS: 47.224479, -93.55056)

**Minnesota Forest History Center**
This Minnesota Historical Society facility tells the story of the great pine logging era in northern Minnesota, explains modern forest management in the area, and features an early twentieth-century logging camp replica. www.mnhs.org/places/sites/fhc/

From the Sylvan Point trailhead, take sidewalks through town passing by the UPM-Blandin Paper Mill to the Itasca County Fairgrounds/Mesabi Trail trailhead (GPS: 47.249811, -93.522642).

*Note: the NCTA's Arrowhead Chapter is working with the City and University of Minnesota to designate a route for the NCT through the city of Grand Rapids. For updates, visit northcountrytrail.org/mnguidebook.*

### 🚶 Map 30 Grand Rapids to Giant's Ridge

**Distance:** 90 miles

The Mesabi Trail is a paved multiple-use, mostly off-road trail that stretches from Grand Rapids to Ely.

For more info, visit www.mesabitrail.com/ or check out their interactive trail map at www.mesabitrail.com/maps-images/interactive-map/. There are several highlights along the Mesabi Trail, including:
- The Hull-Rust-Mahoning Mine, the world's largest open pit iron mine, and other evidence of mining history.
- The boyhood home of Bob Dylan in Hibbing.
- The U.S. Hockey Hall of Fame in Eveleth.
- Many beautiful wilderness sights.

## Map 30 Giant's Ridge to Ely

**Distance:** 41.3 miles

From Giant's Ridge, walk north on County 138 for 5.7 miles before turning east on County 21 (GPS: 47.651021, -92.293194) and following it for 1.9 miles. At the intersection with State 135 (GPS: 47.66004, -92.258255), turn north and follow it for 10.8 miles to the intersection with Minnesota 169/1 at Tower (GPS: 47.804335, -92.281393). Head east on Minnesota 169/Minnesota 1 for 33.8 miles to Ely and the junction of Minnesota 169 and 1. You'll pass through the communities of Tower and Soudan and past Soudan Mine Underground/Lake Vermilion State Park. Tours are available of the underground mine (fee charged, learn more at www.dnr.state.mn.us/state_parks/soudan_underground_mine/index.html)

Note: Camping is available within Hoodoo Point campground (GPS: 47.818947, -92.296509), located 1.4 miles north of Minnesota 169/1 at Tower via County 697, and at McKinley Park (GPS: 47.827688, -92.274058), located 1.8 miles north of Soudan at 169/1 via Main Street and McKinley Park Road.

City of Tower (GPS: 47.805243, -92.274452; www.lakevermilionchamber.com/)

City of Soudan (GPS: 47.81595, -92.238382; www.lakevermilionchamber.com/)

Camping is also available at Bear Head Lake State Park (GPS: 47.794534, -92.07908), which was voted "America's favorite park" in a 2010 contest sponsored by Coca Cola, located 6.8 mi. south of Minnesota 169/1 via Bear Head State Park Road; learn more at www.dnr.state.mn.us/state_parks/bear_head_lake/index.html).

## 🚶 Map 30 Ely to Snowbank Lake Road, Kekekabic Trail Trailhead

**Distance:** 19.7 miles

Walk east on Minnesota 169/County 18 (Fernberg Road). At 0.7 mile you'll pass the Superior National Forest's Kawishiwi Ranger District (GPS: 47.906841-91.829717).

Here, NCT hikers should stop and pick up their Boundary Waters Canoe Area Wilderness (BWCAW) permit for hiking the Kekekabic and Border Route Trails.

After 4.8 miles, look for a road heading north into a parking lot (GPS: 47.931706, -91.755517). A short (less than 1 mile) trail leads from the parking area to a vista of Kawishiwi Falls. This is well worth the side trip.

After another 0.6 mile, look for Fall Lake Road heading northeast. The Superior National Forest's Fall Lake Campground (GPS: 47.950982, -91.722338) is located 1.6 miles northeast.

After 12.9 miles, turn northeast onto Snowbank Lake Road (GPS: 47.954848, -91.485097). Follow this road for 1.4 miles until you see the signs for the Snowbank Lake Road/Kekekabic Trailhead on the north side of the trail. (GPS: 47.968049, -91.46579)

### Official Route

The NCT from Remer to the Kekekabic Trail east of Ely is under development and much of the current official route is road walk. The alternate route described above is recommended.

### Service Towns, Map 30

### Ely

A small former mining and logging town that is now a small (population 3,460) outdoor recreation-oriented city. It is located at the "end of the road" and the edge of the Boundary Waters Canoe Area Wilderness. Ely is home to a variety of canoe outfitter companies, a great outdoor gear store, the International Wolf Center, North American Bear Center, and the Superior National Forest's Kawishiwi Ranger Station. It offers the full range of hiker services. www.ely.org.

### Grand Rapids

A medium-sized city (population 10,900) that is the regional hub for a large portion of northeastern Minnesota. It is a Mississippi River town that features a large paper mill, power plant, and several large lakes. It is also the southern extent of the Mesabi Iron Range. Full range of hiker services. www.visitgrandrapids.com/

**Remer**

A small community (population 370) located in the northeastern corner of Cass County and home to the world's largest bald eagle statue. Long-distance hiker services, including coffee shop, medical clinic, small grocery store, a hardware store, ice cream shop, U.S. Post Office, restaurant, motel/campground, laundromat, and gas station/convenience store. www.remerchamber.com/.

◀ **Map 31**
**Kekekabic Trail (The Kek), Snowbank Lake Road to Gunflint Trail**

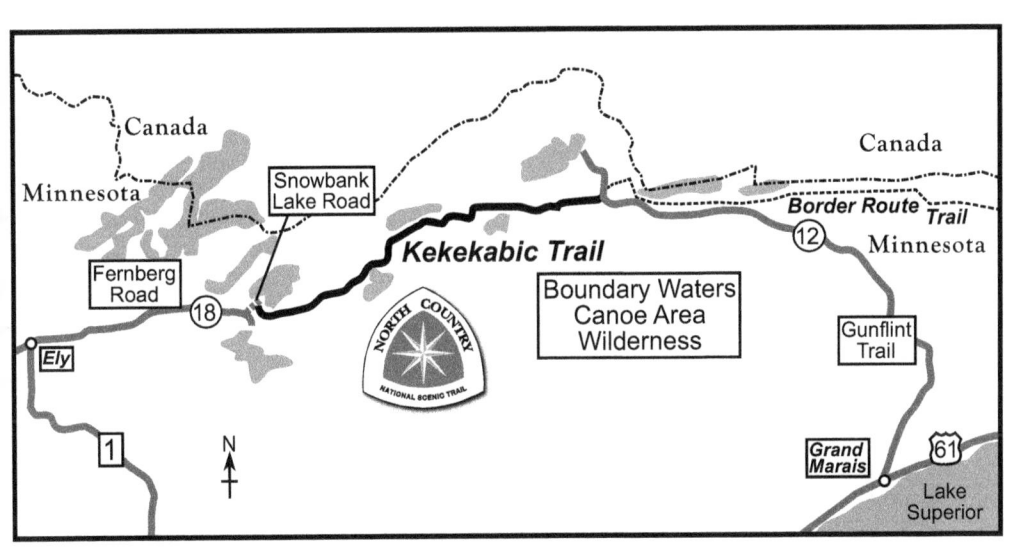

**Distance:** 42 Miles

*Permits are required for hiking the Kekekabic Trail. They are available at BWCAW, Superior National Forest, Kawishiwi Ranger District Station.*

The 42-mile long Kekekabic Trail ("the Kek" for short) is a wilderness hiking trail that runs from the

*Rock and broken rock make up much of the tread of the Kekekabic Trail. Photo by Todd "Tman" McMahon.*

*Hikers often hear only the wind in the trees on the primal Kekekabic Trail. Photo by Todd "Tman" McMahon.*

Snowbank Lake Trail/Kekekabic Trail trailhead on Snowbank Lake Road east to the Gunflint Trail just west of Gunflint Lake.

About 30 miles of the Kek pass through the heart of the Boundary Waters Canoe Area Wilderness (BWCAW), offering unsurpassed remoteness and opportunities for solitude.

The western third of the Kek passes through forest that is mostly intact and includes jack pine, aspen, white pine, and hardwoods.

The central third of the trail passes through the 1999 BWCAW derecho (a powerful blowdown). The Kek was severely impacted by the blowdown and by damage from subsequent forest fires that still make it difficult to stay with the trail in some places.

The eastern third of the trail has also been affected by natural forces, like the 2007 fires at Ham Lake and Cavity Lake. This burned-over area continues to the eastern terminus of the Kek. Some portions of it can be difficult to navigate because of the proliferation of brush growing back following the loss of the forest canopy from the fire.

It is, in part, the wildness of the Kek that leaves it vulnerable to nature's extremes, and it is the extremes that provide inspiration and challenges for hikers.

### Information and Contacts

- Purchase the recently revised Kekekabic Trail Guide at www.northcountrytrail.org.
- Visit the Kekekabic Trail Club (KTC) website at www.kek.org.
- Contact the KTC via email at info@kek.org.

**From the Kek to the BRT**
The Border Route Trail's western terminus is approximately 0.15 mi. west of the Kekekabic eastern trailhead.

# Map 32
## Border Route Trail (BRT), Gunflint Trail to Otter Lake Road

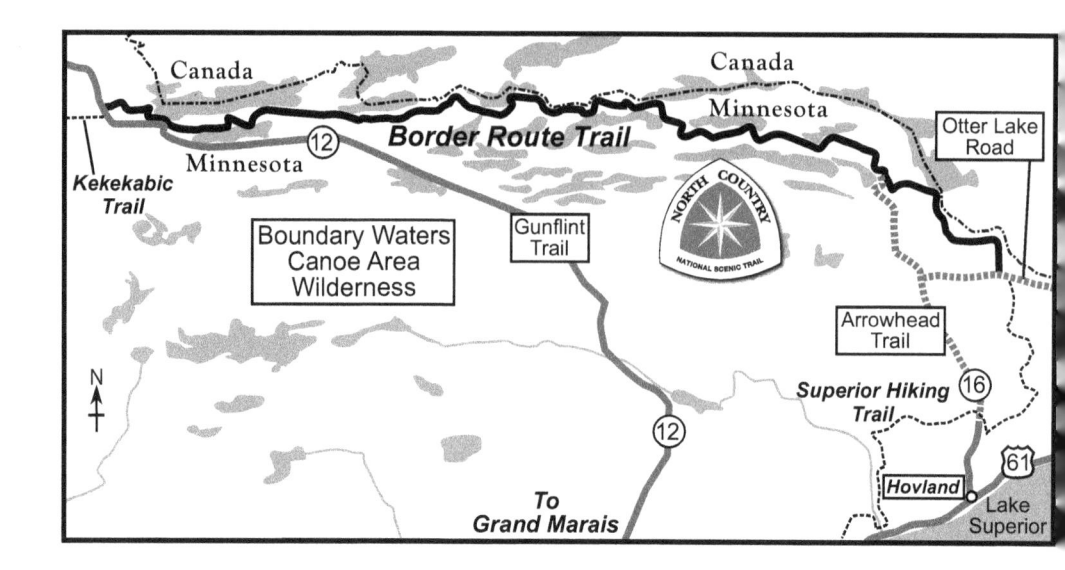

**Distance:** 65 Miles

*Permits are required for hiking the Border Route Trail. They are available at BWCAW, Superior National Forest, Kawishiwi Ranger District Station.*

This wilderness trail's western terminus is the Gunflint Trail's Magnetic Rock trailhead.

It runs to the Otter Lake Road trailhead off the Arrowhead Trail, 16 miles north of Hovland, Minnesota.

The BRT is best known for its dramatic overlooks of Canada, for old-growth forests, and for its route following the chain of lakes located along the U.S.–Canada border that was one of the Voyageur routes from the Great Lakes to the great Canadian interior.

The BRT was built by the Minnesota Rovers Outdoors Club and is now maintained by volunteers with the non-profit Border Route Trail Association (BRTA).

### Information and Contacts

- Purchase the recently revised *The Border Route Trail: A Trail Guide and Map.*

*An iconic Border Route view from a high vantage point on the trail. Photo by Todd "Tman" McMahon.*

*Hikers on parts of the Border Route Trail walk directly on the earth's crust where it has been exposed by glaciers. Photo by Todd "Tman" McMahon.*

- Visit the BRTA's website at www.borderroutetrail.org.
- Contact the BRTA via email at info@borderroutetrail.org.
- Visit the BRT Facebook group page, www.facebook.com/groups/borderroutetrail/.
- Visit the BRT Meetup group, www.meetup.com/Friends-of-the-Border-Route-Trail/

◀ **Map 33**
**Otter Lake Road to Jay Cooke State Park**

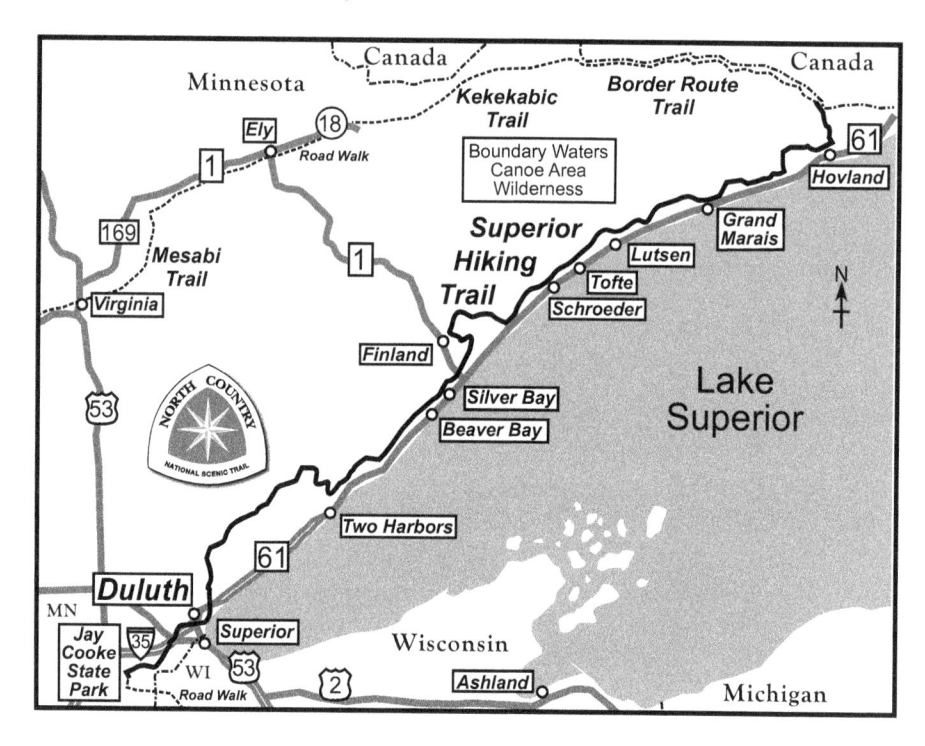

### Map 33 Superior Hiking Trail®

**Distance:** 305 Miles

This footpath follows the rocky ridgeline above Lake Superior's North Shore from Otter Lake Road (BRT trailhead) near the Canadian border to Jay Cooke State Park south of Duluth.

*Superior Hiking Trail volunteers construct "water bars" and wooden steps to help hikers on steep slopes and to protect the path from erosion. Photo by Todd "Tman" McMahon.*

*The water in creeks and rivers on the Superior Hiking Trail frequently tumbles over rock in its hurry to get to Lake Superior. Photo by Todd "Tman" McMahon.*

The SHT is known for easy access via frequent trailheads and road crossings, numerous backcountry campsites, rugged nature, and fabulous scenery viewed from an abundance of overlooks.

The SHT has been named as one of the top long-distance trails in the United States by *Backpacker Magazine* and is generally considered to be Minnesota's premier hiking trail.

It was built and is maintained by the non-profit Superior Hiking Trail Association (SHTA), which publishes the *Guide to the Superior Hiking Trail*, maps, and other merchandise. Purchase the guide and other merchandise from SHTA headquarters office/store in Two Harbors. The guide is also available at SHTA sites online and at online bookstores.

### Information and Contacts

- Visit www.shta.org.
- Contact SHTA at 218-834-2700, hike@shta.org.
- Visit the SHTA Facebook page, www.facebook.com/suphike.
- Visit the SHTA at groups.yahoo.com/neo/groups/hiker/info
- Purchase the *Guide to the Superior Hiking Trail* at bookstores and at www.shta.org.

# Chapter 7
# West and East of Minnesota

## North Dakota

The NCT in North Dakota starts near the Visitor Center at Lake Sakakawea State Park just west of Garrison Dam, which backs up Lake Sakakawea. It enters Minnesota just east of Fort Abercrombie State Historic Site after crossing the Red River of the North. In between, the NCT charts a circuitous course through the Peace Garden State. From the boundary of Lake Sakakawea State Park, it follows roads to reach the McClusky Canal, which it follows for about 70 miles. The route crosses through 32 miles of the diverse habitats of Lonetree Wildlife Management Area. East of Lonetree, it follows the New Rockford Canal for another 60 miles.

A road walk connects the NCT with a 30-mile segment along Lake Ashtabula. Road walks and isolated segments take the hiker through aptly named Valley City and then south through the Sheyenne River Valley. Disjointed segments are found along the way, including at Clausen Springs Recreation Area, Fort Ransom State Park, and the Sheyenne State Forest. A road walk connects the NCT to the Sheyenne National Grassland, where a 28-mile segment passes through tall grass prairie and oak savannah. From the National Grassland, the NCT heads east with isolated segments at the Ekre Grassland Preserve; a 6-mile segment between Colfax and Walcott; and a short segment at Fort Abercrombie.

In general, the NCT in North Dakota features mowed grass or graveled trail through rolling hills within pastures, along the edge of crop fields, or through wooded shelterbelts or bottomland. For updates on trail development, local chapters and events, visit northcountrytrail.org/trail/states/north-dakota/ or www.facebook.com/NCTinND.

## Wisconsin

The NCT in Wisconsin starts just east of Jay Cooke State Park, Minnesota, and features a road walk to Pattison State Park, where it passes the state's highest waterfall (Big Manitou Falls). From Pattison, a road walk links the trail to a contiguous segment of the NCT that stretches from the Moose River at St. Croix National Scenic Riverway to the city of Solon Springs. East of Solon Springs, another contiguous segment goes through a scenic white cedar bog along a long puncheon before following the historic Brule–St. Croix Portage Trail.

The NCT continues through the Brule River State Forest, Bayfield County Forest, and Chequamegon National Forest before passing through the city of Mellen and then scenic Copper Falls State Park, which features several amazing waterfalls. East of the park, the NCT follows roads and isolated segments to reach the Michigan border. For updates on trail development, local chapters, and events, visit northcountrytrail.org/trail/states/wisconsin/ or www.facebook.com/NCTinWI.

## Onward to New York

The NCT from Wisconsin to New York varies widely in scenery and terrain and includes rolling segments winding around the bluffs along Lake Superior in Michigan's Upper Peninsula (UP); flat stretches along canal towpaths and urban pathways in western Ohio; views of beautiful hills and valleys in the Allegheny and Finger Lake regions; and the steep mountains of the Adirondacks. Some highlights along the way include:
- Porcupine Mountains Wilderness State Park in the UP.
- The waterfalls of Tequahmenon Falls State Park in the eastern UP.
- Old Man's Cave in Hocking Hills State Park in Ohio.
- Old-growth pine and hemlock in Cook Forest State Park in Pennsylvania.
- Majestic waterfalls in Watkins Glen State Park in New York.
- The historic Old Erie Canal State Historic Park in New York.

## Best Hikes

Learn more about some of the best hikes along the NCT:
- NCTA website (northcountrytrail.org/trail/states/)
- NCTA Facebook page (www.facebook.com/northcountrytrail)
- The guidebook *The North Country Trail: The Best Walks, Hikes, and Backpacking Trips on America's Longest National Scenic Trail*, by Ron Strickland, available at northcountrytrail.org and bookstores.

# Appendix A
# Map Index and Hiking Checklist

| Map # and Section | Page | I Hiked It! Date |
|---|---|---|
| **North Dakota to Tamarac National Wildlife Refuge** | | |
| 1. Fort Abercrombie State Park, North Dakota Border to Maplewood State Park, Park Office | 54 | |
| 1-A. Maplewood State Park | 56 | |
| 2. Maplewood State Park, Park Office to Vergas | 62 | |
| 3. Vergas to Frazee | 63 | |
| 4. Frazee to Tamarac National Wildlife Refuge | 65 | |
| | | |
| **Tamarac National Wildlife Refuge through Chippewa National Forest** | | |
| 5. Boundary Road Trailhead to Blackbird Wildlife Drive Trailhead | 67 | |
| 5-A. Optional Road Walk, Tamarack National Wildlife Refuge | 68 | |
| 6. Blackbird Wildlife Drive Trailhead to 400th Avenue Trailhead | 76 | |
| 7. 400th Avenue Trailhead to Becker County 35 Trailhead | 80 | |
| 8. Becker County 35 Trailhead to Camp Six Forest Trail Trailhead | 86 | |
| 9. Camp Six Forest Trail Trailhead to Elbow Lake Road Trailhead | 90 | |
| 10. Elbow Lake Road Trailhead to Clearwater County 39 Trailhead | 94 | |

| Map # and Section | Page | I Hiked It! Date |
|---|---|---|
| 11. Clearwater County 39 Trailhead to Anchor Matson Road Trailhead | 99 | |
| 12. Anchor Matson Road Trailhead to 540th Avenue Trailhead | 104 | |
| 13. 540th Avenue Trailhead to Itasca State Park South Entrance Trailhead/Hubbard County 122 | 109 | |
| 13-A. Itasca State Park | 109 | |
| 14. Itasca State Park South Entrance Trailhead/Hubbard County 122 to Spider Lake Road Access Point | 116 | |
| 15. Spider Lake Road Access Point to Hubbard County 4/Halvorson Forest Road Trailhead | 120 | |
| 16. Hubbard County 4/Halvorson Forest Road Trailhead to Hubbard County 91 Trailhead | 125 | |
| 17. Hubbard County 91 Trailhead to Steamboat Forest Road Access Point | 130 | |
| 17-A. Gulch Lake Campground and Day-Use Area | 131 | |
| 18. Steamboat Forest Road Access Point to Akeley Cutoff Road Trailhead; Waboose Lake Loop Trail | 136 | |
| 18-A. Waboose Lake Loop Trail and Campsite | 141 | |
| 19. Akeley Cutoff Road Trailhead to Minnesota 64/East Steamboat Forest Road Trailhead | 145 | |
| 20. Minnesota 64/East Steamboat Forest Road Trailhead to Minnesota 34/Shingobee Recreation Area Trailhead | 148 | |
| 21. Minnesota 34/Shingobee Recreation Area Trailhead to Minnesota 371/Lake Erin Trailhead | 154 | |
| 21-A. Shingobee Recreation Area | 154 | |
| 22. Minnesota 371/Lake Erin Trailhead to Forest Road 3790 Access Point | 160 | |

| Map # and Section | Page | I Hiked It! Date |
|---|---|---|
| 23. Forest Road 3790 Access Point to Woodtick Trail/Forest Road 2107 Access Point, Third Crossing (heading east from Minnesota 371) | 166 | |
| 24. Woodtick Trail/Forest Road 2107 Access Point, Third Crossing (heading east from Minnesota 371) to Forest Road 2100 Access Point | 170 | |
| 24-A. Goose Lake Trail System | 170 | |
| 25. Forest Road 2100 Access Point to Minnesota 84 Trailhead | 176 | |
| 26. Minnesota 84 Trailhead to Minnesota 200 Trailhead | 179 | |
| 27. Minnesota 200 Trailhead to Forest Road 2117 Access Point | 184 | |
| 28. Forest Road 2117 Access Point to Milton Lake Drive/ Forest Road 2324 Trailhead | 188 | |
| 29. Milton Lake Drive/Forest Road 2324 Trailhead to Forest Road 2101 Trailhead at Minnesota 6 | 193 | |
| | | |
| **Chippewa National Forest near Remer to Jay Cooke State Park** | | |
| 30. Chippewa National Forest near Remer to Ely via Grand Rapids and the Mesabi Trail (Recommended route) | 201 | |
| 31. Kekekabic Trail (KTC), Snowbank Lake Road to Gunflint Trail | 205 | |
| 32. Border Route Trail (BRT), Gunflint Trail to Otter Lake Road | 208 | |
| 33. Superior Hiking Trail (SHT), Otter Lake Road to Jay Cooke State Park | 210 | |

# Appendix B

**Camping, Campsites, Campgrounds**

- Please review Chapter 2: Safety on the Trail, before camping in areas that are new to you.
- For additional information about using the trail, see Accessing and Using the Trail in the front of this book, including "Camping along the Trail."
- For trail details, including parking, access, and features, see relevant map sections.

**About Camping on the NCT in Minnesota**

- Dispersed camping (outside of designated campsites and campgrounds; no amenities) is allowed on most public lands along the NCT, and Leave No Trace principles should be adhered to, e.g. camp and dispose of human waste at least 200 feet from a water source. Campfires are allowed but NOT when no burning restrictions are in place (see www.dnr.state.mn.us/forestry/fire/firerating_restrictions.html). Campfires should be contained within a rock fire ring and completely extinguished before moving on.
- Tamarac National Wildlife Refuge: Camping is not allowed; plan hikes accordingly.
- Maplewood and Itasca State Parks: Designated campsites and campgrounds are available. Permits and reservations are required. Dispersed camping is not allowed in state parks.
- See Appendix C: Service Towns for additional camping and lodging facilities.

## Fort Abercrombie, ND, through Chippewa National Forest near Remer

| Map | Campsite Name | Tent sites | Fire Ring | Privy | Bench and/or Table | GPS Coordinates |
|---|---|---|---|---|---|---|
| Map 1 | Abercrombie, ND | The campground is in the city park on Richland County 4, west of Fort Abercrombie. Campground amenities. | | | | 46.447553,-96.725254 |
| Map 1-A | Maplewood State Park* | 3 | X | X | X | 46.53357, -95.949219 Permit required. |
| Map 5 | Boundary Road | 1 | Wide spot at end of gravel road between Tamarac NWR and Hubbel Pond WMA. No amenities. | | | 46.890329, -95.646791 |
| Map 7 | 400th Avenue | 2 | X | X | No | N46 56.066 W95 33.660 |
| Map 9 | Flooded Woods | 2 | X | X | No | 47.04829, -95.47129 |
| Map 10 | Horseshoe Lake | 2 | X | X | No | 47.113372, -95.445927 |
| Map 10 | Pine Island Lake | 2 | X | X | X | 47.148634, -95.439253 |
| Map 11 | Old Headquarters | 4 | X | X | X | 47.166026, -95.411466 |
| Map 11 | Gardner Lake | 2 | X | X | X | 47.1581, -95.338076 |

## Fort Abercrombie, ND, through Chippewa National Forest near Remer

| Map | Campsite Name | Tent sites | Fire Ring | Privy | Bench and/or Table | GPS Coordinates |
|---|---|---|---|---|---|---|
| Map 12 | West Itasca State Park* | 2 | X | X | No | 47.169892, -95.282904 No permit required. |
| Map 13 | De Soto Lake* | 4 | No | X | No | 47.148989, -95.22022 |
| Map 13 | Iron Corner* | 1 | X | X | No | 47.151791, -95.170742 |
| Map 14 | Zingwaak | 4 | X | X | X | 47.145467, -95.088528 |
| Map 16 | Amikwik | 3 | X | X | X | 47.15477, -94.958971 |
| Maps 17, 17-A | Nelson Lake at Gulch Lake* | 8 | X | X | X | 47.159519, -94.836565 Fee required. |
| Maps 18, 18-A | Waboose Lake | 3 | X | X | X | 47.059562, -94.822603 |
| Map 20 | Sprinkle Road Lake | 4 | X | X | X | 47.077758, -94.702236 |
| Maps 21, 21-A | Shingobee Recreation Area | Dispersed camping | No | X (At Warming Chalet) | No | 47.037, -94.644 |
| Map 21 | Crockett Memorial | 2 | X | X | No | 47.03823, -94.629022 |
| Map 22 | Woodtick Impoundment | 2 | X | X | No | 46.994586, -94.513746 |

### Fort Abercrombie, ND, through Chippewa National Forest near Remer

| Map | Campsite Name | Tent sites | Fire Ring | Privy | Bench and/or Table | GPS Coordinates |
|---|---|---|---|---|---|---|
| Map 22 | Hovde Lake | 1 | X | X | X | 47.00765, -94.448359 |
| Map 23 | Gut Lake | 3 | X | X | No | 47.003092, -94.427782 |
| Maps 24, 24-A | Goose Lake (Off-trail) | 2 | X | X | No | 46.990162, -94.328574 |
| Map 24 | Hazel Lake (Off-trail) | 1 | X | X | No | 46.998849, -94.287212 |
| Map 26 | Crown Lake | 4 | X | X | No | 47.046408, -94.184469 |
| Map 28 | Old Pines Lake | 4 | X | X | X | 47.090476, -94.046277 |
| Map 29 | Milton Lake | 1 | X | X | X | 47.134272, -93.933831 |

\* Campground also available at this location. See below.

## Campgrounds

| Location | Drinking water | Showers | Toilets | GPS Coordinates | Information | Additional Facilities |
|---|---|---|---|---|---|---|
| Maplewood State Park, Knoll Loop | X | X | X | 46.522412,-95.947536 | Chapter III; Chapter IV Maps 1 and 1-A | Camper cabins |
| Itasca State Park, Bear Paw and Pine Ridge | X | X | X | 7.223725,-95.183423 | Chapter III; Chapter V Maps 13 and 13-A; Appendix C | Cabins, lodge |
| Gulch Lake Campground and Day-Use Area, Paul Bunyan State Forest | X |  | X | 47.159534,-94.83656 | Chapter V Maps 17 and 17-A | Self registration, boat launch |
| Off-trail: Mabel Lake, Chippewa National Forest | X |  | X | 47.047866,-94.071616 | Chapter V Map 27 | Self registration, picnic area with swimming beach |

| Chippewa National Forest near Remer through Superior Hiking Trail, Jay Cooke State Park | |
|---|---|
| Map 30 | Remer to Ely via Grand Rapids and the Mesabi Trail (recommended route). Visit www.mesabitrail.com/ |
| Map 31 | Kekekabic Trail (Kek). Visit www.kek.org |
| Map 32 | Border Route Trail (BRT). Visit www.borderroutetrail.org |
| Map 33 | Superior Hiking Trail (SHT). Visit www.shta.org |

# Appendix C
# Service Towns

*In an emergency, call 911 from any location.*

**Maps 1–4**

**Fort Abercrombie, North Dakota, to Tamarac National Wildlife Refuge, Minnesota**

- The following services are available in towns listed in map descriptions, plus a few others that might have services and supplies of interest to hikers.
- The nearest commercial airport is in Fargo, ND.
- The nearest major medical services are in Fargo/Moorhead.
- Amtrak runs through Fargo/Moorhead and Detroit Lakes.

| Town | Description | GPS Coordinates Website |
|---|---|---|
| Detroit Lakes | Off-trail, many services. See below, Service Towns for Tamarac National Wildlife Refuge through Chippewa National Forest. | 46.813333, -95.844722 www.visitdetroitlakes.com |
| "Four Corners" Near Rochert | Junction of Minnesota 34 and Becker County 29. Gas station/convenience store/café, liquor store. (Not a town.) | 46.834288, -95.689347 |
| Abercrombie, ND | West of Fort Abercrombie .33 mile. Campground, post office | 46.447222, -96.729444 www.wahpetonbreckenridgechamber.com/visitor_fort.htm |
| Fargo, ND | A major city. Services include medical facilities and commercial airport. Not within hiking distance of the NCT. West of the Red River and Moorhead, MN. | 46.877222, -96.789444 www.fmwfchamber.com |
| Frazee | The city of Frazee (population 1,350) is becoming known for its trails. It features a marked 1.5-mile NCT urban segment and will one day feature the Heartland State Trail (a paved bike trail). Currently, it features the Otter Tail River state water trail, a canoeing/kayaking route.<br><br>Long-distance hiker services include a U.S. Post Office, motel, grocery and convenience stores, restaurants, city beach and park. Be sure to get your photo at the world's largest turkey in Frazee. You can find it in Lions Park off Minnesota 87 by Town Lake. | 46.728333, -95.701111 www.frazeecity.com. |

225

| Town | Description | GPS Coordinates Website |
|---|---|---|
| Moorhead | A major city. Services include medical facilities and commercial airport. Not within hiking distance of the NCT. East of the Red River and Fargo, ND. | 46.873889, -96.767222 www.fmwfchamber.com |
| Pelican Rapids | Located 7 miles west of Maplewood State Park's entrance road. This community features lodging, grocery, medical clinic, library, gas, coffee shop, ice cream shop, hardware store, a fine park on the Otter Tail River, and the world's largest pelican statue. | 46.474444, -96.0831124 www.pelicanrapidschamber.com/ |
| Rothsay | A small community located near the eastern edge of the Red River Valley on I-94. It features lodging, Ole & Lena's Pizza, a convenience store, and café. Rothsay is also known for the world's largest prairie chicken statue. | 46.569167, -96.081389 www.rothsay.org/ |
| Vergas | The small community of Vergas (population 330) has a variety of long-distance hiker services, including U.S. Post Office, small grocery, convenience store, restaurants, city beach and park. Be sure to get your photo taken at the World's Largest Loon, located in the City Park on Minnesota 228 on the shores of Long Lake. | 46.655833, -95.806111 www.vergasmn.com/ |

# Maps 5–29

## Tamarac Refuge through Chippewa National Forest

- The following services are available in towns listed in trailhead driving directions, plus a few others that might have services and supplies of interest to hikers.
- The nearest commercial airport is in Bemidji.
- The nearest major medical services are in Bemidji (Sanford Health clinics and hospital).

---

**Finding Services**

To find specific services, go to maps.google.com and enter the GPS coordinates of the town. The map will show many businesses and services. For more specific information, click on "Search nearby" and enter a term such as "pizza." Nearby locations will appear on the map.

| City/Services | Campground* | Camping Supplies | Gas Stations | General Merchandise | Groceries | Hospital** | Lodging* | Post Office | Restaurants | GPS Coordinates • Additional Information |
|---|---|---|---|---|---|---|---|---|---|---|
| Akeley | X | | X | | | | | X | X | GPS Coordinates 47.001667, -94.728056 www.akeleychamber.com |
| Bemidji | X | X | X | X | X | X | X | X | X | GPS Coordinates 47.473611, -94.880278 • Major medical center (Sanford) • Commercial Airport www.visitbemidji.com |
| Detroit Lakes | X | X | X | X | X | X | X | X | X | GPS Coordinates 46.813333, -95.844722 www.visitdetroitlakes.com |
| Dorset | | | | X | X | | | | X | GPS Coordinates 46.956389, -94.9525 • Tiny town, many restaurants (summer). www.dorsetmn.com |

| City/Services | Campground* | Camping Supplies | Gas Stations | General Merchandise | Groceries | Hospital** | Lodging* | Post Office | Restaurants | GPS Coordinates • Additional Information |
|---|---|---|---|---|---|---|---|---|---|---|
| Frazee | X | X | X | X | X | X | X | X | X | GPS Coordinates 46.80896, -95.82298 www.frazeecity.com |
| Grand Rapids | X | X | X | X | X | X | X | X | X | GPS Coordinates 47.233333, -93.529167 www.visitgrandrapids.com |
| Hackensack | | | X | X | X | | | X | X | GPS Coordinates 46.928889, -94.521667 www.hackensackchamber.com |
| Itasca State Park | X | X | | X | | | X | | X | GPS Coordinates 47.194648, -95.165012 • DNR Emergency Services • Park Information: 218- 699-7251 • See also Chapter III, Maplewood and Itasca State Parks www.dnr.state.mn.us/state_parks/itasca/index.html |

| City/Services | Campground* | Camping Supplies | Gas Stations | General Merchandise | Groceries | Hospital** | Lodging* | Post Office | Restaurants | GPS Coordinates • Additional Information |
|---|---|---|---|---|---|---|---|---|---|---|
| Lake George | X | | X | | X | | X | X | X | GPS Coordinates 47.239722, -95.2075 parkrapids.comneighborhoods/lakegeorge.htm |
| Laporte | | X | X | | X | | | X | X | GPS Coordinates 47.213889, -94.755 laportemn.com |
| Longville | X | | X | X | X | | X | X | X | GPS Coordinates 46.985278, -94.214167 www.longville.com |
| Nevis | X | X | X | X | X | X | X | X | X | GPS Coordinates 46.964167, -94.844444 www.nevischamber.com |
| Park Rapids | | | X | | X | | X | X | X | GPS Coordinates 46.900694, -95.073111 parkrapids.com/neighborhoods |
| Ponsford | | | X | | X | | | X | | 46.9699602, -95.383611 |

| City/Services | Campground* | Camping Supplies | Gas Stations | General Merchandise | Groceries | Hospital** | Lodging* | Post Office | Restaurants | GPS Coordinates • Additional Information |
|---|---|---|---|---|---|---|---|---|---|---|
| Remer | X |  | X | X | X |  | X | X | X | GPS Coordinates 47.055833, -93.913889 www.remerchamber.com |
| Walker | X | X | X | X | X |  | X | X | X | GPS Coordinates 47.099722, -94.581111 www.leech-lake.com |

* Campgrounds and lodging are X'd only when there are facilities in the town itself. However, there are many resorts, resort campgrounds, and park campgrounds outside of towns.
** Many small towns in Minnesota have medical clinics. Only towns with hospitals are X'd.

**Maps 30–33**

**Chippewa National Forest near Remer to Jay Cooke State Park**

See Chapter 6 Maps.
- Some towns and services are described for each trail (Mesabi, Kek, BRT, SHT).
- Resource information is provided for identifying additional towns and services.
- The nearest major medical center and airport are in Duluth.

# Appendix D
# Loop Trails for Easy-Access Shorter Hikes

**Fort Abercrombie, ND, through Chippewa National Forest**

**Chapter 4 Maps 1–4**

**Chapter 5 Maps 5–29**

Loop trails are an excellent way to try out the NCT in Minnesota. The ones listed here have trailhead parking associated with the NCT, are generally easy terrain—gently undulating—are varied in length, and wend through a variety of forest types from re-growth to old-growth. See map section for terrain information.

- Please review Chapter 2: Safety on the Trail before hiking a trail that is new to you.
- For trail details, including campsite amenities, parking, restrictions, permits, access points and features, see relevant map sections.

| Loop Trail/ Map Number | Length | Privy | Camping Facilities | Potable Water | Kiosk with Information | Picnic Table, Fire Ring | Description (See map for parking information.) | Checklist: I Hiked it! |
|---|---|---|---|---|---|---|---|---|
| Map 1-A Maplewood State Park | Variable | X At park office & Trail Center trailhead. | X | X | X | X | Terrain is mostly level to rolling with some short, steep hills. Multiple loops. For detailed maps, obtain brochure at the park or at www.dnr.state.mn.us/state_parks/maplewood. State Park permit required. | |
| Map 5 Tamarac Lake, Tamarac National Wildlife Refuge | 2.0 miles | X At trailhead. | | | X | | Terrain mostly level, gently undulating. | |
| Map 5 Old Indian Trail, Tamarac National Wildlife Refuge | 2.25 | | | | | | Terrain is gently undulating. Mileage includes trailhead spur. | |

| Loop Trail/ Map Number | Length | Privy | Camping Facilities | Potable Water | Kiosk with Information | Picnic Table, Fire Ring | Description (See map for parking information.) | Checklist: I Hiked it! |
|---|---|---|---|---|---|---|---|---|
| Maps 13, 13-A, 14 Itasca State Park | Variable | X Throughout park. | X | X | X | X | Terrain is mixed with some challenging hills. Multiple loops. For detailed maps, obtain brochure at the park or at www.dnr.state.mn.us/state_parks/maplewood. State Parks permit required. | |
| Maps 17, 17-A Gulch Lake Campground and Day-Use Area | Nelson Lake: 1.4 miles; Lake 21: 1.3 miles | X At campsite. | X | X | X | X | Terrain is mostly level. Two loops that form a figure eight with some overlap. | |
| Maps 18 & 18-A Waboose Lake | 3.9 miles from Waboose Lake public lake access. Slightly longer from Akeley Cutoff Road Trailhead. | X At NCT campsite. | X At NCT campsite. | | | X At campsite. | Terrain is gently undulating with some ascents and descents. | |

| Loop Trail/ Map Number | Length | Privy | Camping Facilities | Potable Water | Kiosk with Information | Picnic Table, Fire Ring | Description (See map for parking information.) | Checklist: I Hiked it! |
|---|---|---|---|---|---|---|---|---|
| Maps 21, 21-A Shingobee Recreation Area | Variable | X At chalet. | X At NCT campsite. | | X | X | Terrain mostly level. Multiple loops. For detailed maps, obtain brochure at the Chippewa National Forest Ranger Station in Walker or at www.co.cass.mn.us/maps/pdfs/trail_maps/shing.pdf. | |
| Map 22 Lake Erin | .6 miles | X | | X Hand pump | X | Picnic table, no fire ring. | Terrain is gently undulating. | |

# Appendix E
# Winter Use

The NCT is open year round. In the winter it is available for hiking, snowshoeing and backcountry cross-country skiing as snow cover permits. See below for trailheads that are maintained in winter and for sections of the trail that are groomed for cross-country skiing.

**Trailheads Maintained in Winter**

- Chapter 4 Maps 1–4 Abercrombie, ND, to Tamarac National Wildlife Refuge. See contact information at map entries.
- Chapter 5 Maps 5–29 Tamarac National Wildlife Refuge through Chippewa National Forest

| Map | Trailhead |
| --- | --- |
| 5 | Becker County 29 at Pine Lake |
| 5 | Old Indian Trail |
| 6, 7 | 400th Avenue |
| 9, 10 | Elbow Lake Road |
| 10 | Minnesota 113 |
| 10, 11 | Clearwater County 39 |
| 13, 14 | US 71 at Itasca State Park South Entrance |
| 20, 21 | Minnesota 34/Shingobee Recreation Area |
| 21 | Cass County 50 |
| 21, 22 | Minnesota 371/Lake Erin |

- Chapter 6 Maps 30–33 Chippewa National Forest near Remer to Jay Cooke State Park. See contact information at map entries.

## Groomed Cross-Country Ski Trails on the NCT

There are many other groomed cross-country ski trails in northern Minnesota. Those that share the NCT are listed here.

| Map | Trailhead |
| --- | --- |
| 5 | Becker County 126 to near Tamarac Lake |
| 13 | Intersection of Nicollet and Eagle Scout Trails to intersection of NCT and Ozawindib Trails |
| 21 | Just east of Minnesota 34 to just west of the Anoway Bridge. |

# Appendix F
# Restricted-Use Areas

**Tamarac National Wildlife Refuge**

The refuge is only open to day use between the hours of 5:00 a.m. and 10:00 p.m. No overnight use is allowed! Because of this, long-distance NCT hikers should plan accordingly to make it through the refuge in one day. Backcountry camping is available at the south end and the east end. A shorter, road-walk alternative outside the refuge is mapped (Map 5-A) for those unable to make it the 14 miles across the refuge in one day. No shuttle service is available.

Pets are welcome, however, they must be leashed or kept under control at all times. Trapping does occur on portions of the refuge for wildlife management purposes through the winter months and pets, especially dogs, could unintentionally be caught.

For more information, visit www.fws.gov/refuge/Tamarac/visit/rules_and_regulations.html.

**Greenwater Lake Scientific and Natural Area**

Greenwater Lake SNA is closed to overnight use (no camping) and pets, picnicking, and swimming are prohibited. NCT users must not disturb any plants, animals, rocks, fossils, or other natural elements so that they "can fulfill their life cycle and role in the environment." For more information, visit www.dnr.state.mn.us/snas/detail.html?id=sna00977 or www.dnr.state.mn.us/snas/rules.html.

**Itasca State Park and Maplewood State Park**

Regular park admission requirements apply for NCT users (e.g. daily or annual sticker required for parking at one of the two NCT trailheads within the park) but hiking within the park does not require a permit. Camping is only allowed in designated campgrounds or at backcountry campsites for which fees are charged. The West Itasca State Park campsite is maintained by the NCTA and no fees are charged for camping. The others, DeSoto Lake (Itasca Park Site B03 and B04) and Iron Corner Lake (Itasca Park Site B06) are fee sites. Some of these backcountry sites can be reserved. For more information, visit www.dnr.state.mn.us/state_parks/rules.html.

**Chippewa National Forest**

No fees or permits are required to use the NCT within "the Chip" but fees are required to camp at nearby developed campgrounds. NCT users may camp anywhere on National Forest lands, although they should be at least 200 feet from the trail or water source. Leave No Trace principles should be adhered to (see Accessing and Using the NCT in Minnesota).

# Appendix G
# Recommended Reading

Bjerkness, Odell M. and Tim E. Holzkamm. 1988. *A Good Dose of Bad Medicine: The Story of the Bad Medicine Lake Community and Surrounding Area* (Ponsford, MN: Bad Medicine Lake Area Association). Local account of the Bad Medicine Lake area, just south and east of the Laurentian Lakes portion of the trail.

Brower, J.V. 1904. *Itasca State Park: An Illustrated History.* Minnesota Historical Collections, Vol. 11. (St. Paul: Minnesota Historical Society). A history of Itasca State Park by one of the park's founders—pdf copy available online.

Cooley, Myron. 1894. *Outings and Innings in Northern Minnesota and Along the North Shore of Lake Superior* (Detroit [Lakes], MN: Record Steam Print). An early collection of hunting and fishing stories from northern Minnesota, including the Tamarac Refuge—pdf copy available online.

Densmore, Frances. 1928. "Uses of Plants by the Chippewa Indians" in the *Forty-fourth Annual Report of the Bureau of American Ethnology to the Secretary of the Smithsonian Institution,* 1926–1927 (Washington, D.C.: GPO. Reprint, Dover publications.

———. 1929. *Chippewa Customs.* Smithsonian Institution, Bureau of American Ethnology, Bulletin 86 (Washington, D.C.: GPO). Reprint, Minnesota Historical Society. Ethnographies largely based on the author's fieldwork on the White Earth Indian Reservation.

Dobie, John. 1959. *The Itasca Story* (Minneapolis: Ross & Haines). The story of how Itasca State Park came to be.

Dunn, Anne. 1995. *When Beaver Was Very Great: Stories to Live By* (Midwest Traditions).

Graves, Kathy Davis and Elizabeth Ebbott. 2006. *Indians in Minnesota* (Minneapolis: University of Minnesota). Fifth edition of an informative text prepared for the League of Women Voters of Minnesota.

Hazard, Evan B. 1982. *The Mammals of Minnesota* (Minneapolis: University of Minnesota). Field guide.

Heinrich, Bernd. 2003. *WinterWord: The Ingenuity of Animal Survival.* New York, Ecco.

Hilger, M. Inez. 1951. *Chippewa Child Life and its Cultural Background.* Smithsonian Institution, Bureau of American Ethnology, Bulletin

146 (Washington, D.C.: GPO). Reprint, Minnesota Historical Society. Ethnography based, in part, on the author's fieldwork on the White Earth Indian Reservation.

Holland, Ren. 2004. *The Edge of Itasca: Life at the Mississippi Headwaters and in Early Itasca Park Communities* (Little Falls: The Book Lode, LLC). A history of settlement in the Itasca State Park area, mainly in communities adjoining the park.

Jasken, Jim. 2011. *Kayaking A Moonbeam: The Sugar Bush Reader... Up North Balm for the modern overloaded mind* (Xlibris). Essays, poetry, and short stories highlight unique ways to view issues and explore the provincial Minnesota personality.

Johnson, Deane L. 2014. *The Best of Itasca: A Guide to Minnesota's Oldest State Park* (Adventure Publications).

Minnesota Historical Society. n.d. *Itasca State Park Oral History Project.* MHS Archives, St. Paul. In 1993, oral history intern Amy K. Rieger, working for the Minnesota Department of Natural Resources, did 27 interviews with people who had associations with Itasca State Park. She spoke with architects, directors, long and short time employees, including Civilian Conservation Corps workers, visitors, and people who lived near the park. Also included are sound recordings of two Itasca State Park programs presented by Ben Thoma, Park Naturalist, "Walk Through Time" and "People of Itasca." In 1994, Thoma, then retired, interviewed an architect and people restoring buildings at the park. In 2000, he did a series of interviews with 17 other people associated with the park. To access the Itasca State Park Oral History Project, visit collections.mnhs.org/voicesofmn/index.php/10002540

Phillips, Gary L., William D. Schmid, and James C. Underhill. 1982. *Fishes of the Minnesota Region* (Minneapolis: University of Minnesota Press). Field guide.

Strickland, Ron. 2013. *The North Country Trail: The Best Walks, Hikes, and Backpacking Trips on America's Longest National Scenic Trail* (University of Michigan Press).

Tekiela, Stan. 1999. *Wildflowers of Minnesota: Field Guide* (Cambridge, MN: Adventure Publications).

———. 2002. *Trees of Minnesota: Field Guide* (Cambridge, MN: Adventure Publications).

———. 2004. *Birds of Minnesota: Field Guide* (Cambridge, MN: Adventure Publications).

———. 2005. *Mammals of Minnesota: Field Guide* (Cambridge, MN: Adventure Publications).

Tester, John. 1996. *Minnesota's Natural Heritage.* (University of Minnesota Press).

Watrin, Rev. Benno. 1930. *The Ponsfordian 1880–1930* (Park Rapids, MN: Press of the Park Rapids Enterprise). A short history of the community of Ponsford, including part of the area the Laurentian Lakes trail passes through.

Wilcox, Alvin H. 1907. *A Pioneer History of Becker County, Minnesota, Including a Brief Account of Its Natural History* (St. Paul: Pioneer Press). Reprint, Becker County Historical Society. An early history of Becker County.

# Appendix H
# Meetup Groups, Social Media, Contacts

**Meetup.com**

NCT chapters and affiliates in Minnesota utilize the online site Meetup.com to announce hikes and to share event information with members and friends. The Meetup sites are open to the public and there is no charge for joining them. They are a good way to get to know the NCT in Minnesota and its friends, members, trail adopters, and volunteers. To stay in the loop, sign up for email notices of hikes, trail workdays, and NCT events. Maps, directions, contact information, and enticing descriptions are offered.

*Friends of the Border Route Trail*, Border Route Trail Association
www.meetup.com/Friends-of-the-Border-Route-Trail/

*Hike the North Country Trail in Western Minnesota*, Laurentian Lakes Chapter
www.meetup.com/HikeNCTinMN/

*MN Arrowhead North Country Trail Hikers*, Arrowhead Chapter
www.meetup.com/Arrowhead-NCT-hikers/

*Paul Bunyan & Chippewa Forests NCT Hiker*, Itasca Moraine & Star of the North Chapters
www.meetup.com/Chip-NCT-hikers/

Red River Valley Outdoors Meetup group, Fargo-Moorhead
www.meetup.com/Red-River-Valley-Outdoors/

**Social Media**

Twitter: @ nctrail
On youtube.com, search "North Country Trail"

# Contacts

## *National*

National Park Service
nps.gov/noco; 1-866-HIKENCT

North Country National Scenic Trail
www.northcountrytrail.org

North Country Trail Association on Facebook
www.facebook.com/northcountrytrail

## *Minnesota*

The North Country Trail in Minnesota, Facebook
www.facebook.com/NCTinMN

Guide to the North Country Trail in Minnesota, updates and news
northcountrytrail.org/mnguidebook

## *Chapters*

Arrowhead Chapter
northcountrytrail.org/arw
arw@northcountrytrail.org

Itasca Moraine Chapter
northcountrytrail.org/itm
itm@northcountrytrail.org

Laurentian Lakes Chapter
northcountrytrail.org/llc
llc@northcountrytrail.org

Star of the North Chapter
northcountrytrail.org/stn
stn@northcountrytrail.org

## *Shared and Utilized Trails*

Border Route Trail Association (BRTA)
info@borderroutetrail.org

www.borderroutetrail.org
www.facebook.com/groups/borderroutetrail/

Kekekabic Trail Club (KTC)
www.kek.org
info@kek.org

Mesabi Trail
www.mesabitrail.com/

Superior Hiking Trail Association (SHTA)
218-834-2700
www.shta.org
www.facebook.com/suphike
hike@shta.org
volunteer@shta.org

# Appendix I
# Editorial Team
## Guide to the North Country National Scenic Trail

**Matthew R. Davis** is the North Dakota/Minnesota Regional Trail Coordinator for the North Country Trail Association. He has thru-hiked and worked on the Appalachian Trail and, with his family, maintains a section of the NCT within Itasca State Park.

**Susan Carol Hauser** is an editor, natural history writer, and essayist. Her books include *A Field Guide to Poison Ivy, Poison Oak and Poison Sumac*, and *A Field Guide to Ticks*. She is a member of the Itasca Moraine Chapter of the NCTA.

**Bruce M. Johnson** is president of the Itasca Moraine Chapter of the NCTA. He is a resident of Park Rapids, Minnesota, where he lives with his wife, Linda. He has been active locating, flagging, building, and maintaining the NCT across Hubbard County since 2006. In 2011, he was awarded the Trail Builder of the Year award. Bruce and Linda maintain a section of the NCT.

**Linda D. Johnson** is a retired math teacher living with her husband in northern Minnesota. After a career of teaching in American Schools overseas, she enjoys the peaceful life by a lake in the woods. She is an active member of the Itasca Moraine Chapter of the NCTA.

**Todd "Tman" McMahon** has hiked more than 550 miles of the North Country Trail in Minnesota and over 700 miles of the Ice Age Trail in Wisconsin. He received the NCTA's Outreach Award in 2013 for his work publicizing the NCT at Canoecopia, Outdoor Adventure Expo and his Internet site, "I saw Tman." As a member of the Heritage Chapter of the NCT, he is building trail in Copper Falls State Park near Mellen, Wisconsin.

**Ray Vlasak** is president of the Laurentian Lakes Chapter of the NCTA. He has been a member since 1989 and became actively involved after retiring in 1999. A founding member of the Itasca Moraine Chapter (2001), he was instrumental in forming the Laurentian Lakes Chapter (2007). He served on the NCTA Board of Directors from 2010–2013 and has earned the NCTA Vanguard Award, Chapter Honor Award, NCTA Leadership Award, and the United States President's Call to Service Award.

# Acknowledgments

This guidebook was constructed step by step with the help of the same people who built the trail—also step by step, who maintain it, and who use it and love it. With grateful appreciation, the following are acknowledged:

Trail adopters and volunteers who hiked and re-hiked sections, making notes, checking cell signals, writing up stories, offering suggestions: Kit Arnquist, Ruth Bergquist, Larry Best, Katie Jo Blau, Richard Chamberlain, Matt Davis, Mary Donnellan, Alison Edgerton, Dave Edgerton, Jim Eisele, Laurie Hanson, Roger Hanson, Carter Hedeen, Rhoda Jackson, Bruce M. Johnson, David Larsen, Harlan Liljequest, Arvan Matheny, Willis Mattison, Jerry McCarty, Melinda McCarty, Todd "Tman" McMahon, Eric Mickelson, Tom Moberg, Marvin Mortensen, Gary Narum, Philip Nimps, Brian Pavek, Jeri Rakness, Darrel Rodekuhr, Karen Stenberg, Beth Trout, Jerry Trout, Ray Vlasak.

NCTA Minnesota Chapters, their officers, volunteers and members, for their work and support: Arrowhead, Itasca Moraine, Laurentian Lakes, and Star of the North.

Photographers Ron Alden, "Windigo Doug" Boulee, Matthew R. Davis, Carter Hedeen, Florence Hedeen, Bruce M. Johnson, Deane Johnson, Todd "Tman" McMahon, Marcus Schaffer, Karen Stenberg, Beth Trout, Jerry Trout, and Ray Vlasak, as well as Ryan Rodgers <www.ryan-rodgers.com>, and Bart Smith <www.walkingdownadream.com/home.html>.

Proofreaders Kathy Meyer, Gary Narum, Mary Nordeen, Stacy Davis and others for their precision reading.

Itasca Moraine Chapter Volunteer Beth "Tick Tock" Trout for hiking 105.3 miles of the trail with a mileage wheel.

Itasca Moraine Chapter President Bruce M. Johnson for hiking the trail from the Tamarac National Wildlife Refuge through the Chippewa National Forest, proofreading, filling in blanks in copy, and for wheeling trail, correcting a draft of the guide as he went along.

Laurentian Lakes Chapter President Ray Vlasak for generous attention to detail in the guide, close reading of the manuscript, writing up missed sections, wheeling trail, and other invisible work.

Sue Nokleby and Paula Peters, Paul Bunyan Mushroom Club, for help with mushroom identification.

Regional Trail Coordinator for Minnesota and North Dakota, North Country Trail Association, Matthew R. Davis for precise information, knowledge of the trail, encouragement and support for the guide, and his own generous nature.

Essayists Barry Babcock, Nancy Brennan, James Cotter, Bob La Fleur, Deane L. Johnson and Harvey Tjader for their knowledge, their wisdom, and their way with words.

Luke "Strider" Jordan for honoring his dream of a thru-hike on the NCT, for persevering through ice and snow, for keeping a journal, and for permission to use excerpts from it in this guide.

Anishinabe Storyteller Grandmother Anne Dunn for her story, her trail statement, and her understanding of the forest.

Author Will Weaver for his lyrical, perceptive, and encouraging Foreword.

Map Illustrator Todd "Tman" McMahon for the fine maps, with additional thanks to Matt Kania, Map Hero, for shepherding Todd at the beginning of the process.

# Index

Akeley, 27, 228
Anoway Stream, 155, 158
Arrowhead Chapter, 13, 24, 244, 245

Bemidji, 27, 228
Bois de Sioux River, 78
Border Route Trail, 13, 14, 24, 208, 244, 245
Boundary Waters Canoe Area, 204
Boy River, 183, 184

Camping, Campsites, Campgrounds. See Appendix B, 218-223
Chippewa National Forest, 13, 66, 200, 215, 217, 240
Cross-country Ski Trails, 238
Crow Wing River, 112
Crown Lake, 180, 182, 221

De Soto Lake, 110, 113, 114, 220
Detroit Lakes, 27, 225, 228
Divide (geographic), 25, 83, 84, 89
Dorset, 228

Elbow Lake, 78, 96, 97, 102
Elk Lake, 112
Ely, 13, 198, 210, 223

Fort Abercrombie, 54, 213, 219, 224, 225
Four Corners, 65, 225
Frazee, 27, 225, 229

Gage Lake, 123
Gardner Lake, 99, 103, 219
Giant's Ridge, 202, 203
Gilfillan Lake, 109, 115
Golden Spike, 120, 123
Goose Lake Trail System, 170, 171, 173, 217
Grand Rapids, 27, 229
Greenwater Lake Scientific and Natural Area, 80, 86, 239
Gulch Lake Campground and Day-Use Area, 131, 135

Gunflint Trail, 205
Gut Lake, 166, 168

Hackensack, 27, 229
Hazel Lake, 170, 174
Heartland State Trail, 148, 152, 153
Hiking Checklist. See Appendix A, 215-217
Horn Lake, 113
Horseshoe Lake, 94, 96, 141, 143
Hovde Lake, 160, 166

Iron Corner Lake, 239
Itasca Moraine Chapter, 13, 24, 244, 245
Itasca State Park, 27, 47, 50, 51, 105, 109, 115, 222, 229, 239

Jay Cooke State Park, 200, 210
Juggler Lake, 94, 96

Kekekabic Trail, 13, 14, 24, 205, 246
Kirk Lake, 108

Lake Twenty-one (21), 131, 135
Lake Erin, 160, 163
Lake George, 27, 120, 230
Lake Itasca, 51, 109, 115
Laporte, 27, 230
Laurentian Divide, 25, 89, 98
Laurentian Lakes Chapter, 13, 24, 244, 245
Leech Lake, 27, 153
Longville, 27, 230
Loop Trails. See Appendix D, 233-236

Map Index, See Appendix A, 215-217
Maplewood State Park, 27, 47, 48, 56, 63, 239
McKenna Lake, 113
Meetups, See Appendix H, 244
Mesabi Trail, 201, 202, 246
Milton Lake, 193, 196
Milton Lake Esker, 193, 194, 195
Mississippi River, 51, 53, 84, 109, 115

Morrison Lake, 109, 112

Nelson Lake, 131, 135
Nevis, 27, 230
Nicollet Lake, 112
North Country National Scenic Trail, 11, 24, 245
North Country Trail, *See* North Country National Scenic Trail
North Country Trail Association, 13, 24, 245
North Dakota, 12, 27, 54, 213

Old Headquarters, 102
Old Indian Trail, 67, 73
Old Pines Lake, 190
Otter Tail River, 65, 78

Park Rapids, 27, 230
Paul Bunyan State Forest, 141
Paul Bunyan State Trail, 153, 154, 158, 160
Pelican Rapids, 27, 226
Pine Island Lake, 94
Pine Lake, 67, 71, 73
Ponsford, 230

Red River, 27, 83, 84
Red River Valley Outdoors Meetup Group, 244
Remer, 27, 231
Restricted-Use Areas, *See* Appendix F, 239-240
Robertson Lake, 125, 129

Rochert, 65, 225

Schoolcraft River, 120, 125
Service Towns, *See* Appendix C, 224-232
Shingobee Connection Trail, 151, 153, 154, 160
Shingobee Recreation Area, 154, 157
Shingobee River, 157, 158, 159
South Chippewa Lake, 76, 78
Spur Lake, 125, 128
Star of the North Chapter, 13, 24, 244, 245
Stocking Lake, 166, 169
Superior Hiking Trail, 13, 14, 24, 210, 246
Swift River, 184, 187

Tamarac Lake, 67, 72, 73
Tamarac National Wildlife Refuge, 27, 67, 71, 76, 79, 239
Ten Lake, 148, 153, 158
Tepee Lake, 125, 129, 169
Thorpe Tower, 136, 139
Tioga Trail, 202
Trailheads. *See* Appendix A, page 215-217

Vergas, 27, 63, 226

Waboose Lake, 141, 142-147
Watershed, 89, 95, 112, 115
Winter Use. *See* Appendix E, 237-238
Wisconsin, 12, 27, 210, 214

# Journal/Notes

# Journal/Notes

# Journal/Notes

# Journal/Notes